COLLECTED WRITINGS OF E W ROGERS

VOLUME 2

Collected Writings of E W Rogers - Volume 2

COLLECTED WRITINGS OF E W ROGERS
VOLUME 2

Compiled by Mervyn Wishart

John Ritchie Publishing
40 Beansburn, Kilmarnock, Scotland

ISBN-13: 978 1 914273 16 2

Copyright © 2022 by John Ritchie Ltd.
40 Beansburn, Kilmarnock, Scotland

www.ritchiechristianmedia.co.uk

All rights reserved. No part of this publication may be reproduced, stored in a retrievable system, or transmitted in any form or by any other means – electronic, mechanical, photocopy, recording or otherwise – without prior permission of the copyright owner.

Typeset by John Ritchie Ltd., Kilmarnock
Printed by Bell & Bain Ltd., Glasgow

Contents

Foreword 9
The Fall..19
The Life of Faith - Exemplified in Elijah (1 Kings 17)............28
The Consecration of the Priests 35
The Cleansing of the Leper 40
A Meditation on Love...44
Peter's Utterances (Matthew 16:13 to 17:8).........................49
"When Ye Come Together In One Place" 56
Luke 10..59
Sundry Thoughts on Luke 12 63
The Lord Jesus Christ - His Unique Person 67

Matthew's Gospel - Jesus the Christ 71
Preface 72
Introduction..74
On the Differences in the Four Gospels 76
The Author...78
Structure of the Gospel...79
Part 1
1   The Genealogy (Chapter 1:1-17) 84

2	The Circumstances of His Birth (Chapter 1:18 - 2:23)...87
3	His Forerunner (Chapter 3)..94
4	Is He Competent To Rule? (Chapter 4)..........................98
5	The Laws of the Kingdom (Chapters 5-7)....................102
6	Messianic Miracles (Chapter 8:1 - 9:35)......................113
7	The Offer of the Kingdom (Chapter 9:36 - 10:42)........118
8	How was the Message Received? (Chapter 11)..........123
9	The Rejection of the King (Chapter 12)......................126
10	An Unexpected Move (Chapter 13)..............................131
11	Paradoxical Events during the King's Absence (Chapter 14)..136
12	The King's Loyalists (Chapters 15-16)........................138

Part 2

Outline of Chapters 17-25 143
13	The Transfiguration (Chapter 17:1-13).........................144
14	Replies to Questions (Chapters 17-18).......................146
15	More Questions (Chapters 19-21) 153
16	Still More Questions (Chapters 22-23)........................160
17	When Shall These Things Be, And What Shall Be The Sign of Thy Coming? (Chapters 24-25).............169

Part 3

18	The Trial and Death of Jesus Christ (Chapters 26-28) 183
19	The Resurrection and its Sequel (Chapter 28) 197

The Epistle to the Ephesians

The Purpose of God 202
Paul's Prayer 211
What a Change!... 216
The Jew and the Gentile.. 224
The Mystery 232
Ministry in the Church.. 239
Gathered Threads 245
Some Practical Lessons 251

Paul's Pastoral Epistles - Introduction 258

The Epistle of 1 Timothy

1 Timothy 1 263
1 Timothy 2 267
1 Timothy 3 272
1 Timothy 4 277
1 Timothy 5 281
1 Timothy 6 285

The Epistle of 2 Timothy

2 Timothy 1 289
2 Timothy 2 295
2 Timothy 3 300
2 Timothy 4 303

The Epistle to Titus

Titus 1 309

Titus 2 313
Titus 3 317

The Epistle to Hebrews - Him That Endured

Foreword 322
Introduction 324
Chapter 1 - Authorship 327
Chapter 2 - The Aim of the Epistle 330
Chapter 3 - God Speaks in His Son 336
Chapter 4 - What is Man? 346
Chapter 5 - Rest 357
Chapter 6 - Our Great High Priest 365
Chapter 7 - The Perfect Sacrifice 373
Chapter 8 - Earnest Warnings 386
Chapter 9 - Faith 397
Chapter 10 - Will Ye Also Go Away? 406

Foreword

Mr Ebenezer W. Rogers
(1893-1977)
Precious Memories

He was known to all as Mr E.W., a form of address which he welcomed and encouraged even the young believers to use. I had noticed this name in assembly magazines listed amongst the speakers at conferences in England and Scotland. However, it was at the Annual Conference in Lurgan in October 1946 that I first heard him speak. What I did not know at that time, was that while Mr E.W. was a very well-known minister of the Word throughout the British Isles, and was often called to speak at conferences abroad, this was the first time he had been invited to the Lurgan Conference. Scotsmen of course were welcome, they were almost kin to us, and we had had several faithful preachers from Wales whose ministry had won many hearts; but an Englishman, and coming from London too!

Speaking personally, I was thrilled to be there as this was my very first time to attend Lurgan Conference as a believer. My parental home was at the rural end of Union Street in Lurgan. The Gospel Hall stood half-way along Union Street. Directly across the street from the Gospel Hall was the Salvation Army Hall, kindly loaned for the Conference Bible Readings. At the town end of Union Street was Lurgan Town Hall, which the Town Council leased to the assembly for the Conference Ministry meetings. I had been taken to the Conference since I could walk, but things were different now because two months before this Conference, on Monday night the 5th August 1946, a young man of 17 summers had got saved. This was my first Conference as a believer.

If truth be told, and had I any choice in the matter, I would have preferred to listen to one of our preachers from Ulster. I had heard most of them in my unsaved days and thought that many of our local preachers could do better than an Englishman. However, saved just a few weeks and the joy of salvation filling the soul, I was prepared to listen to this new voice.

Every seat was filled long before the time for the meeting. Preliminaries completed, at the appointed hour Mr E.W. stood to his feet and was introduced to the gathering. Though slightly below average height he had a natural dignity that carried authority; his voice reinforced that authority as he handled the Scriptures most reverently. As he began his exposition a hush fell over the company as they realised that here was a man who knew his Bible and could unfold the deepest truths with simplicity and clarity. Few who were present would forget the teaching of that passage: it was written clearly in the tablets of memory.

Any prejudice had long since melted away. This Englishman had clearly given his life to the study of the Word of God – it seemed to be a part of him. With divinely given ability he handled the truth reverently and with a total competency that reached through to the minds, and then the hearts, of the audience. As I heard him on other occasions down the years I recognised that his mastery of the subject was always complete; he had the ability to handle every question with honesty and fairness, even when the questions came from those who did not agree with his interpretation. His courtesy was unfailing, even with 'awkward' brethren who appeared from time to time. To the genuine seeker his patience was inexhaustible, but I felt sorry at times for the debater who tried to trick him into some faulty deduction. This was not cold, clinical exposition. In those first studies, when we came to the words 'But we see Jesus' (Heb. 2:9), there was warmth in his voice that drew worship from those present at the Bible Reading that we would never forget.

At this point my personal impressions rush back, as I see the teacher *par excellence* leading a Bible Reading as it should be led. He became an inspiration and a pattern that I can recall with absolute clarity, even after seventy years. The picture that came to my mind that day, and was summoned up immediately when I was asked to write this foreword, is the picture drawn by Oliver Goldsmith of the village schoolmaster in *The Deserted Village*. In my memory I still see him just as I first saw him, a solitary figure dominating a gathering of over 400 men and teaching from the Word of God with clarity and authority. Even those who did not agree with his interpretation were compelled to re-examine their case. Every eye was upon him. With Bible open in his left hand from which he read clearly from time to time, his voice unstrained yet filling the hall, and his right index finger moving swiftly from Bible to audience, he applied scriptural truth to the conscience of his hearers. With no thought of disrespect to the audience, for I was one of them, the lines I had read in school came to mind;

> *Beside yon straggling fence that skirts the way,*
> *With blossomed furze unprofitably gay,*
> *There, in his noisy mansion, skilled to rule,*
> *The village master taught his little school . . .*
> *The village all declared how much he knew:*
> *'Twas certain he could write, and cipher too;*
> *Lands he could measure, terms and tides presage,*
> *And even the story ran that he could gauge.*
> *In arguing too, the parson owned his skill,*
> *For even tho' vanquished, he could argue still;*
> *While words of learned length and thundering sound,*
> *Amazed the gazing rustics ranged around;*
> *And still they gazed, and still the wonder grew,*
> *That one small head could carry all he knew.*

I was one of the 'rustics' who watched for the first time a competent scholar who, without reference to any notes, opened my understanding, and I believe the understanding of many in that audience, to the worth of the Hebrew Epistle and the greatness of our Saviour. There was no question who was the schoolmaster as we sat at his feet. As questions poured in from every side, courteously, skilfully and yet perfectly in command of the whole situation, he guided the audience through the difficult passages. In my judgment he was one of the most able teachers of his day. I saw it that first day and have enjoyed it over the years. He had enthusiasm and certainty in the truth he taught, and, in this way of teaching it, he was the master. He really loved the cut and thrust of debate. No hesitation, repetition, retrogression or diversion was allowed as the truth was brought out of the selected passage.

When I saw Mr E.W. handle the Bible Readings, I thought of him as a superb teacher. When I gathered with around 800 others in Lurgan Town Hall that same evening, I was thrilled to see him move to the rostrum and show himself gifted as a powerful preacher of the Word. He began his message with the first walk he had taken through Lurgan town: Market Street, Main Street, Queen Street, naming the religious buildings that had caught his eye. The audience could follow his steps and then pause before each building. First the Roman Catholic Chapel, then the majesty of the Anglican Church in the very centre of the town, then Methodist, Congregational, Presbyterian, Quaker, Baptist, Salvation Army, Gospel Hall. The question before the audience was: where could the young believer find a spiritual home amidst this denominational confusion?

To find out, Mr E.W. took us through the Acts of the Apostles and the first thirty years of church history. With a masterly touch he brought out the absolutely unique character of the local assembly, as distinct from any denominational gathering. The same Holy Scripture, applied by the same Holy Spirit that led the sinner to the person of the Saviour, could and would, if we allow it in this later day, lead us to the place where saints could find fellowship; and there He would be found, as He promised (Matt. 18:20). It was a ministry used of God to establish many young believers who had been saved recently in the truth of assembly fellowship. It was a life changing ministry for many of us.

Down through the years I have often thanked God for the privilege of hearing Mr E.W. at the height of his powers as a teacher and a preacher. I owe much to him. From those very first meetings, I personally had a deep longing to be able to handle the Word of God as he did. I have my notes from those meetings and have used them in five continents, acknowledging tribute to him.

Mr E. W. brought dignity to the platform. He normally stood entirely motionless, except for that wagging schoolmaster's index finger and the movement of his lips pouring out words that brought clarity to his subject. Then the pause, as he allowed a new facet of the subject to grip the minds of believers. Due to health problems in early years he was entirely self-taught, including Greek, Hebrew, and shorthand. In his working life as a Civil Servant, he moved up the ranks to the head of The Patent Office where the very principles of detailed analysis, descriptive conciseness, and dogmatic definiteness, that set him apart amongst teachers and preachers, marked him for responsibility in his daily work.

In 1951 he retired early from the Civil Service to give more time to the Lord's work. In this period he made many trips abroad, especially to join Mr J.M. Davies in work in India where his missionary daughter was working for the Lord. His major work, however, was done throughout the British Isles, and very especially in the large Bible Readings of Netherhall in Largs, Ayr, Eastbourne and many other centres, where Mr Albert Leckie was his usual partner. God used him mightily in the preservation of assembly truth in the 20th Century. When I heard him that first time, little did I think that when age caught up with him I would be asked to partner Mr Albert Leckie in those same Bible Readings. I must have learned a little from the man I regarded as the outstanding teacher of my time.

After being asked to write this foreword, the very next morning a book which I had ordered some time before arrived by post. It was a copy of the Seventieth Anniversary Edition of the *Precious Seed* magazine. Turning over the pages of the March-April Issue of 1947, I found a letter from Mr E.W. Rogers to the Editors. It was in answer to their request for his impressions of his recent visit as an invited speaker at the Lurgan Conference in October 1946, rumoured to be numerically the largest in its history. I was thrilled to read the letter and learn something I had not previously known - that this was his very first time to be present at the Lurgan Conference.

Mr E.W. responded most heartily: 'I had often heard of the Lurgan Conference but not until October 1946 was I able to give myself the pleasure of being at it. It was a time never to be forgotten. The sight of so very large a number of brethren only, all gathered together in earnest desire to learn more of the Word of God with the view of making themselves more efficient in the ministry of that Word, will long be remembered. Nor will the brethren themselves easily forget the steaming hot mid-day meals given by the kindly and diligent labours of a band of very hard working sisters. They did admirably, for every one of us had a hot meal: the relay system worked splendidly as the meals were passed from the cookhouse to the consumer.' Speaking very warmly of the discussion, he sums up: 'There were no unprofitable wordy and prolonged debates. The Lord helped all wonderfully to be restrained.' He goes on to say, 'If I criticised at all it would be as to the hardness of the forms and the narrow width thereof. For 2.5 hours to sit on such was itself an achievement – seeing that none complained.' In that letter he said he would be very happy to go back, if asked. He was asked, and he did go back many times in the following years.

I have often found profit in the writings of our beloved brother. Illumination on scriptural teaching, education in spiritual training, and elucidation in spiritual exercise can always be drawn from the writings of a man who had made such a deep impression upon a young believer and set a pattern that, despite much failure, may show features that glorify the Lord. If so, it will be because he had a very good teacher – the best. There are very few preachers whom I have heard over the years who could handle the Scriptures so consistently, that every time I heard their voices it was to my own spiritual enrichment.

Mr E.W. fills this unique place in my memory, and in his writings I can still hear his voice and still see the finger point, and I know it will be to spiritual profit. I am thrilled that our brother Mervyn Wishart has undertaken the Herculean task of republishing them. These volumes published by John Ritchie will be a vital step in the preservation of the writings, as well as making them readily available to another generation. I know they will be of incalculable value in setting forth practical assembly truth, to the clarification and preservation of which our brother gave his life in devoted service. There will be few assemblies in the UK where his voice was not heard and appreciated.

I am not personally acquainted with the many overseas trips he made to reach assemblies who needed help. I do know that I followed him in meetings in Gospel Halls across South Africa from Johannesburg through Cape Town to Port Elizabeth a few years later, and the memory of his teaching was still fruitful, fragrant and fresh. Families were still talking of the help he had been in establishing them in the truth of the assembly position, and helping them to deal with the many problems that were already dividing assemblies in that land. He did this with grace and yet with truth. I know these writings will contribute to that same purpose. We do pray that the Lord will continue to use them for the good of His people and for His own glory.

Jim Allen
Newtownabbey, Co. Antrim, N. Ireland.
June 2019

The Fall

Man's present state – not always so

That man, who is both sinful and mortal, was not originally created thus by the Holy and Eternal Creator is certain, since all that God does partakes of the nature of what He is. It follows, therefore, that the present condition of man is one into which he fell, and it is the purpose of this paper to consider the only Authorised record of such fall. The validity of that record is due to its Divine revelation and inspiration.

To be read literally

It may be emphasised that this Record should be read literally and, whatever may be its deeper meaning lying beneath the surface, it should be regarded as simple history. To treat the Record as mere allegory will involve one in logical difficulties with other parts of Scripture as *e.g.*, Romans 5:12, 1 Timothy 2:13, 14.

Headings

In order to aid in the understanding of this chapter the subject may be considered under four heads, suggested by the words of the Lord Jesus to the Pharisees when He rebuked them for overlooking the weightier matters of "Law, Judgment, Mercy, and Faith" (Matt. 23:23).

LAW

The prohibition

The created pair, Adam and his helpmeet, placed in the Garden of Eden, had imposed upon them by their Creator and Benefactor but one restriction, viz: that the "Tree of knowledge of good and evil"[1] was forbidden, and its fruit was not to be eaten by them. The reason for this law was not that that tree was of special use to God, nor was it intrinsically pernicious to man, but it served as a means of enforcing the claims of God in His own creation, and reminding the creature that he was not independent, but dependent on God; that he was not the owner of the garden but simply the tenant. It was as the imposition of a peppercorn rent (a nominal rent sometimes imposed today for retaining legal rights) asserting God's rights in the garden and over the creature, and reminding Man of such rights.

The *modus operandi*

The Devil, who approached the woman (note, not the man) in the Serpent[2] (John calls him "that old serpent, the Devil, Satan"), first cast a *doubt* upon God's word. The woman, who lent her ear to the Serpent (it should have been given to her husband), thereupon *distorted* God's word by both adding to and detracting from it. The Serpent in response *denied* God's word, and the woman thereafter *disobeyed* it.

---

[1] So called because of its resultant effect upon the disobedient participants.
[2] It is the consistent witness of Scripture that the animal or human tools used by Satan are themselves always subjected to consequential judgment, e.g., Judas, The Beast (Rev. 19), The Swine, etc.

Such is the downward course of the Fall. (Who can doubt it was a Fall? What folly to speak of the Ascent of Man!) From doubt to distortion; from distortion to denial: from denial to disobedience: and all this the result of negotiations with the Devil, who is liar and deceiver.

Hath God said?

To doubt God's word and to question its plain force and meaning is the thin end of the wedge that ends in disaster.

Perverted orthodoxy

To distort God's word, though it may have the appearance of orthodoxy, is to libel God and to deceive self. These two things the woman did. She added to God's word by inserting the detail "touch," which made God appear harsh and arbitrary. She also detracted from God's word by *substituting* for the word "shall" the word "lest," deceiving herself into the belief that the penalty might not prove altogether inevitable. No marvel that God speaks so sternly later concerning those who "add to or take from" His own written utterances.

"Ye shall not die."

To deny God's word of necessity issues from the former two, for Doubt entertained leads to a wresting (Distortion) of the Scriptures to serve one's own sinful desires, resulting in a plain contradiction of their obvious meaning (Denial). This was the course followed here. Satan asserted that it was God's jealous regard of His own position that led Him to deprive His creatures of the higher rank of the equality with God[3] which,

---

[3] See Revised Version, "as God"

by taking of the fruit of the tree, they could achieve. In a word, he attributed to God motives other than kindness towards the creatures who were surrounded by every evidence of His kindness. Satan's own earlier aspirations of pride had resulted in his fall (1 Tim. 3:6). He, therefore, would now adopt a similar procedure to secure the fall of the woman, and, through her, of the man also, thus again (see chap. 1:2) spoiling the handiwork of God.

It was true, as Satan said, that "their eyes were opened," but it was to their own nakedness, and not to their elevation.

"She took and gave."

To disobey God's word is the final downward step which secured, as it always does, the execution of God's forewarned calamity. The woman threw open the avenues called (a) "the lust of the flesh" (b) "the lust of the eye" and (c) "the pride of life," and observing the tree was (a) good for food, (b) pleasant to the eyes, and (c) useful to make one wise, she, being deceived by the Devil, took, although without economic necessity, and gave to her husband who, "hearkening to the voice of his wife"[4] and knowing right well what he was doing, did eat also (see 1 Tim. 2:13, 14). For him to eat was to disobey the voice of God: for him not to eat, was to forfeit the partner given him by God. What was to be done? He loved his wife and for her sake he took from her hand the forbidden fruit, and shared with her the consequences.

---

[4] Note how Satan confuses God's order. Man should have hearkened to God and the woman to her husband but, as it was, the man hearkened to his wife and the woman hearkened to the serpent.

JUDGMENT

God's law cannot be broken with impunity: judgment of necessity must follow disobedience, since the moral government of God in His own creation must be upheld. Accordingly, in this Record we discover judgment falling on the Devil, the Serpent, the Woman, the Earth, and the Man.

The Conqueror conquered

God's judgment on the Devil is stated in Genesis 3:15. It is God's counter-move to the Devil's move. The Devil used a woman to bring sin into the world; God will use a woman to bring the Redeemer into the world. The Conqueror of the woman is to be conquered by the Seed of the Woman. This was fulfilled when the Redeemer, "born of a woman", came into conflict with the Devil at Calvary. There He suffered, but there the Devil was conquered. The heel of the Conqueror suffered as it was placed in victory upon the head of the Serpent.[5] Other parts of Scripture show that the Devil's eternal doom is to be sealed by the Lord Himself, Who at Calvary potentially defeated him, and is later to consign him to the lake of fire.

The Animal Serpent

The animal *serpent* too was permanently judged for, whatever Millennial blessings will be shared by the brute creation, the judgment which here originally placed it on its belly with dust as its food will not even in Millennial days be removed (Isa. 65:25).

---

[5] The picture is of a Victor standing erect with his heel on the serpent's head, whilst the tail of the serpent is lashing that heel.

The Woman's penalty

The judgment upon the *Woman* is plain and self-evident in connection with which should be read 1 Timothy 2:15. In sin the woman took the lead, but God originally intended that man whom He formed first should in all earthly matters have priority. How eloquently does Paul's inspired utterance tell that in the midst of judgment God remembers mercy.

Creation fallen

The *Creation* was subjected to vanity and made the subject of the curse for the sake of man, since God would not have fallen man in an unfallen creation. When man is restored, Creation will be restored (Rom. 8:21). In the meantime, the thorn, sweat and sorrow persist, in the midst of which man has to work in order to provide the physical means of subsistence.[6]

The Man's penalty

On *Man* death has ensued: from dust he came, to dust he goes.

How touching that our sinless Lord in His sufferings partook of all these.

A sinless substitute

"They put on Him a Crown of *thorns*."
"He *sweat* as it were great drops of blood."
"My soul is exceeding *sorrowful*."
"Thou has brought Me into the *dust* of death."

---

[6] It may be questioned whether the present economic troubles are not largely due to the avoidance of manual work by so large a number of black-coated employees.

He thus bore the judgment of man's sin, and died for the sinner.

So God's Word came true: "In the day thou eatest thereof thou shall surely die". Separation from God was spiritual death, immediate and felt; "to dust thou shalt return," involved physical death, ultimate but real.

MERCY

In the midst of judgment God remembers mercy and throughout this Record it shines.

The Cry

"Adam, where art thou?" is the cry of God for His hiding, naked, fearful creature – not of a vindictive proprietor about to arrest the thief, nor of a judge revelling in the opportunity to strike, but of one who, delighting in communion with man, sorely felt the loss of it when man fled and hid. The Call, "Where art thou?" was a call of Mercy.

Even though the Man blamed God – "the Woman Thou gavest me" – His mercy is not stayed. How full of mercy is verse 15.

The Conquest

By Him Who is to come through the "Woman Thou gavest me," the destroyer is to be destroyed: the deceiver is to be taken by his own craftiness. Sin and the Devil are not always to prevail. A Deliverer and Deliverance are announced. What mercy!

The Costs

Although man tried to cover himself by his own efforts,

God substituted coats of skin,[7] coats instead of breeches, skin instead of withering leaves – nay more, a slain substitute suffering death to cover the death-deservers. What Mercy! Foreshadowing God's mercy in the slain Lamb of Calvary by Whose death all naked sinners may be clothed.

The Barrier

How merciful too of God to bar the way of the Tree of Life! That the sinful first man and woman and all their sinful posterity should live concurrently for ever on earth would make society intolerable. Even the death of some is a mercy to the living that are left, and perhaps to the dead themselves.

Ere that Tree of Life could be eaten by man that revolving sword must first be met and stayed, and He Who met it was our Blessed Lord Jesus Christ against Whom the sword was drawn at Calvary. Now redeemed sinners have right without fear or risk to that Tree of Life (See Rev. 22:14, R.V.).

FAITH

Life instead of death

God speaks in verse 19 of dust and death, and man immediately in the next verse calls his wife's name, "Eve", *i.e.*, "living". God pronounces death, but man speaks of life, this strange response being not so much a reply to verse 19 but faith's grasp of the truth of verse 15. God says Redemption is to come through the Woman. "Here," says Adam, "is the Woman, and I believe God that through her Seed sin's judgment will

---

[7]The skin of the burnt offering was for the offering Priest (Lev. 7:8).

be removed, I therefore call her Eve – living": such was the confession of faith.

Wherever faith is found God always answers, and accordingly God's immediate response is to cover the guilty pair. So it always runs – "Death" – Sin's Penalty (v. 19): "Eve" – faith's utterance (v. 20): "Coats" – God's response. And gladly did man part with his leafy effort for God's adornment.

The Life of Faith

Exemplified in Elijah (1 Kings 17)

The contents of this chapter can briefly be summarized by the text, "The just shall live by faith." Herein is presented a man whose life was maintained by daily faith in the Living God.

Elijah comes on the scene as suddenly as a meteor flashes through the heavens: he is God's man for the moment. The declension of Israel was at its lowest. The "most provoking" king that ever sat on Israel's throne was in power. An unholy matrimonial alliance had been effected. Idol worship had been established: God's word had been defied, and Jericho had been built with its foreshadowed bitter consequences. In such circumstances, the man of God emerges from seclusion with the thunder-clap announcement that "There shall not be dew nor rain these years, but according to my word." Mark those last two words – "My word" – an extraordinary claim for man to make, but explained by James, who informs us that "Elijah" though "a man of like passions with ourselves" prayed that it might not rain, and it rained not. His was a -

Prayer of Faith

Resultant upon a knowledge of God's word through Moses, that departure from Him would be visited by drought and famine. It revealed that Elijah was in the mind of God. He, thoughtless of his own safety, but zealous for God's glory, pleaded that even such a severe judgment might come if, perchance, it would bring the apostate people back to Himself. Elijah, by faith, spoke to Ahab without equivocation – "There shall not be" – for he believed that that for which he prayed he would receive. He was confident that both God's word and the people's condition justified his petition.

The answer to his prayer would, inevitably, expose Elijah also to the privations that the nation would suffer. Moreover, his declaration to the King would further expose him to his relentless revenge. These two dangers, however, but furnished the opportunity for Elijah to prove his God, and for God to display His care and power on behalf of His servant. "Go, hide thyself by the brook Cherith" was the direction given to the man of God. "Beside those still waters" he was to live a -

Life of Faith

In which he would be secure both from enemy and famine. There the God of creation used the unclean ravens as His messengers commanding them to do His bidding with unremitting regularity. Elijah's daily food was free, whilst others were concerned with soaring prices; he, thereby, preserving a healthy independence of all. His food was plentiful – bread and flesh both morning and evening – whilst others were faced with increasing scarcity. It was regular, whilst others under the stroke of judgment were not sure of the next meal. All this was the blessed outcome of the "obedience of faith" which led him to take that separate low-lying place ('Cherith' means 'separation'), not in a vaunting superiority but in humble dependence (see Prov. 30:17). There he proved Jehovah to be "his shepherd," and there he "did not want."

Our day largely corresponds to Elijah's: it has always been and ever will be till the Lord Himself reigns, that God needs men to testify for Him against current sins. Such testimony will involve suffering and privation, but He is ever the God of miracles Who, in the most unlikely ways, supplies the needs of His witnesses.

Attempts have been made to destroy the miraculous, and to explain the ravens as being the Arabians, but whilst the Hebrew word may be difficult, it is plain that God's end in hiding Elijah would have been defeated had the Arabians discovered his whereabouts, for news would rapidly travel. Moreover, what need would there be for the Arabians laboriously to make the visit twice a day to him, since an adequate supply could have lasted for many days? Besides, was such a supply of food available? No, the simple reader may safely believe that God used the ravens to feed His servant.

When the antitype of Ahab is in power, that is when the Man of Sin rules, there will be Elijahs bearing witness to the true God, and who will then experience the same care and power – "I am Jehovah: I change not."

Whatever is of earth, however, is bound ultimately to "dry up" albeit that in the meantime God, in sovereignty, might use it. Such happened to the brook. In drinking from that brook Elijah appeared to be living on his capital, but He who knew all beforehand had already made arrangements for the maintenance of His servant. He is to go to Zarephath and there, by divine command, to be sustained by a widow woman. How strange, how humiliating, for this hardy, strong, hairy, bold, ascetic man to be dependent on a widow. No, he was not. He was dependent on God: the widow was but God's servant for the benefit of Elijah, although she was "mistress of the house". This man of God was to prove by experience that "Jah is my God" (as "Elijah" means). It was a "path of righteousness" whither he had been led "for His name's sake".

The incidents connected with Elijah's journey to, and stay with, the widow at Zarephath display the -

Work of Faith

"Faith without works is dead," but true faith:

> *"Is a living power from heaven*
> *Which grasps the promise God has given."*

Accordingly, although it appeared to be an utterly absurd procedure, he goes thither. No fear seems to have entered his heart lest, since the place lay near to wicked Jezebel's father, he should discover him and disclose the news secretly and maliciously to his daughter.

Such was the condition of the people that, although there were "many widows in Israel" in those days (a solemn state), God would not allow one of them to be entrusted with the care of His servant. Was it that not one was willing so to do? Was there no faith in Israel then?

The providential dealings of God in the lives of His people are always instructive. When Elijah arrived at the city, the widow was about "gathering of sticks" to make a cake for herself and her son (she puts herself first) and thereafter to die. Why, indeed, trouble to make or eat the cake if that inevitable death were soon to follow? But, Elijah being in the right place – it was to him the "path of righteousness" – and having now been assured he has found her of whom the Lord spake (for the woman making no reference to her husband was manifestly a widow), concludes that it is at her house he is to stay, and by the word of the Lord the three are to be maintained. Thus faith is operative: *he obeys* in going to Zarephath; *he seeks* for the widow through whom he is to be maintained, and *he abides* at her house, not as a "paying guest" but as the "messenger of Jehovah".

The woman's faith, too, is active. She believed the promise concerning the miraculous multiplication of both meal and oil, although it was the *failing* brook that had sent the man of God to her. She staggered not at the promise through unbelief. Scientific impossibilities had no place with her. Unhesitatingly she complies with that strange injunction, "Make a little cake for me first." Hitherto, she had put herself first: now she "sought first the Kingdom of God and His righteousness" and other things were added to her. She honoured the Lord with the first-fruits of her meagre substance, only to prove that her barns were filled with plenty and her presses burst out with new wine. The Lord would ever say to us – *Me first*.

It was faith, too, that led her to go to the barrel and cruse day by day and to use therefrom, not grazing at the bottom with misgiving, but daily drawing upon the ever-existing supply, knowing that the word of the Lord abideth for ever, and it was His word that was preached in the good news brought to her.

Oh for a like faith in God in these days. Why should it not be? He is the same yesterday, and today, and for ever; His ways are everlasting. Tables are still spread in the wilderness; heads are still anointed with oil; cups still flow over.

Faith is more precious than gold that perisheth, and if this latter be tried with fire so that it may be freed from dross and impurities, it is no wonder that God deems it necessary to try the faith of His people. Hence the next scene presents the -

Test of Faith

He tested the faith both of Elijah and the widow. The son of the woman dies, although it seemed to be that it was to prevent that very thing that the supply of meal and oil was maintained. How strange that this boy should die in the midst of plenty! It would not have appeared strange had he died through famine. Why has God allowed this untoward event just now? It was, indeed, "the valley of the shadow of death".

Elijah, however, was at Zarephath (a workshop for the purpose of smelting and purifying metals) and faith – so valuable in God's estimate – had to be tested. If he had prayed that it should not rain, and it rained not, why should he not pray again to his God that this boy should revive? Getting alone with God – leaving in heart and mind this world altogether – going "aloft" to scenes in which earth had no place, he speaks to God about, and for, the boy, and his prayer is heard. The lad revives. Faith has triumphed. It has known what it is to be alone with God, away from the running brook, the visiting ravens, the distressed widow. Elijah was alone with God, not to speak to Him about maintaining life, but doing the even greater miracle of restoring life. And he triumphs.

The woman's faith also must be tested and purified. She, too, could not understand why the God who had multiplied the food supply should not resist the incursions of death. Why has God allowed her boy to die?

Her conscience is exercised: foregoing sin comes back to her memory with vivid force. Had the God who had proved Himself merciful to her now become vindictive and punitive? Had His servant whose arrival had meant life and peace to her now become a messenger of death and judgment? She could not understand it: she must leave it.

She does not know God as Elijah does. She speaks of Him as, "Jehovah thy God" and cannot say with Elijah, "Oh, Jehovah my God". Nevertheless, she feels a peculiar safety in leaving the child with this "man of God," but her inactivity is a great trial to her. She would like to be in the upper chamber to see how things are faring; to hear the prayer; to be able to do something herself. What a trial this enforced inactivity was to her, and is to us! But she can do no more. She can only hope and wait for Elijah's God to restore the boy whom He had already so far fed.

But faith in the last instance always triumphs. The -

Triumph of Faith

Is seen in the handing of the child by Elijah to his mother – "See thy son liveth". She was one who "by faith received her dead back to life again" (Heb. 11:35). It is always so. Faith conquers despite universal declensions, famines, starvations and death. Indeed, faith reckons that with God all things are possible and, therefore, it wins through. It is sure that "goodness and mercy will follow" throughout life's day, to be crowned with eternal residence in the "Father's house".

The Consecration of the Priests

The opening chapters of the book of Leviticus are occupied with a detailed statement of the various sacrifices prescribed by God to be offered for the people, all of which speak of the death of Christ in its many-sided characteristics.

Chapters 8 and 9, however, deal with the consecration of the priests, for God would emphasise that He has provided for His people both *sacrifice* and *priest*.

While under law the sacrifice and priest were distinguished, now our Lord Jesus Christ is both. When He died He "offered Himself" to God, thereby being the sacrifice: now in resurrection He is a "priest after the order of Melchizedek".

The believer, furthermore, *should be* a sacrifice, whilst he also is a priest. He *should* "present his body a living sacrifice": He is one of the "kingdom of priests": one of that "royal priesthood".

Priesthood is not a privilege reserved exclusively for those who are appointed by men and who wear special garb: nor is it a matter of high spiritual attainment: priesthood is the common possession of all believers in the Lord Jesus Christ, each having the right of direct approach to God without the intermediation of any other save Christ Himself, the Great High Priest.

In these chapters Aaron is sometimes alone and certain things apply exclusively to him, while at other times he stands associated with "his sons" and certain things apply to both. Thus, too, Christ in some matters stands unique, and exclusive, whilst in others "His people" are joined with Him. The reader would be well repaid to examine the chapters in view of this.

Here the Christian may "look back" on his own history and see set out in type facts which are now historically true of him: he too may "look up," and see here set forth things which are operative now: he, further, may "look on" and see set forth events which yet shall be.

The Look Back

Four things were done to the priests: they were washed, clothed, sprinkled, and anointed. The washing rendered them clean preparatory to the clothing; the clothing was the external indication of the new office about to be held; the sprinkling with the blood was the bond which now held them under obligation to God in that office; while the oil was the duly appointed means of their installation into that office.

Of the Corinthians it is said, "But ye have been *washed*"; and to the Lord Jesus is praise ascribed thus: "Unto Him that loveth us and hath washed us from our sins in His own blood". The Lord Jesus spake to His own thus: "Ye are clean".

The priestly garments constituted suitable *clothing* for the activities of the priests. So, too, the "best robe" constituted

The Consecration of the Priests

suitable clothing for the presence at the Father's table. The believer is *"in Christ"*: "graced *in* the Beloved".

Peter speaks of the believer as "being *sprinkled* with the blood of Jesus Christ" and the writer to the Hebrews encourages his addressees "to draw near to God having the heart sprinkled from an evil conscience and the body washed with pure water".

The oil with which the priests were *anointed* speaks of the Holy Spirit who is the "unction" possessed by all believers, each having been sealed on the moment that faith became operative with that Holy Spirit of Promise.

All Christians then are washed: clothed: sprinkled and anointed.

The washing removes the uncleanness: the clothing confers beauty: the sprinkling incurs obligation: the anointing imparts competency.

The Look Up

The priests were instructed "not to go out for a period of seven days," a type of the separation of the believer from the world for the whole period of his earthly course from conversion onwards.

They further were provided with food: the "breast" and the "shoulder" of the sacrifice, speaking respectively of the love and power of Christ, are available at all times for the sustenance of the believer. These two things are joined together, for while some earthly friends would help (they have the breast), they are unable to do so (they have not the shoulder); while with other people it is the reverse; in the case of our Lord Jesus who died for us, however, both love and power are conjoined for the help of His own. He *can* and *will* help.

They were instructed to "boil and then eat it" corresponding to "roasting what is taken in hunting": or to "chewing the cud": or to "turning these things over in the heart".

Another thing which was to characterise them during these whole seven days was "that they should keep the charge of the Lord", that is, obedience. It should be the consistent conduct of the believer during all his life. Disobedience is a most expensive thing: it lost for Adam and his race the original bliss of Eden: it cost Moses entrance into the land; it cost David his prestige and domestic happiness; it cost the prophet his life; and in all cases it demands a heavy price.

Again "their hands were filled" with that with which they should worship God. None there had empty hands, yet how often it is that we "come before the Lord empty". As sinners it was good that we said, "Nothing in my hand I bring", but this should never be on our lips as priests; our hands should be filled with the excellence of our Lord who died and rose again, which we may present before God for His own pleasure and our own acceptance.

The Look On

Chapter 9 shows "Moses and Aaron" coming out to the people, a type of Christ as King (Moses) and Priest (Aaron) coming out from heaven to earth to the relief and blessing of His earthly people the Jew.

When they came out "the glory of the Lord appeared", and

when our Lord comes out He will "be manifested in glory" and the believer will be with Him.

They thereafter "blessed the people", foreshadowing that that down-trodden afflicted people, the Jew, as today they are, will then on His appearance be "blessed" by Him, their national status being re-established and they being made the head of all nations.

Thereupon the people "shouted and bowed themselves", the song of praise issuing in the silence of worship, and when the Lord appears later He will not only be the subject of the song of the redeemed, but He will also be the object of their worship and adoration in silence.

The Cleansing of the Leper

The disease of leprosy is a type of sin. Leprosy affects a man's body; sin affects both body and soul. Leprosy affects a man for time; sin affects him for eternity. Leprosy will put a man in his grave; sin will send a man to hell.

So grave a matter is sin in the eyes of God that He gave His only begotten Son to deal with the matter effectively and finally by His being made sin.

So grave a disease was leprosy that God furnishes in two long chapters (Lev. 13 and 14) instructions concerning its discovery in an individual, house, or garment, and rules of action both for the leper himself, and for the priest on his cleansing.

It is significant that no cure for leprosy is prescribed. It was not curable; when all was out, the leper was pronounced clean, as when there is full confession today God freely forgives the sinner. God in grace *gives* cleansing both from leprosy and from sin. (See Rev. 1:5).

The Evidences of Leprosy

In order to diagnose rightly the trouble the following guides were furnished the priest.

He was to look for a trouble *"deeper than the skin"*. This sin is. It is a disease with which one is born (Psa. 51:5). It shows itself in the child and in the aged man and at all stages in the interim. Criminal tendency is a trouble "deeper than the skin," and all other milder forms of wrong show that the spring thereof is in the heart and nature; not on the surface.

Again, he was to look for *"raw active flesh"* – an open sore – ugly to look at. The fallen nature of man in the New Testament is called "flesh" and when active it will display itself in that which is "raw" or ugly: for all manifestations of sin are ugly, and the closer one lives in communion with God the more ugly does it appear.

Again, he was to look for *"White hair"* – the sure sign of decay and death approaching, for the "wages of sin is death". It is the inevitable issue. The white hair was the outward indicator of approaching dissolution.

Lastly, he was to look for a *"yellow thin hair"*. Why yellow? Blue is the heavenly colour; green is the earthly colour; but since there is only one other place, "yellow" must be the hellish colour. This is confirmed by the fact that the Hebrew root of the word "yellow" is "burning" – and hell is the place of burning. It is the manifestation in the individual of what is devilish.

Pronounced A Leper

When the man is pronounced a leper there are things which he has not to do, as others he has to do.

He was *not to attend his hair* – it was to be let go loose. Why? Well, what is the use of decorating the flesh and brushing the hair and keeping up a good exterior if the interior is corrupt? It would be a repetition of the "whited sepulchre"; or "washing the outside of the platter but leaving the inside"; reformation instead of regeneration.

Again, he was to *rend his clothes*. By so doing he would acknowledge he was virtually a dead man, and thus mourned his death. He had been exposed to the eye of God and nothing could be hid. Why then use raiment? It must be rent.

Further, his upper lip was to be covered with his hand and *he was to cry, "Unclean, Unclean,"* as did Isaiah in his notable sixth chapter. In separation and solitude, he was compelled to own his state. It is the condition of a soul under conviction.

Lastly, he was *to dwell in a separate house,* outside the camp; for the sinner is outside of the circle of God's blessing and the communion of His people. He is of them that are without.

The Cleansing of the Leper

In respect of this certain ceremonial laws were given by God, compromising –

> Two birds.
> Two offerings.
> Two materials.
> Two actions.

The *two birds* speak of Christ dead (the slain bird) and Christ risen (the bird let loose). Only by that can the sinner be cleansed from his sin. He has washed us in His blood; and given assurance thereof in that He has been raised from the dead.

The two *offerings* are respectively the burnt offering meeting God's claims and the sin offering meeting man's need. It is only as this is understood that the sinner can be assured of his cleansing. He must know that the death of Christ has satisfied God's requirements and is adequate to meet his need.

The *two materials* are "blood and oil" each put on ear, hand and foot, sanctifying the person henceforth. The blood speaks of the blood of Christ; the oil speaks of the Spirit of God. The believer today should recognise that he has been cleansed by the blood, and the Spirit of God who indwells him should control the whole mind (ear), doings (hand) and walk (foot) of life.

The *two actions* are "washing" and "shaving". "Washing" to remove defilement: "shaving" to cut off fleshly activity, the hair. This involves the use of water and razor, both of which speak of the Word of God. Water is a cleansing agent; the razor is a cutting agent, and both should be used by each believer, not on another, but on himself, cleansing the garments (walk) and judging the flesh.

A Meditation on Love

The hallmark of practical Christianity is love: its absence renders worthless any profession which one makes of being Christian.

He who journeying to Jericho has fallen victim to robbers and thereafter has been the object of the gracious ministrations of the Good Samaritan is enjoined to, "Go and do likewise" to any others who may, in any way, be in need of mercy. This is the essence of Christianity: love received resulting in love bestowed.

It is to this effect that John writes in his first Epistle. He affirms that -

Love is the proof of the genuineness of our profession.

This is His commandment – this is His golden rule – that we "should believe in the name of His Son Jesus Christ, and love one another, as He gave us commandment," that this is our bounden duty. Inward faith in Christ should be accompanied by outward evidence in love: each believer should love the other: not merely *a* loving *b* (for that is but 50%) but *b* loving *a* also. It is useless for any to say, "I love God" (that is the Trinity, the Father who gave the Son, the Son who gave Himself, and the Spirit who indwells each one that believes) if simultaneously he hates his brother, for such verbal profession and actual conduct are mutually contradictory, and totally incongruous with each other. "He that loveth not his brother whom he hath seen is utterly unable to love God whom he hath not seen." The golden rule enunciated by the lawyer (*vide* Luke 10:27) relating to these two "things which God hath joined together" and which should never be put asunder, applies here, that "he who loves God love his brother also". A mere verbal profession of Christianity is inadequate: it must be accompanied by practical proof.

John, furthermore, observes that, since "God has so loved us, we ought (that is, we owe it) to love one another," for failure to love incurs a debt as real as failure to pay for goods received.

Love is the display of the nature of God

for "no man hath seen God at any time" (that is, God in His essential being), and the only thing that man can see of God is, either what was seen historically in Christ, or what has since been seen in His people. "If we love one another," God's love has reached its goal in our case (that is the force of the word "perfected" in ch. 4:12). The design of that love was that it should find, not a terminus in us, but a junction from whence to flow out to others. Quarrelling and its allied evils furnish a shocking display of the corruption of the flesh, which, as with Abraham's and Lot's servants, is calculated to stumble the unbelieving Canaanites, Perizzites, and others who witness it. Who can measure the damage that has been done to unbelievers, as well as believers, through the absence of love?

Love is the evidence of the possession of divine life.

It is very satisfactory if a young convert finds his assurance of life in the basic utterances of our Lord (*vide* John 3:16; 5:24; 10:28) with which promises none can afford to part at any time.

But the older Christian should find additional confirmation of his possession of eternal life in his own active display of love. "We know that we have passed from death to life because we love the brethren," that is, because there is that within us which irresistibly goes out in affection to every born again soul who, by reason of such birth, is in the family of God. "Everyone that loveth is born of God" – it is the indubitable evidence of life. It is this which makes us so quickly feel at home with erstwhile strangers.

If any one should find himself harbouring an unkind spirit to any believer, he may well question his own possession of eternal life. Christians may not see eye-to-eye on certain things; some may even be linked up with systems and people with which it would be impossible to have fellowship; but this could constitute no hindrance to active love, rather it should furnish the opportunity for its display in seeking their deliverance and good.

Love is not an idle ideal: it is that which is real and active.

Love is practical.

"Let us not love in word and tongue" – it is not to be mere surface talk, but "in deed and in truth". Such love will show itself in a concrete form when a case of genuine need comes under one's notice, and it lies within our power to help. If there be failure to render that possible help, the Apostle enquires, "How dwelleth the love of God in him?" (3:17). It comes very near to "wasting our Master's goods" (Luke 16:1) when they are not used to alleviate distress, and it is a matter of the most solemn moment when, as with the rich man and Lazarus, the need is brought before us, but luxury and plenty mark ourselves whilst the beggar starves. If the Lord "laid down His life for us, we ought to lay down our lives for one another," although in His case it entailed vicarious death, and it could not involve that for us. He gave all He had for the good of others, thus leaving us an example that we should follow His steps.

But John tells us, further, that -

Love is obedient.

This is a day of compromise, when it is generally supposed that we can serve our brethren's best interests and display real love to them by "agreeing to differ," and "not insisting on minor details," but mutually omitting to refer to matters where agreement of judgment thereon does not exist, and so acting as if divine principles were of no consequence. Chapter 5:2 points the very opposite way. Love insists on compliance with the Father's commandments, and insistence which is imposed on one's self, and encouraged in others. It is not unknown for children in an earthly family to act contrary to the father's wish thereby incurring his displeasure, although some of the children may have been culpably disobedient, and others may have been unwittingly so. So, too, there are many of God's dear children who are ignorant of His will and, as a result, their conduct in ecclesiastical and other ways is not in accordance with His commands. These need instruction. On the other hand, there are others of His children who "know their Lord's will" and non-compliance in their case becomes a serious matter, calling for discipline. The best interests of our fellow Christians are served when we are insistent on obedience to the Father's will for ourselves. We render them no kindness (although we may deceive ourselves into thinking that we do) when, for their sake, we act contrary to the Word of God.

It is not uncommon to hear that "Love is blind," and although the phrase is largely used in a restricted sphere, yet it conveys a certain measure of truth. The "blindness and deafness" alluded to in Isaiah 42:19 have their spring in His love to others. But John in chapter 2:11 emphasises that it is hatred which is blind, for -

Love has sight.

The one who hates his brother is unable to foresee, whither such hatred will lead him. Had Cain been able to see beforehand the issue of his hatred toward Abel, would he not have abandoned it forthwith? Had Christians foreseen the damage incurred in later years by their petty strifes would they not gladly have abandoned their disputes? Love, however, has sight. There is no risk in its exercise. It stumbles none. It works no ill.

The Lord grant that we all may be marked again by that which characterised the early Christians of whom it was said, "See how these Christians love one another".

Peter's Utterances

(Matt. 16:13 to 17:8)

1 – Moral Order In Scripture

The arrangement of the contents of Scripture is not haphazard, and without design, but each and every part is in its right place. Sometimes chronological order is sacrificed to other interests, and dispensational or moral order is observed.

In the passage under review three incidents are recorded, the first of which relates to the Person of Christ, the second to His Death, and the third to His glory. This order is right and in accordance with the statement of Peter who, referring to Christ, spake of the "sufferings and the glory that is to follow". Again, prior to the display of the glory of which chapter 17 speaks, reference is made to the building of the church in chapter 16, which, of course, is the proper order. The display of that glory will be in union with the then completed Church (John 17:22).

What has been said as to the arrangement of this section is true of the whole of Matthew's Gospel, and all the rest of Scripture. The sixty-six books are a perfect model of method and system.

"From that time forth" (16:21) is a suggestive time indicator. The Lord Jesus communicated new information to His disciples always at the appropriate moment, either when they were able to bear it, or when it was essential for them to be informed thereof, and the circumstances justified His divulging it. A *bona fide* offer of the Kingdom having been made to Israel by the King Himself (chapter 10), and such offer having been refused by the representative religious elders, the Pharisees, who ascribed His miracles to Satanic origin (chapter 12), there was nothing now left but to hold in abeyance Israel's blessing; to withdraw the offer of the Kingdom; to cease announcing Jesus "as the Christ" (16:20), and to reveal to His apostles the inevitability and necessity of His death (v. 21). The obduracy of Israel did not defeat the purposes of God: it served to develop them by introducing a new thing, the Church, which is now being formed consequent on the rejection of the Kingdom by Israel. This is touched upon in chapter 13:1, wherein we are informed that "Jesus left the house (of Israel) and sat by the seaside (the Gentiles)". The whole subject is treated at length in Romans 9 to 11, where we are told that the natural branches (Israel) have been broken off (set aside) and the wild branches (the Gentiles) have been grafted in.

2 – The Deity of Christ

James has a great deal to say concerning the tongue, and these three incidents in Peter's history demonstrate the truth of his remarks. Therewith he made the great confession. Therewith he contradicted flatly the statement of the Lord concerning the inevitability of His death. Therewith he made a suggestion that robbed the Lord of His unique glory, putting Him on a level with others who were but men. "Out of the same fountain" there came forth these utterances. "My brethren, these things ought not to be." Consistency is a very desirable moral trait to be assiduously encouraged.

Public opinion as to the Person of Christ was not unanimous. Some said this, and some said that. No wonder, for "no one knoweth the Son but the Father," and anything that is known of the Son is by the revelation of the Father. Peter, in giving his own personal confession, affirms that the despised Nazarene, with Whom he companied, and Who had no exterior signs of pomp and power, is the Messiah foreshadowed in the Old Testament. The difficulty in reconciling His humility with the prophesied glory, which had puzzled John Baptist and concerning which he made enquiry, did not prevent Peter's confession of faith.

He affirmed that the Lord Jesus was not man only. That Messiah to come should be Man the Old Testament Scriptures had made plain: they also affirmed unequivocally that He is God, as is witnessed by His prophetic name of Immanuel. This Peter here confesses. He acknowledges His manhood in calling Him, "Christ" and acknowledges His deity in calling Him, "Son of the Living God". Co-equal with the Father, possessor of the same nature, displaying the same attributes, He was self-existent as was His Father – "the *living* God". Doubtless Peter did not enter into the full significance of his words, but they embodied a truth which had dawned on his soul, and which he had grasped by faith. "Fortunate" (blessed) man! The "Flesh and blood" of the Lord might have stumbled him: the Father's revelation was the source of this bold confession.

3 – The Death of Christ

"To him that hath shall be given," and this revelation concerning the Son was followed by the revelation concerning the Church. Before the Church could be built, however, Jesus must die, and this He categorically stated in verse 21. The place, manner, instruments, and issue of His death are all briefly enumerated. Peter, in the warmth of his love for the Lord, but "not knowing" the counsel of God, said, "Be it far from Thee, Lord," or, "Pity Thyself" – "this shall not be to Thee". Thus he flatly contradicts the Lord. The Lord affirmed it was imperative, inevitable, necessary. Peter, on the other hand, says, "It shall not be". Little did Peter suspect that the Adversary was using him to test the Lord, and that this was but another of the very many wiles of the enemy which he had employed in order to defeat, if possible, the purpose of God by deflecting the Lord Jesus from the path that God and He knew must be trodden. Satan knew that his own defeat had long ago been determined, and hence by all means he must, if possible, prevent either the advent and/or the obedience of the Son of God. The former he was not successful in achieving; nor would he succeed in the latter, despite such endeavours as the one here. Peter in saying this was not evincing an interest in Divine things – the holy claims and righteous demands which a holy law inexorably required to be satisfied – but he was displaying an interest in human things – the safety, security and ease of the "flesh and blood" of the One Whom he loved. The Lord takes occasion of this to point out to him that the "way of life" lies via the cross, not only for Him but for all who would follow Him.

4 – The Glory of Christ

His third utterance was on the occasion of the Transfiguration when, charmed with the scene of glory high up on the mountain away from the thronging multitude below, he proposes that a settlement should at once be effected there. Glory without the cross was the proposal of the Devil at the Temptation, which recurs here in another form. He who combined in His Being two holy and perfect natures (the Christ, the Son of the Living God) is put by the very man who made that confession on a level with Moses and Elijah. Illustrious as they are, they are not to be compared with Him. It is true that Peter placed the Lord first, and Moses and Elijah after Him, but He was far above them and should have stood alone. "This is My Beloved Son" – the others were but servants. "If Thou wilt!" (chap. 17:4); but how could He will that glory should be then and there established, while for sinners no redemptive provision had yet been made! How could He so will when His desire was always, "Not My will, but Thine be done?" He "in whom God had been well pleased" could not, and would not accept of His own volition such a proposal. In Peter's whole utterance there is that which is commendable and there is that which is reprehensible. His putting the Lord first, and deferring to His will is commendable; his desire that he should make permanent that glory, and that in tents, is not commendable.

5 – The Words of Scripture

The utmost care should be taken to observe the precise words of Scripture. Carelessness in this direction results in misinterpretation and resultant erroneous doctrine. This section affords two important examples of verbal precision.

"And I also say unto thee," that is, in addition to what "My Father" has said, "that thou art a stone (*Petros*), and on this rock (*petra*) I will build My Church," a congregation of people out of all nations, and the power of the unseen world shall not succeed in retaining for ever in its grasp any one of those who compose it.

Although endeavours have been made, even to alter the text as well as to destroy the important difference between *Petros* and *Petra*, yet it cannot seriously be refuted that the passage teaches that the Lord Jesus Himself is the bed-rock (*petra*) foundation of the Church, and the Apostle Peter is a stone (*petros*) built thereon. Indeed, Peter's own remarks in the second chapter of his first Epistle are the best commentary on this passage.

Peter was to be an instrument in commencing the building work through stating the terms on which sins could be remitted (loosed) or sins would be punished (bound). To him was given the key to open the door to the Jew, and the key to open it to the Gentile. These he used respectively on the day of Pentecost (Acts 2) and in Cornelius' house (Acts 10). Acts 2:38 and 10:43 are the Scriptural explanations of the doctrine of absolution here stated.

The phrase "on earth" should not be overlooked. It defines the time and the sphere of the activities of Peter in "binding and loosing". This he did (not does) on earth (not now in heaven). This "binding and loosing" are now matters of history, so far as Peter is concerned. He has no such function at present in heaven.

We should ever be careful in dealing with Scripture not to allot to the wrong party its sundry statements. There is enough in it for all, and the one who handles Scripture wisely will never, by *applying* to the unbeliever the terms of a verse designed for the disciple, overlook and fail to emphasise its true bearing upon the proper party. How often has chapter 16:26 very rightly been urged upon the timeserving sinner, yet it is a word for the timeserving disciple! It is sound common sense. The word "soul" is better read, as in the R.V., "life". To gain all here, and then to lose one's life, is to lose all. To forfeit things here for the sake of the Lord and the Gospel is to find life now, and a reward hereafter (v. 27). True discipleship will lead us to take our place with Christ on the other side of Jordan, the cross ever standing between us and the world, resulting in our daily recognition that self has not claims, it having been crucified with Christ. This is "denying self" and "bearing the cross daily".

"When Ye Come Together In One Place"

Nothing that is of consequence, connected with the gatherings together of the people of God, is omitted from the Scriptures. The believer, therefore, may expect to find, and will do so, in the Scriptures *adequate ecclesiastical guidance.*

Its *simplicity* is striking, when compared with the elaborate paraphernalia of Christendom, comprised as this latter is, partly of shadowy and antiquated Judaism, and partly of corrupt Paganism.

No *distinctive title* of a sectarian nature is given to the companies, nor is any distinctive rank or title given to any of its public ministers.

The *geographical place* of the gathering is unimportant. Everything depends upon the name of the Person to Whom the saints are gathered. Saints are not now expected to gather at Jerusalem in an ornate temple or consecrated building. A barn has been known to suffice.

Ministry of the Word amongst them is not restricted to the humanly ordained, but is exercised under the direction of the Spirit of God, through whatever channel that Spirit equips for the purpose. This presupposes the recognition of but One Head, the Risen Lord in Heaven, and altogether precludes a pre-arranged Church "service".

The *Ordinances* are not multitudinous: they are but two in number. First baptism, occurring once in the life of the believer, and that immediately after his conversion. Secondly, the Lord's Supper, recurring every first day of the week, from which the believer is not supposed to be absent without good cause. Another has well said, "We have no more right to change this order than we have to change the ordinances."

The *monetary needs* of the saints, and those addicted to the ministry, are met not from the purses of the ungodly, nor indeed from the State Coffers, but out of the liberality of the saints. This should be effected by way of collection on the first day of the week.

It is not a matter of mere custom that the men have their heads uncovered, and the sisters have their heads covered: nor that the man's hair is short, and the sister's hair is long. This is according to Divine prescription, and has its lessons, both for the saints and the angels.

The silence of *sisters*, and the restriction of oral ministry, and public prayer, to the brethren is also not without instruction.

It is not a democratic undisciplined company, but one which has been furnished by the Lord through the Spirit with *guides, pastors and teachers;* and when occasion arises for the exercise of discipline their guidance and instruction will be invaluable, although the exclusion of any individual from the company (as in the case of reception) is effected by the whole gathering, and is not restricted to the decisions of any given few.

It is regrettable that not all of the Lord's people follow these simple paths. The Lord give us all a heart of love and yearning for such!

Many, alas! do not enjoy the liberty that pertains to such simple assemblings through their desire for, and endorsement of, that which is less dependent upon the Spirit and more subject to human arrangement. "New carts" have a wonderful fascination. "Devising" things "out of one's heart" is a subtle snare. Security from failure is not to be achieved by departure from Scriptural precept. Man cannot devise anything which is more safe than that prescribed by God.

He who calls *"Jesus, Lord"* should do the things He says. For, "How call ye Me Lord, Lord, and do not the things I say?" Our obedience will encourage others to obey: but compromise not only bespeaks weakness in one's self, it also engenders weakness in others. It is a short-sighted policy to forego insistence on certain Divine principles in order to win others. This is a prevalent evil. Its tendency is inevitably to propagate the idea that certain things enjoined by the Lord may altogether be safely ignored by the saints, although the fact is that nothing can be overlooked save without great spiritual loss, and incurring the Lord's sore displeasure.

May the Lord preserve His people from this error.

Luke 10

The incident concerning the murmurs of Martha because of the conduct of Mary falls between that of the Good Samaritan parable, and the request of the disciples to be taught how properly to pray. This arrangement is according to the Spirit's guidance and is most instructive.

In the parable of the Good Samaritan the host of the inn is requested to "take care" of the wounded traveller, but lest such service to Christ should degenerate into "carefulness" and "trouble" the incident of Martha and Mary is inserted as a warning.

Here Martha is seen addressing the Lord in a most unsuitable way. Although she calls Him, "Lord," yet her utterance, "Dost Thou not care?" is altogether out of place, and her bidding the Lord to tell another what to do is not proper. To safeguard against such things, and to afford positive guidance as how to pray properly, the next incident, (embodying what is usually known as "the Lord's Prayer"), is furnished. Instead of "me" twice recurring as in the case of Martha's petition, "Thy" is several times repeated firstly, and thereafter "us" occurs.

Thus this episode has *two links*, one connecting it with what precedes and the other with that which follows. (a) Serve Christ and take care of the wounded but rescued travellers, but beware lest that service becomes a source of trouble and distraction. (b)

Neglect not prayer, but see that first things are put first, and that God and His interests have priority over your interests.

It may be observed that Martha was the **hostess** entertaining the Lord, whilst Mary availed herself of the opportunity to become a **scholar** sitting at the feet of the Lord. Every Christian may be both. He may be host: He may make his home the place where he entertains the Lord not as a casual visitor but as a permanent guest. This should be the regular practice. If the Lord were in our home, in bodily form, would His holy eye observe with approval the books, pictures, ornaments, newspapers, etc., or, would they furnish occasion of reproof? He also may be scholar for no place is so suited to private instruction direct by the Lord Himself as the home. In the solitude of the room and its quietness His voice through the Scriptures may be heard as one abides prayerfully at His feet.

It is true that the work has to be done, whether it be in home, office, workshop, or elsewhere. No Christian should neglect his daily mundane duties, but he should see that they do not exclude the all-important exercise of the soul waiting at the feet of the Lord to hear His word. The conjunction *"also"* should not be overlooked. "Mary also sat at the Lord's feet." She knew the work must be done and doubtless helped Martha to do it, but she recognised that not all her time should be spent in work, some of it must be spent in listening; she knew the spiritual was greater than the material. She worked but she *also* sat at His feet. Martha worked only.

It is interesting to observe that the R.V. alters the word "Jesus" to "Lord", showing that Mary recognised that He at whose feet she sat was One Whose authority should be respected and Whose word should be obeyed: she recognised

Him as her Lord. Martha, on the other hand, merely called Him, "Lord", but by her utterances displayed that her heart failed to understand its true significance. It is quite easy for the believer to use the correct phraseology and to speak of Jesus, as always he should, as the Lord Jesus Christ, and yet in heart and life to fail in acknowledging His Lordship. "Why call ye Me, Lord, Lord, and do not the things I say?" "If I then, your Lord and Teacher, have washed your feet; ye ought also to wash one another's." The real acknowledgement of the Lordship of Christ is not by lip but by deeds of obedience.

Yet observe again Martha was "cumbered" or "distracted". There was so much to do that her eye lacked a definite object. Mary on the other hand had her eye solely on her Lord. Even when at work the eye of her heart was on Him and her feet thereafter hastened to Him. If work is the object it will become troublesome: if Christ is the object work will become easy, for the eye should not be on the service for Christ, but on Christ for Whom the service is.

Mary's eye being on the Lord she soon left her sister and joined the Lord, which caused Martha to murmur. "She has left *me*": "tell her to help *me*." This revealed Martha's heart that she thought more of herself than of Christ, whilst it showed also that Mary thought more of Christ than of her sister or herself. Martha put herself first: Mary put the Lord first, and it is only by doing this latter that peace can be enjoyed. "Seek *first* the Kingdom of God and His righteousness," and then all material necessities will be added. Away in Elijah's day there was a mother who was about to make a cake for "*me* and my son," and then to die. She put herself first, but the man of God said, "Put someone else before yourself, and make a little cake for me *first*, and then see what will happen," which thing she did with marvellous results. For it is he who puts Christ first who sees His power, hears His voice, and knows His love.

The Lord would not comply with Martha's request: He would not take way from Mary that part which she had chosen, for whilst service of the particular nature that Martha rendered, or that which we may render down here, is bound to pass away with the passage of time, "Communion" which Mary chose and which we may have survives the passage of time, and continues throughout eternity. It is the better, and it is the more durable part.

Sundry Thoughts on Luke 12

The suitability of this chapter for the present day will be felt by most, for it is a day when the visible resources of men are being severely tested. Wages are cut: dividends are reduced: business is declining, and the children of God are feeling the effects of these things, as are others. In such circumstances how precious are the truths of the chapter under review!

It should not be overlooked that it commences with a warning against hypocrisy, for surely nothing tests the faith of a person and discovers whether that one is genuine or spurious, honest or hypocrite, as either adversity of circumstances on the one hand, or persecution by men on the other. In times of persecution the hypocrite is discovered, and to save his skin he renounces his confession. In times of adversity, too, the hypocrite is discovered, and the real thoughts of the heart become verbal expressions of the lip. "Beware of the leaven of the Pharisees which is hypocrisy" – appearing one thing, and being another; for surely the testing time will come.

Nevertheless for him whose heart is true toward God there is every cause for courage and confidence, for the Lord would remind His own that the *three Persons* of the Holy Trinity are exercised on the behalf of, and for the good of, such. As to God, twice He is spoken of as, "Your Father," all His attributes being operative in the power of parental love. As to Christ Himself, He calls His own, "My friends" and "Little flock," for He is that friend "that sticketh closer than a brother," and He is the Shepherd who never fails His sheep. As to the Holy Spirit, He is mentioned by name Who in the hour of necessity and emergency will assist the one in need.

In the light thereof, how significant and forceful are the three warnings: -

Fear not, Worry not, Covet not.

"Fear not men" for their power is limited to the material and to the body: they cannot touch the soul. "Fear not circumstances" – your Father has settled His good pleasure to give you the kingdom, in His own time and manner.

The words translated in the A.V. as, "Take no thought," and in the R.V. as, "Take no anxious thought", are well represented in the English word "worry". If before hostile men, do not worry how to address them; or how to answer their charges; and what to say in positive testimony, for the Holy Spirit will give the words appropriate for the moment. "Worry not" as to circumstances, for you cannot alter them no more than it is possible to increase your age, or your stature.

"Covet not" should you see others with more than you possess, or should you see the circumstances of others, as you suppose, less adverse than your own. Learn the lesson from the rich farmer: that quantity of goods does not determine either length or happiness of life, for he had *plenty* of goods, but not *plenty* of time to enjoy them.

Sundry Thoughts on Luke 12

It is no new grumble that another has more, for the appellant brother grumbled to the Lord concerning his brother who had more than he. The Lord, however, was not here to remedy social inequalities, but with a master-stroke reached the root of the matter without circumlocution when he spoke of covetousness. This was the spring of that young man's complaint.

But the Lord not only warns: He encourages, and that by drawing attention to the lessons of nature. These are threefold: -

The sparrow, the raven, the lily.

The sparrow is little thought of by men: two are sold for a farthing: one is thrown in if you buy two farthings' worth, for five are sold for two farthings, YET should one fall to the ground the Father knows and cares. So each hair of the head is numbered, and when one comes out in the comb, your Father knows.

The raven is like the unemployed. It sows not (as the farmer did), it reaps not (as the farmer did), and has no barn (as the farmer had): and some of the Lord's people can't work: for others there is none to do: as to having behind them a store for the rainy day, they cannot accumulate it or gather into barns. But the raven is fed by a faithful God, and so too will these be.

The lily of the field clothed that eastern grass with beauty, as the daisy and buttercup clothe the western green carpet. And if God so clothes the grass of the field which is "here today and gone tomorrow," how much more will He not clothe us who do remain a little longer than that!!

So then let us take courage! And heed three exhortations – to have our: -

Loins girded, Lights burning, Eyes looking.

"Let your loins be girded," ready to go, and to leave all behind us. But should the Lord determine that we are to stay a little longer then "let your lights be burning," you in your small corner and I in mine; although do not settle down and forget He is coming, but "Let your eyes be looking" and "Be ye as men that watch for their Lord".

The Lord Jesus Christ - His Unique Person

It should ever be remembered in considering this great theme that "no man knoweth the Son but the Father," that His Person, as the curtains in the tabernacle, is "a cunning work," and that Scripture states things concerning Him, to which (even if our intellects fail to reconcile) faith should bow in submission.

The word "Person" is a reminder that the One of Whom we are to consider is not the product of mental fancy, or the imaginary subject of ancient literature, but is a present, real, tangible, living Person Who once was on earth and now is in heaven.

And this Person is "Unique," He stands alone – there is none like Him. "Whom have I, Lord, in heaven but Thee? And there is none on earth that I desire beside Thee." "What is thy beloved more than another? ... He is altogether lovely, the chiefest among ten thousand." As the perfume of old was unique, and God prohibited anything like it being made, so too the Lord Jesus Christ is unique, and of Him we may say, "Who is like unto Thee?" He is God's "only begotten Son" – a term which is not to be interpreted as if the Son of God had a beginning of days, but one indicating uniqueness. "I have one beloved Son" – and only one. There was not another. The Greek word here used, translated "only begotten", is the equivalent of the

Hebrew word translated in Psalm 22: "Darling", and literally means "only one". As there was only one tabernacle, so there was only one Eternal Son. Of Him we may say, as another said of a sword, "There is none like *Him*."

This blessed Person is the chief theme of Scripture from beginning to end. The difficulty which confronts me is to know exactly where to start and where to finish. Let us, however, adopt this method.

To take a citation from each of the three main sections of the Old Testament Scriptures as divided in the days of our Lord and as divided now in Hebrew Bibles: one from the Law: another from the Psalms and another from the Prophets.

Firstly then, turn to -

Genesis 3:15

In this verse is contained in germ the truth concerning the Person of the Lord Jesus Christ which is later in Scripture more fully developed. The expression to the woman, "Thy seed," indicates that He who should come would be as to His human nature, born of a woman: but not by a generation of a human father; therefore He would be unique in that respect: Moreover He would conquer the Devil, and, having regard to the fact that the whole of the human race has been conquered by him, the Lord Jesus would stand unique in that further respect. By these prophetic terms man was taught to look for a Man, Someone from their own race, Who was more than a man and Who was destined to defeat the enemy of man. In the conquest it is hinted that the Conqueror would suffer somewhat. We can look back now upon that prophecy in the light of its historical fulfilment and understand that the Victory and Defeat were simultaneous in the Cross and that the Unique One, more than man but truly man is He Who hung thereon.

Our second extract shall be from the book of Psalms.

Psalm 110:1

"The Lord said unto my Lord," by the side of which we may place the remarks of the Lord Himself when contesting with the Pharisees. David, the human author of the Psalm, affirms that Jehovah spake to another who was then his (David's) Lord that Other – Adonai – being the Messiah. Yet later Old Testament prophecies show that the Messiah was to be the Son of David. If, therefore, David in his lifetime called this Person who was then existent his Lord, how is He his son, since human sonship involves posteriority? If He was before him, how can He be after him? The answer is that His being Lord of David is by reason of His eternal deity (He then existing though not in bodily form); and His being the Son of David is effected by His humanity, having been born of David's line and subsequent to David.

Our next extract is from -

The Prophets

In chapter 4 of Isaiah this One is called the "branch of the Lord" and "the fruit of the earth" – an assertion that He embodies in Himself two full and perfect natures – as "the branch of the Lord" affirms His deity, so the "fruit of the earth" affirms His humanity. Look again at chapter 7:14. "Behold a virgin shall conceive, and bear a son, and shall call His name Immanuel." His being born of a virgin ensures sinless but real humanity: His being called Immanuel affirms His deity, for that name means "God with us". Yet again chapter 9:6. "Unto us a child is born, unto us a Son is given". Here the same combination is met with; the "child born" denoting humanity, the "Son given." denoting Deity, for He must have had being, and have been Son, prior to His incarnation in order to be then given. And once more, in chapter 11:1, He is called the off-spring (or shoot) of Jesse which denotes He comes out of Jesse and after him: thus affirming His humanity. In verse 10, however, He is called the "root of Jesse" which means He was before him and Jesse sprang out of Him – thus asserting His deity.

Thus the consensus of information obtained from these Old Testament specimen citations is that One was to come Who would have all the marks of sinless unique Humanity for He would be truly man, though not born as other men with double parentage, but only single. But He would bear the evidence of higher origin, He being eternal in existence and God in essence. There are other points but these are salient.

Jesus the Christ

A Survey of Matthew's Gospel

Preface

The aim in writing this book is to present to the reader a panoramic view of the contents of the Gospel of Matthew. An endeavour has been made to show that it is a consistent argument throughout, and not a haphazard collection of incidents, miracles and speeches of the Lord Jesus. Everything in the Gospel is in its right place.

No attempt has been made to treat exhaustively any chapter or passage. Details are not examined: the main theme of the Gospel is traced from chapter to chapter. The reader must look elsewhere for a close examination of its verses, as they are not dealt with in this book.

The reader will not find here, it is believed, an extreme form of dispensationalism, nor will he find that dispensational teaching has been jettisoned altogether. An effort has been made to give it its proper place and a key with which to open up the meaning of the Gospel.

The author's desire is that the reader may be led to study afresh this part of God's Word and to search for himself to see whether what he reads herein is so. The Lord will give understanding to the willing mind.

Many thanks are due to Mr. James Hislop, M.A., B.Sc., who has very kindly read the original manuscript and made most helpful suggestions.

May God graciously use this book to the glory of His Son, Jesus, and the confirmation of the faith of all who read it.

Oxford

Introduction

'The book of the generation of Jesus Christ.' With these words Matthew opens his Gospel: words which would cause no surprise to a Christian or strike him as unusual. Yet to a Jew, both of Matthew's day and ours, the words would be astonishingly significant. Not long before Matthew's Gospel was in circulation Jesus had been crucified outside the wall of Jerusalem, and though it had been alleged that He was alive none of His enemies had seen Him after His death. They did not admit His claim to Messiahship, and because they regarded Him as a deceiver and an impostor they persuaded Pilate to consent to His crucifixion. But now here is a man daring to write a treatise, which opens with the two words in juxtaposition: 'Jesus', which is the name of the Person concerned, and 'Christ', which denotes His office.

It is plain that Matthew judged Him to be in the right and His enemies to have been in the wrong; he accepted His claim to Messiahship with all that it involved. He is prepared to put it in writing so that there can be no misunderstanding of his view of the matter. He believes in Jesus, he accepts His claims. In his Gospel he will tell you why he does so. He is not governed by prejudice, nor has he any unworthy motive which leads him to side with One Whom the Jewish world then regarded as a man not fit to live. He has good reasons for the attitude he has adopted, and in his Gospel he sets these out. However, he acknowledges that mere human judgment and logical reasoning is insufficient to apprehend the true Person of Christ. More than that is needed. In due course we shall learn what that 'something more' is.

The Gospel cannot be said to have this, however, as its prime object. Matthew has a larger purpose. He writes for his fellow nationals, the Jews, so that they may have before them all the facts and reach their own conclusions from the evidence which he produces. He desires that they should change their minds and repent of their national crime and be willing even now to receive Jesus Christ, so that 'the times of refreshing' might be brought in for them, and that there should be a restitution of all things. Universal blessing awaits the repentance of the Jew.

Matthew assumes that his readers, his fellow nationals for whom in particular he writes, know their Scriptures and he, therefore, quotes freely from them. They can judge for themselves whether those Old Testament Scriptures and the history of Jesus accord with each other, and what bearing such agreement has on the claims of Jesus.

Although it may appear that the mission of the Lord Jesus Christ in the world was a failure, and His claims were utterly discredited, resulting in His death as a malefactor, yet Matthew shows that it was part of a vast scheme which God was then beginning to work out and which He is continuing till this present day. Far from being frustrated or defeated, the death of Jesus was a vital, integral part of that scheme, without which the scheme itself could never have been effected. His death did not end all; it was followed by His resurrection and investiture with universal authority. Matthew tells us what that scheme is.

He does not write at random. His material is carefully collected and arranged, and his argument is logical throughout. He, of course, writes by the Spirit's inspiration, and we have in his Gospel far more than mere human reasoning, but his method is, as we have said, logical and his arguments are irresistible. His method differs from that of his fellow evangelists. His chief aim is to attest the Messiahship of Jesus, while that of Mark was to present Him as God's Perfect Servant. Luke depicts Him as the Perfect Man and John shows Him to be the eternal Son. The four records give us a full-orbed idea of the glories of the Son of God, the Lord Jesus Christ. They accord with Ezekiel's symbols of the lion, the ox, the face of a man and the flying eagle. Matthew presents Him as holding the highest office and Mark as holding the lowest. Luke presents one side of His Being, as sinless Man, and John gives the other side, His full deity. Thus we have a complete picture.

Whether Mark's Gospel should be first in the New Testament canon or Matthew's is a moot point. Certainly if we consider how far back each evangelist goes, we shall suppose that Mark's Gospel should come first, for he cites Isaiah, whereas Matthew takes us back to Abraham: Luke goes further back still to Adam, and John yet further still, to eternity past. But this seems to be of little importance: the contents of each book is of far greater consequence than their place in the canon.

ON THE DIFFERENCES IN THE FOUR GOSPELS

It would appear to be, we may believe, an unwitting attempt to defeat the purpose of the Spirit of God in giving us four Gospels to try to harmonise them. The Person of Christ is so inscrutable to the human mind that only by representing Him in this fourfold manner can we be given a glimpse of His glory. Everything in each Gospel is recorded consistently with the particular object before the Spirit, and details which serve that object are included and other details which do not serve that purpose are excluded. This accounts for some items being found in only one Gospel. It also accounts for the differences in details in recording the same incident. Even the arrangement of the record is given with this in view, and consequently the chronological order of the events is often ignored. We cannot on any account assume that the historians fell into error: they were safeguarded from that by the Spirit of God who inspired them and what they wrote, and brought all things to their remembrance in accordance with the Lord's own promise on the night in which He was betrayed. It is to be anticipated that there are difficulties that we cannot solve, seeing that it is God's word. Had it been the word of a mere man, we might have been able completely to understand it; but God, being infinite, it is to be expected that His writings will partake of that same character. How then can finite man apprehend the infinite? Moreover, if in the interests of a special object some details are omitted in order to make the record serve the particular purpose in view, is it not likely that, did we know such omitted details, we should find there has been no inaccuracy and certainly no misrepresentation? Furthermore, often by putting all the records together we can form a complete picture which, had it been presented as a whole, would never have conveyed to us the distinctive teaching of each writer. We may confidently assume then that Scripture has no mistakes.

But the interpretation of Scripture, being that of fallible man often is mistaken and, consequently, great men differ in their explanation of certain passages. In such cases we must be content with stating our convictions and leave the reader to judge for himself.

THE AUTHOR

It is not categorically stated that Matthew wrote this Gospel, but internal evidence helps us to approve as correct the common and ancient tradition that he was the writer. For example, in the list of the names of the apostles his name is placed after that of Thomas, and not before it as it appears in the other lists given by Mark and Luke. In recording his call by the Lord Jesus, details are omitted by him which are given by others. He does not say, 'he left all', nor does he say that it was he who made the feast in his own house. One can understand these omissions on the assumption that Matthew is the writer. The Spirit of God would work in him the grace of humility, which would prevent him from self-praise. He magnifies the mercy that had been shown to him, a publican. He tells us that publicans are usually found in bad company, such as 'publicans and heathens', 'publicans and sinners', and 'publicans and harlots'. He would have us join him in extolling the wondrous grace that had shown mercy to such as himself.

As a tax gatherer he was *persona non grata* with the Jews, and as a Jew he would have no bias in favour of the Gentiles. He was pleased to serve them in such a capacity for the enrichment of himself at the expense of his fellow-nationals. If then he undertook to write a record touching the Lord Jesus, no one could accuse him of a bias in favour of the Romans. He was peculiarly fitted to write impartially and fairly.

There are differences in his record from what the other evangelists tell us, but such differences are not mistakes or contradictions, nor are they impossible of reconciliation with the other statements had we more information and facts. They tend rather to show the independence of Matthew and preclude any thought of his collusion with the other writers. Besides, we must never forget that all were inspired, and that the Spirit of God had instruction to impart by the particular manner in which He caused the writers to present each incident. The omissions of Scripture are like pauses in music, they add to its harmony. Some of the differences we shall note in their proper place. Were the records false, or had they been specially altered with the intent of deceiving the readers, it is far more likely that they would have agreed in all details. The differences in these independent and honest treatises are *prima facie* evidence of their genuineness and accuracy. The Spirit of God would save them from error.

THE STRUCTURE OF THE GOSPEL

The watershed of the Gospel is the incident in chapter 16 which took place at Caesarea Philippi. Peter is the only one who makes an accurate confession of who the Lord Jesus is: He is 'the Christ, the Son of the living God'. From the fact that some said He was Elias, others that He was Jeremias, others that He was one of the old prophets raised from the dead, it is evident that none of the people knew Him to be who He really was. They all seemed confused and uncertain, even the other apostles. Peter stands out in grand solitude as he makes this magnificent confession.

The Gospel may be regarded as a mountain peak and this incident its summit. What comes before it is the scaling of the mountain on one side from Bethlehem to Caesarea Philippi; what follows is the descent on the other side from thence to even lower than the point of starting, namely to Calvary. In the ascent Matthew records the words and deeds of the Lord Jesus as he produces evidence in proof of His claim, which claim as we have seen Peter confesses. In these chapters there is no mention made of His coming death. Seeing, however, that that claim was generally rejected, from chapter 16 verse 18 the clouds gather. He forecasts His crucifixion, which would be effected by the Jews with the aid of the Gentiles and instigated from within the small circle of the apostolate (see 16:21; 17:22; 26:21).

This brings us to the end of chapter 25. The remaining chapters record His trial, death and resurrection. It is all so amazingly orderly.

Any open-minded person, who is willing to be convinced, must acknowledge that Matthew has made out his case that the Man called Jesus, Who was born in Bethlehem, brought up in Nazareth, Who worked as a carpenter and later went about as a preacher, ultimately crucified as a felon, was indeed 'Jesus Christ'.

The Main Argument

If a person claims that he is entitled to certain privileges or rights, such as, for example, if a person claims to be a king and entitled to sit on the throne, it is only reasonable that he should submit evidence in support of that claim. So too with 'Jesus Christ'. If Matthew, as the penman of the Holy Spirit, claims that Jesus is entitled to David's throne, and to be the recipient of and administrator of the promises made to Abraham, and that He is the one of whom the ancient prophets wrote, it is only proper that he should furnish evidence in support of that claim. This he does.

What is the first question any pious Jew would be likely to ask? Surely it is: Is His genealogical tree satisfactory? Can Jesus trace His descent indisputably to David and to Abraham? Does it give *prima facie* evidence of the validity of His claim? This Matthew deals with in chapter 1.

He would next ask: Were the circumstances attending His birth such as agreed with the prophetic forecasts of the Old Testament Scriptures? This he answers in chapter 2.

Next, did He have the prescribed Forerunner, seeing that the prophets envisaged such a one prior to the coming of God's King? This Matthew deals with in chapter 3.

But seeing that a person may have *prima facie* evidence in support of his claims and yet be personally altogether incompetent to rule, a further question arises: Is He competent to rule? This Matthew answers in chapter 4.

Then by what laws will He rule? These are set out in chapters 5 to 7.

Finally, did He do the prescribed Messianic miracles? If we read chapters 8 and 9 we see clearly that what the prophets said He would do, He did.

At chapter 9 verse 35 we may draw a line and mark it, 'Evidence closed'. Matthew had given such evidence in support of his contention that Jesus is the Christ that, surely, all fair-minded people must admit that he has proved his case. But, as we have said, it needs more than a convinced mind to receive Jesus. If the will is at enmity to God, no amount of evidence will convince. 'Convince a man against his will, he's of the same opinion still.'

Accordingly, in chapter 10 Matthew records the offering of the King and the Kingdom to Israel: the offer was limited to them and restrictions were imposed. The message was to be given to none other. How was that offer received?

Chapter 11 answers this and it gives us details. Some were honestly perplexed; others were undecided and vacillating; yet others were definitely unbelieving; a few, however, childlike in their simple but not unintelligent trust, accepted the message.

Nevertheless, the religious leaders of that day, as they always do, dominated the thinking of the common people, made false accusations and, despite the greatness of Jesus, totally rejected Him. This is recorded in chapter 12.

Was God defeated then? Was the mission of Jesus Christ an utter failure? Chapter 13 records how God had other plans, not hitherto revealed ('mysteries', as the New Testament calls such plans) which were to be brought into operation consequent upon the rejection of the King. This chapter 13 and later chapters develop. But more of that anon.

Sufficient has been said to show that, far from Matthew writing at random, he sets things out in logical sequence, satisfactorily answering the reasonable enquiries of a thoughtful and open mind. He shows why the Jewish nation has lost its place of privilege among the nations, and what God is doing until the time when they are as a people prepared to accept His King, and are thereby ready to be re-instated.

Matthew is throughout his Gospel occupied with Christ in relation to earth. The Spirit of God used Paul to tell the saints about Christ in relation to heaven and of a heavenly people, but that is not Matthew's chief line of things. He is primarily writing with the nation of Israel in view, though he often tells how the branches of the 'greater than Joseph' have gone over the wall and reached unto the Gentiles. Though he has to record the blindness and hardness of heart of that people, their unbelief and rejection of Jesus their true Messiah, yet he is able to show how God carries on His work on earth notwithstanding the setting aside of Israel. Chapter 13 gives us the mysteries of the kingdom of heaven.

During the period of the absence of the King, certain paradoxical events take place on earth and these are set out in historic-pictorial form in chapter 14. During the same period, also, Matthew shows how certain moral principles should be observed by the loyalists of the true King. These are set out in the same historic-pictorial way in chapters 15-16.

Thus we reach the summit of the mountain. We have reviewed the evidence, the offer of the kingdom, the rejection of that offer, the new move taken by God consequent on that rejection, and the things that are to mark the period of the King's absence. What conclusion have you reached? Men generally were blinded and have made various wrong suggestions. Peter stands alone as the great confessor of 'the Christ, the Son of the living God'. He thereupon tells Peter of His Cross, His church and His coming.

The later part of the Gospel is no less orderly, though the sequence may not be so apparent; but we will defer setting this out until we have considered this first part in more detail.

Part 1

1. THE GENEALOGY (Chapter 1:1-17)

The very first question that needs to be dealt with is: Is His genealogical tree satisfactory? It is basic. If His genealogical descent cannot be traced back to Abraham and to David, then His claim is false and we need proceed no further. This is fundamental.

Both Matthew and Luke furnish us with a genealogical tree and, while there are some difficulties which yet await resolution, in the main it would seem that Matthew gives us Joseph's line and Luke gives us Mary's.

It clearly establishes certain principles in the ways of God's moral dealings with men. For example, it establishes the principle of *sovereign election*, a vast subject but this is not the place to go into it. But note how God chose Abram, one of three brothers; He chose Isaac and not Ishmael, who was born some years before; Jacob was chosen and not his twin brother Esau, despite the fact that he was the elder; Judah was chosen and not Reuben the senior. Solomon too, who was by no means David's eldest son. The lesson is that God's ways are not ours, nor His thoughts ours. God sets aside the first man, for the first Adam failed. Everything now with God is linked with the second man, the Lord from heaven.

This genealogy further clearly demonstrates the working of the *sovereign grace* of God, in that it does the unusual thing of introducing five women. Tamar, the unsavoury history of whom may be read in Genesis 38. Rahab the harlot, and we must not reduce the utterly sinful nature of this woman's character in order to justify her inclusion here. 'Where sin abounded, grace doth much more abound.' Paint her as black as you may, God's grace went out to her in this wondrous fashion and made her a forebear of the Messiah. Ruth the Moabitess, who but for the grace of God would have forever been barred from inheritance among His people. There is the one who is circuitously called 'her that had been the wife of Urias'. Matthew thereby, taught by the Spirit, emphasises her guilty participation in David's adultery. She was as much to blame as he. Oh, how wonderfully have the branches of this 'greater than Joseph' gone over the wall, not only of nationality but of sin. And finally there is Mary, the poor village maiden, young and tender, but bowing to the will of God and accepting its inevitable reproach, who became the most blessed of all women, the mother of our Lord.

This genealogy further demonstrates the fact of *Divine government*. We have all the generations given in the first series of fourteen; but while the second and third series are given in the same numerical fashion (perhaps as an aid to memory), it is not said that all are there. Some individuals have been omitted. This is not by accident but with design. Nor is the design maleficent but instructional. Ahaziah, Joash and Amaziah are omitted. Ahaziah's mother was that wicked woman Athaliah whose desire it was to destroy all the seed royal. By these omissions we are reminded that God in His government visits the iniquity of the fathers unto the third and fourth generation (see 2 Chron. 22:10; Exod. 34:7; Gal. 6:7).

Again, the genealogy evidences the superintendence of *Divine providence*, which, despite all the vicissitudes of history and all the Satanic attempts to defeat the purpose of God by destroying the nation, as Haman desired, or the seed royal, as Athaliah intended, continues its unhindered course until the goal is reached and 'the birth of Jesus Christ was on this wise' and Christ has come.

As to the difficulties in this genealogy which still await elucidation, it may be remarked that the genealogies as given both by Matthew and Luke have stood the critical test of centuries and no one has been able successfully to upset them and prove the claim of Jesus on this ground to be invalid. Even were it so, His claim rests also on other grounds, but for the moment we limit ourselves to this.

The omissions referred to could be readily discovered by examining the already existing genealogies in the Old Testament. Matthew certainly knew that they were available to his readers. His setting out of the genealogies in three parts of fourteen generations each, with the careful insertion of the word 'all' in the first set and its omission from the second and third, was not designed to mislead or deceive. He did not accommodate the genealogy to his purpose, omitting awkward and damaging items. He could not have so easily misled any, seeing that the earlier genealogies were available. The fraud would have become apparent. Matthew was not tampering with the genealogy, nor making the claim of Jesus to appear valid although he knew it was otherwise. The genealogy he gives is in perfect accord with the previous ones given by other inspired writers.

Rationalists such as F. W. Newman have attacked this, but irrefutable replies have been given to such attacks. J. N. Darby deals at length with his assault in his *Irrationalism of Infidelity* and all would be well advised to read what he has to say touching this. The present writer is incompetent to settle all the difficulties attaching to the genealogy, but he is content to know that it is in inspired Scripture and therefore is part of God's word to man. It is moreover reassuring to know that it has withstood the assaults of the enemies of Christ for two millenniums.

In addition to this, there are so many evidences of strict accuracy in the genealogy. Note how Matthew in opening the chapter calls Him 'the son of David, the son of Abraham'. Why select these two only, unless it be that they are carefully chosen? For Jesus is heir both to the promises made to Abraham and to the throne given to David. Observe, too, how carefully he frames his sentence, avoiding the word 'begat' when speaking of Joseph: 'Joseph, the husband of Mary, of whom was born Jesus'. Joseph was not the actual father, but the legal father of Jesus. He was Mary's husband at the time of the birth and so Jesus was born in wedlock and legally entitled to succession through Joseph. The genealogy is a masterpiece of careful selection, thoughtful arrangement, and accurate phrasing.

2. THE CIRCUMSTANCES OF HIS BIRTH (Chapter 1:18-2:23)

The next question to be considered is: Were the circumstances of His birth in accordance with foregoing prophecies? From chapter 1:18 to the end of chapter 2 Matthew cites various Old Testament prophecies and shows how they were fulfilled in the history of Jesus. Some of those which he cites are perfectly plain, such as that which relates to His virgin mother and that which relates to the place of His nativity. Others at first sight do not appear to be so clear, and their application to Him seems strange; but it must not be forgotten that the Spirit of God was the author of these Old Testament prophecies as well as the author of the New Testament writings, for 'all scripture is God-breathed'. It is, therefore, to be expected that He might unfold a meaning in what had previously been written, though for a long time that meaning had remained hidden.

Matthew is very precise in his writing. Here he uses ἵνα when the prophecy has been altogether fulfilled, there he uses the word οὕτως when there was but a partial fulfilment, and yet again he uses the word τότε when the instance was but a case in point illustrating the prophecy. This embodies a great principle which should guide all students, for Old Testament prophecy may be capable of more than one interpretation.

Before we consider these citations from Old Testament Scriptures, we may remark how Matthew regards these writings. They were, he tells us, 'spoken of the Lord'. He was the source. And they were spoken 'through the prophets'. They were but the channels. The prophets were not authors; they were inspired penmen. They often wrote beyond their understanding and frequently their writings had deeper meaning than the outer and plain meaning, which only the true author could in His own time reveal. It is this that explains such apparently strange applications of certain prophecies.

Note further how Matthew presents the person of Christ. He is Jesus; Immanuel; the King; the Christ; a Governor; My Son; a Nazarene. These names imply both His deity and humanity, His royalty and humility, of all of which we cannot here speak particularly.

Observe, too, the regular way in which Matthew speaks of Him in the phrase 'the young child and His mother' (2:11,

13-14, 20-21). Christendom depicts the Madonna and the Child, giving the child the second place and the mother the predominant place both in picture and legend. This is so to the present day, but the old order is better and proper. The young child is the object of worship, not the mother. It is to Him the gifts are presented. The mother truly has a blessed lot, but at most she is the channel through whom the Son of God came into the world.

Nor should we omit to mention the providence of God. He foreknew the flight into Egypt and the expense that such a journey and stay would entail, and He made provision for it in the gold which the wise men from the east brought as part of their gifts to Him.

The citations are:

Isaiah 7:14. It was but natural that Joseph should have had misgivings in the circumstances in which he found himself, and that he should have sought guidance as to what to do from the Holy Scriptures. His purpose to divorce Mary (for the betrothal contract was as binding as formal marriage) was justifiable under the Law of Moses in the circumstances of unfaithfulness which his eyes seemed to tell him must have taken place. He loved Mary too much to make her a public example. His way out of the difficulty was to divorce her privately and not to publicise the ground on which he was taking divorce proceedings. He would 'put her away privily', but God spoke to him in a dream. He was to take Mary to wife and *he* was to name the child, not the mother. Thus the child would be born in wedlock and would be legal heir to the throne of David. Yet the child was not Joseph's. There was no consummation of his marriage until the child was born; until Jehovah the Saviour as Jesus had become flesh. Afterwards there was a family of full brothers and sisters of which Joseph and Mary were the parents.

All this agreed with Isaiah's prophecy. Let the scholar and unbeliever argue as they may over the Hebrew word translated 'virgin', there can be no reasonable doubt that the Greek translation παρθένος accurately represents the Hebrew word '*almah* and that the facts as given historically by Matthew are in full agreement with it. The virginity of Mary and her motherhood of Jesus prove at once the deity and humanity of her child.

We do not hear any more of Joseph. Israel's throne had been cast down temporarily and it will be restored when the rightful occupant returns to earth. That One must be both God and Man: Immanuel, God with us. The whole of the context of Isaiah's prophecy should be read in the light of this. Attempts were made to put another on that throne (see Isa. 7:6) but God said, 'It shall not stand, neither shall it come to pass,' for that throne is reserved for His true Messiah, Jesus, and none other.

Micah 5:2. The Lord Jesus not only had the right mother but He was born in the right place. Micah had identified the particular Bethlehem (for there were several), the one in the land of Judah, as being the place of His nativity. Insignificant as this village was, it was to produce the great Shepherd-Governor of God's people. It would not be the public arrival of a monarch in pomp to his capital city; that was to come later. There was first to be this unheralded arrival, of which but a few godly souls would be aware, before He rode triumphantly into the capital city; just as it will be when He next comes. He will come to the air for His own and later to the earth to take His Kingdom.

Yet more: as astronomical signs preceded His first coming and the star in the east was seen, so also will it be at His second coming (Matt. 24:29). The birth of that babe is none other than God coming into this rebellious part of His universe with the ultimate view of readjusting it to make it conformable to His original purpose. Then Israel, who are set aside and are now Lo Ammi (not My people), will be acknowledged as 'My people' - the very words used in Matthew 2:6. They will be spiritually fitted to accept Him whom they as a people have for so long rejected.

What a strange scene confronts us here. Gentiles worshipping the child, while the Jews are troubled about His alleged arrival. Should they not have rejoiced at His birth? The heavenly hosts did, and the godly few were thrilled and filled with high hopes. Even the Gentile wise men journeyed and sought for Him, and finding Him worshipped. It is all so like the present time when He is 'by the many still neglected, and by the few enthroned'. Some of these few have discovered Him after a long quest; like the wise men following a gleam of light. Whilst others have been suddenly enveloped by divine light; as were the shepherds when watching their flocks. Yet no matter in what way the godly have found Him, all bow down and worship.

Hosea 11:1 (see Matt. 2:15). The nation of Israel had once been in Egypt and had been brought out of it by God's mighty arm. Crossing the Red Sea, they entered the land. Here the Lord Jesus is retracing their history in His own Person. They had been God's failing servant; He was God's perfect servant. Therefore, like them, He went from 'the land' into Egypt, and He came up out of it. Like them, He went through the waters and into the wilderness. He identifies Himself with them in many ways, as Matthew observes in his record. This is an important key to the understanding of his Gospel - the relation of Jesus to His own earthly people. It explains how God will find a righteous basis on which to restore them to His favour and to His purposed earthly blessing; for they cannot be blessed apart from Christ, nor will Christ enter into His earthly rights apart from them.

Hosea's prophecy primarily refers to the nation, but hidden beneath it the spirit of prophecy is seen to be the testimony of Jesus. In Himself, in perfection, He goes over again the way by which the nation had come. Had the Spirit of God not used this passage in this sense, doubtless we should never have discerned its inner meaning, but it is a hallmark of Scripture that not all the truth lies on the surface.

What was it that took Him down to Egypt? It was the murderous plan of Herod to destroy Him. But behind Herod was that old serpent, the devil, whose defeat by the Seed of the Woman had been foreshadowed as far back as Genesis 3:15. He had in devious ways sought to prevent His first advent, but had failed. 'The birth of Jesus' was an accomplished fact: He was here. Hence he would seek to destroy Him and this is but one of several attempts made during His earthly sojourn, but it failed. It must be so, for His hour had not yet come. He would not die till He had finished the work the Father had given Him to do; but steps must be taken under divine guidance to secure Him in babyhood from the cruelty of that Edomite. Hence His father took the young child and His mother to Egypt and finds that God had, through the wise men, provided for their sustenance there.

Jeremiah 31.15 (2:18). While the true King is absent in Egypt, the nation is in trouble in the land. It is remarkable how history repeats itself. It will be so later on when Israel in unbelief returns to the land before the arrival back of their Messiah. Jeremiah's prophecy prefigures the Great Tribulation, yet it foreshadowed this dreadful sorrow that overtook that village of Bethlehem. It reminds one of the days of Pharaoh and his cruel edict concerning the male children that were born to the Israelites, in which time Moses was born and drawn out of troublesome waters by divine providence and according to His plans for their future deliverance. Here is a greater than Moses, spared the sword of Herod while the people are lamenting, weeping and mourning greatly. Rachel suffers but Benjamin is born.

The citation of this prophecy demonstrates the great principle that one prophecy may have more than one meaning and within it may be embodied several meanings. It is the cause of much loss and confusion of thought when this principle of interpretation is not understood.

A Nazarene (2:23). It would be difficult definitely to say to what particular prophecy Matthew refers. He may have had more than one in mind, for he mentions 'prophets' in the plural. He may have had traditional utterances that had come down to his day, for he uses the word 'spoken'. It may have been verbally transmitted prophecy. Certainly, the name of the village of Nazareth seems to lend ground for the suggestion that the word sprang from it. 'Can any good thing come out of Nazareth?' Philologists have had much to say about this word. It seems to be related to 'a crown', and to have to do with 'separation', and is cognate with the word 'Nazarite'. It may also be related to '*netzer*', the Hebrew word for 'branch'. Maybe we shall be safe in embracing all these ideas, for they all had their fulfilment in Jesus. In a spiritual sense, if not a literal, He was a true *Nazarite* who did not fail in His vow. He was harmless, undefiled, and though He walked in and out among sinners He was separate from all their sinful ways. On His head was the *crown* of creatorial authority, which the first Adam forfeited by sin. He is five times called 'the Branch' in the Old Testament (Isa. 4:2, 11:1; Jer. 23:5; Zech. 3:8, 6:12). One thing is certain, 'Jesus the Nazarene' was a term of reproach and contempt, as is seen by the reply of the posse that came to arrest Him in the garden.

Matthew thus answers the second question. Citing from Isaiah, Hosea, Micah and Jeremiah, he shows beyond the slightest shadow of doubt that the circumstances attending the birth of Jesus accorded precisely with these foreshadowings. The normal human chance of their so doing was exceedingly remote; the likelihood of all these things being fulfilled in one person, and at one and the same time, was altogether out of the question. But so it came to pass.

3. HIS FORERUNNER (Chapter 3)

Yet another question must be asked. Did Jesus have the prescribed Forerunner? Malachi had written, 'Behold I will send My messenger, and he shall prepare the way before Him' (3:1). Isaiah had also spoken of a voice crying in the wilderness, 'Prepare ye the way of the Lord, make His paths straight.' Did the claim of Matthew that Jesus is the Messiah fail in this respect? No, for John Baptist was that Forerunner of whose ministry we are given an account in chapter 3.

He came into the wilderness preaching, 'The kingdom of the heavens is at hand'. Daniel's seventy weeks (that is, weeks of years) were shortly to expire; only a few more years remained. The King was already present and it was for John to prepare the people to receive Him. He, indeed, was a voice crying in the wilderness: he was in a scene where there was no fruit for God. His whole manner of life declared that he was in sympathy with the feelings of God concerning the state of His people. He wore sackcloth, his food was the plainest. He had but one purpose in life and that was to prepare a people for the Lord who was following him.

His was a ministry of law. The axe was already at the root of the tree, soon to be applied. When that axe fell it would send scurrying hither and thither the vipers who lay under its shade. They would flee, knowing that as the axe man follows his felling work with fire, so they would - or should - flee from the wrath to come. Mere ancestry is worthless. What counts with God is the fruit of the life; fruits that are the proper accompaniments of repentance. It was useless to claim Abraham as their father. They were a generation of vipers, and were of their father the devil. Sin had to be confessed, and the multitude was doing so; but this 'generation' of Sadducees and Pharisees were mere imitators, their heart was far from God.

The people were confessing their sins by being baptised of John in Jordan, taking their place in the river of death and judgment. The silences of Scripture are significant. John put them in the river but there is no mention made of their coming up out of the water. They did so, of course, but the Scripture is silent on the point, for John's was a ministry of law and this brings sin to light and imposes judgment on it. John could go no further. If there is to be release from judgment it must be brought in by Jesus, for all that law can do is to condemn and punish. Neither the rationalism of the Sadducees nor the ritualism of the Pharisees will deliver from sin's just recompense.

John's ministry made manifest the sinner's dire need of

Christ. And Christ in turn would become the touchstone of the whole human race. The world is His 'floor' and everyone will be winnowed out when He rises in judgment. Those who, like wheat, have life within will be gathered into His garner; those who are but chaff and are dead will be burned with unquenchable fire. This passage does not imply the annihilation of sinners; it rather connotes their eternal punishment, for as the fire is not quenched, neither is the sinner put out of being altogether - each continues.

John preached law; but the One who followed him is the Lawgiver. To Him alone belongs the right to judge. All judgment has been given to the Son for He is Son of Man.

Matthew here treats the matter panoramically, as is his wont throughout his Gospel. He does not go into details; they must be looked for in other parts of Scripture. Often, in one passage, he presents two or more things, each of which may be separated by long intervals of time. This is so in the very passage before us, for the gathering of the redeemed into the garner will take place long before the judgment at the Great White Throne. Again, the baptising 'with the Holy Ghost' took place on the Day of Pentecost, when the risen and ascended Christ fulfilled His promise and sent the Holy Spirit from heaven to indwell His people on earth. But the further item, 'and with fire' awaits fulfilment in the yet distant future. In one sentence, 'the acceptable year of the Lord' and 'the day of vengeance of our God' are conjoined; but, while the former has for long been running its course, the latter has not yet begun.

None knew better than John himself his own inferiority to Christ. He was the voice; Jesus was the Word. He was a lamp; Jesus was the light. He was the herald; he was not the King. He was the axe man; he was not the landowner. He baptised with water, the Lord would baptise with the Holy Spirit and with fire. His was but a preparatory work.

We have already seen that the Lord Jesus identified Himself with the nation of Israel in their history and this is so when He was baptised by John. He had no sin to confess, He did not need to be baptised. But linking Himself with that people, He would do as the others had done and go into the waters of Jordan and thus identify Himself with them. He is here anticipatively, as later He was actually, 'numbered with the transgressors'. It is to be remarked that He took the initiative: John did not come to Him but He approached John. John rightly demurred, but the Lord said, 'Suffer it to be so now, for thus it becometh us to fulfill all righteousness.' Do not overlook that pronoun 'us' - John and the Lord. This was to be the terminus of John's ministry and in that manner was he to close it. His goal had been to bring the people to Christ and prepare them for Him. He was the forerunner and the porter, introducing Christ to the people.

The Lord Jesus was to begin His public ministry in this manner. Although the Lord was not a sinner, John was quite right in baptising Him in these circumstances; and although the Lord needed not to make this confession, He was fulfilling righteousness in being baptised. In His case, mention is made of His coming up out of the water: a thing which we noticed is not said of the others. Death had no claim over Him for He was sinless. It could not hold Him. The whole scene was symbolic of His actual death on the Cross, His burial in Joseph's tomb, and His resurrection therefrom. As here so then. After His coming up from the grave the Spirit of God came down to dwell in His people, as here He abode upon Him.

All three Persons of the Holy Trinity are active here. The Father attests His pleasure in the Son, whose private life of thirty years He had witnessed (of which but one item only is disclosed to us). The Spirit abides upon Him, a thing that had never taken place before; for when the Spirit moved men on earth He clothed them for the time being and then left. None was so perfect that the Spirit could abide upon them. The whole scene graphically adumbrates Calvary and Pentecost, and the uniting of the believer with the Father, Son and Holy Spirit.

4. IS HE COMPETENT TO RULE? (Chapter 4)

Although a person may have a hereditary claim to a throne and other things which justify the claim, yet if he personally is incompetent to rule he should not be entrusted with government. Is then Jesus, whose genealogical tree we have seen to be satisfactory, whose circumstances of birth accorded with prophecy, and who had the prescribed forerunner, competent to hold the reins of government?

The record of the Lord's temptation given in Matthew's fourth chapter proves that He is, for it shows how He overcame the one who was responsible for all the misrule in the world. He overcame the devil, binding the strong man and thereafter spoiling his goods.

He is the last Adam who, in the midst of conditions far different from those of the garden of Eden, stood firm. The first Adam fell when tempted of Satan, although he had plenty and was not hungry, he was in a garden not a wilderness, and there was at the time of his testing the whole of creation at his feet, nor were there any wild beasts. Everything was favourable to him and there was no excuse for his trespass. On the other hand, everything was unfavourable to Jesus. He was hungry, in a wilderness, and with the wild beasts - yet He fell not.

Luke gives the order of the temptations differently from Matthew. He follows the principle of the lust of the flesh, the lust of the eye and the pride of life, of which John writes in his epistle. Matthew, however, records them in principle, as they occurred to Israel when they were in the wilderness. Firstly in the matter of bread (Exod. 16); secondly in the matter of temptation concerning water (Exod. 17); and thirdly in the matter of worship (Exod. 32). He is here retracing Israel's wilderness history, showing Himself perfect in contrast to their sad imperfections. They murmured because they had no bread; they tempted the Lord and limited the Most High because they had no water; and in the absence of Moses they got Aaron to make a golden calf to which they bowed down and worshipped. The Lord thus once more identifies Himself with that people.

Why did Satan tempt Him? He knew nothing of the purpose of God which was being worked out in the pathway of the Lord, so what was behind his actions? Surely he desired to verify the Father's declaration that He was His Son. He tempted Him with the view of finding out what to him was an unknown quantity - can He really sin? The tempter was not omniscient, he had to make trial and discovery. What an immense triumph it would have been for him had he got the Son of God to sin! But he knew not God.

The temptation was a very real thing to the Lord Jesus. It was no play-acting. The Lord was not playing a role and merely creating an impression. He was truly man, and His bodily needs and the adverse circumstances made the subtlety of Satan and his wiles felt all the more keenly. To Him the repugnancy of the sinful suggestions made by Satan had a far more severe impact on His holy being than it would have had on any fallen man. His perfection and holiness did not in any wise reduce the reality of the test. The issue showed Him to be One who was able not to sin as well as One who was not able to sin. It was a moral inability as well as a spiritual triumph.

The scene is pictorially set forth in the notorious victory of David over Goliath. He used but one stone out of five taken from the brook. The Lord Jesus used but one of the five Pentateuch books contained within the volume of 'the Law, the Psalms and the Prophets': He only quoted from Deuteronomy. As David first stunned and then beheaded Goliath, so the Lord Jesus overcame the devil at this temptation. He was, as it were, stunned, and 'departed from Him for a season'. Later by His death, He put out of action 'him that had the power of death', using the devil's own sword to complete His victory. He destroyed the devil (Heb. 2:14).

The word of God was hidden within the heart of the Lord Jesus. He was guided by it and without it He would do nothing. The devil here shows himself to be unaltered from the time of Adam's fall. The parallel is plain. In each case the word of God was doubted. There Satan said, 'Hath God said?', and here he said, 'If Thou art the Son of God ...' In each case it was distorted. There Eve added to the word (for God had said nothing about touching the tree); and took from it (for God had said, 'Ye shall die', but she said, 'Lest ye die'). Here Satan omitted from his quotation from Psalm 91 the important words 'in all thy ways'. It is both an old and a modern tactic of Satan. However, God's word was not denied here, nor was it disobeyed: the victory was complete.

He was tested 'in all points' - that is, in every class of temptation - 'as we are, sin apart'. This experience gives Him a competency to sympathise with those who are tested. Not merely with His apostles who had continued with Him in all His later trials, but with us in our day; for in heaven His earthly experiences are evergreen in His memory.

The victorious issue of this temptation revealed who He really was. He was not only superior to all men and stronger than the devil, who was called elsewhere 'the strong man', but He was above all angels, for at this time they came and ministered unto Him. He was their Lord.

The enmity of Satan to Christ is relentless. If subtle wiles will not achieve his end with the Son of God he will use fiery darts against His forerunner, until such time as he finds himself at liberty to do so against the Lord Himself. John, therefore, is cast into prison (4:12). Jesus moves from Nazareth to Capernaum where, in the midst of their spiritual darkness, He fulfils yet another prophetic word concerning Him, and He shines there as a great light. This is the seventh prophecy cited.

The imprisonment of John, far from shutting His mouth, is but an impetus for Him to begin to preach and continue the same message as His forerunner had been proclaiming. Indeed, He embarks upon His public life work. He preaches, He calls His apostles, for He knew His plans, and therefore made preparations for the continuation of His work after He Himself had returned to heaven. His words are confirmed by His deeds: they show that He was 'a man approved of God by miracles and wonders and signs which God wrought by Him' (Acts 2:22).

Having overcome the one who was responsible for all the misrule, sin and misery in the world, it is as nothing for Him to spoil his goods: overcoming demons and healing those who had become victims in a spiritual or physical way to the consequences of the introduction of sin into the world by the devil. It is no marvel that crowds followed Him; He has given indisputable evidence of His competency to rule the world in which Satan had wrought so much havoc. He can undo the works of the devil. He, indeed, is One who can be safely followed, even if it involves leaving one's nets and one's relations (4:19-20).

5. THE LAWS OF THE KINGDOM (Chapters 5-7)

Our next enquiry is: By what laws will He rule? These are set out in what is commonly called The Sermon on the Mount, in chapters 5-7.

There has been much misunderstanding touching this part of Scripture. For instance, it has been asserted that this Sermon does not apply to the Christians today. We are told that it relates to the Jews, and pertains either to days that succeed the Rapture of the saints, or else to the Millennium. But is this so? It certainly seems strange that so large a territory of Holy Writ should relate to so short a space of time as that which will succeed the Rapture and precede the Second Advent of the Lord to earth. This period must be at least seven years, though it may be considerably more; we do not know. But it cannot very well be of the same length as that which has already elapsed since the Lord went to heaven. Is it likely therefore, that His instruction in this Sermon should be limited to so short a period?

It cannot apply exclusively to the Millennium, if for no other reason that there will not be persecution of the godly in those days. Doubtless the laws of the Kingdom which are here set out will apply then, when the King is on earth and His Kingdom has come, but it plainly cannot be limited to those days. It envisages times of stress and persecution and these will not occur in the Millennium.

To what period then does it relate and to whom does it apply?

The laws relate to 'the kingdom of the heavens', a phrase peculiar to Matthew's Gospel. The kingdom of the heavens is the same thing as 'the kingdom of God'. The terms are used interchangeably, as will be seen by comparing the Gospels. It is untenable to say that the kingdom of God contains only the genuine, but the kingdom of the heavens embraces the true and the false. The mustard seed and leaven parables, which doubtless speak of the evil influences operative in Christendom, are found both in Matthew and Luke, as descriptive both of the kingdom of the heavens and the kingdom of God respectively. The one phrase denotes the ruler, God; the other the headquarters of rule, heaven - much as men used to speak of the empire of the Queen and the empire of Great Britain.

Matthew uses the phrase 'the kingdom of the heavens', because the Jews for whom he writes chiefly would never confuse heaven with God. They were monotheistic; they were not sun worshippers. But Luke, who writes as a Gentile, speaks of 'the kingdom of God', for the Gentiles might very well fall into the error of confusing the heavens with God and worship them and not Him.

The kingdom of the heavens did not commence, as some have affirmed, when God gave government into the hands of Nebuchadnezzar. He was made to know that the heavens do rule; not that they commenced to rule when Israel lost their place with God. As a matter of fact, away back in David's day, God had His throne in the heavens (Psa. 11:4). Solomon, too, called upon God to hear 'in heaven' (1 Kgs. 8:39).

Moreover, it is a 'kingdom of all ages' (Psa. 145:13 margin) and is not limited to any one or few ages of earth's history. As soon as there was a man on earth for God to rule from heaven, as soon then did the kingdom of God and the kingdom of the heavens commence. This was not affected by Israel's Theocracy, when God dwelt between the cherubim; it was always true that 'God dwelleth not in temples made with hands'. His presence was to be seen there, but it is impossible for the omnipresent God to be limited by the confines of an earthly tabernacle.

It should further be noted that entry into both the kingdom of God and into the kingdom of the heavens is in the same manner. 'Except a man be born of water and of the Spirit, he cannot enter into the kingdom of God' (John 3:5). New birth is essential. So also, 'Except ye turn and become as little children, ye shall in no wise enter into the kingdom of heaven'. The same condition is laid down. It is not overlooked that the one is passive and the other active: the one tells us what God does and the other what man should do. But we are concerned here with the point of likeness, not the differences.

Furthermore, the moral features of each are the same. 'The kingdom of God is not eating and drinking, but righteousness, and peace, and joy in the Holy Spirit' (Rom. 14:17). So in the

Beatitudes of the Sermon, we find righteousness and peace and joy mentioned in that very order (Matt. 5:6, 9, 12).

The phrase is not always used with precisely the same connotation. It is most important that we should consider in what sense it is employed and that will be determined by the context. Sometimes it refers to a sphere of merely nominal profession, and as an example see chapter 5 verses 19-20. There is clearly a mixture of the true and false. Sometimes it is a sphere of vital reality (13:44). At other times it relates to a sphere where moral features are to be seen, such as chapter 5:3 and chapter 18:3. And yet again, it may refer to a future manifested kingdom, for example chapter 8:11. So that each passage must be carefully read and the particular aspect of the kingdom considered. There can be no true understanding of this matter if these things are ignored.

There are many other titles of the kingdom. In all cases they relate to the one kingdom, although the emphasis is placed differently. It will repay the reader well to ponder the following passages: Matthew 13:41; Revelation 1:9; 2 Timothy 4:1; Ephesians 5:5; Revelation 11:15; 12:10; Colossians 1:13; Matthew 13:43. Of course, when heaven and earth are reunited in harmony and 'the tabernacle of God is with men' (Rev. 21:3), the title 'the kingdom of the heavens' would no longer be appropriate; it would then be 'the kingdom of God'. All these observations are essential if the Sermon on the Mount is to be understood correctly and the parties recognised to whom it relates.

What is the relation of the Church, which is the body of Christ, to the Kingdom?

It is IN the kingdom, though it did not commence till Pentecost (Acts 2) and it will be taken away long before the kingdom has come on earth. Therefore, the church and the kingdom are not commensurate either as to duration or as to personnel. But the church is in the kingdom. Seeing that this is so, it cannot fairly be said that the laws of the kingdom do not apply to it. They apply as much to it as to any others who are in it, although not of this present dispensation. All who at any time acknowledge allegiance to the King are expected to obey His laws.

It is freely granted that the Sermon on the Mount does not speak of the special mysteries of which Paul writes. But there is nothing in the sermon that is incongruous with such mysteries. We must remember that believers of the present era are members of the body of Christ as to privilege; children of God as to relationship; but sons of the kingdom as to responsibility. Our peculiar privilege does not nullify our common responsibility. Any system of teaching that tends in this direction is not only false but dangerous. We should eschew it. The fact is that the Sermon on the Mount is supradispensational and cannot be restricted to any one period. They are laws that should be obeyed by all the subjects of the kingdom no matter at what stage of history they live.

If any alleges he prefers the Sermon on the Mount to the law of Moses, he knows not what he says. The former is far more severe in its obligations and penalties than the latter. The former regards the thought and look as equivalent to the deed; not so the latter. The former imposed the punishment of Gehenna (5:22) on body and soul, whereas the latter had only to do with corporal punishment. Read as a test of what man should be, it can only utterly condemn him and make him feel as the man of Luke 5:12, 'full of leprosy'. His safest course is to cast himself on the Lord for mercy. Had he received his deserts it would have gone ill with him.

In the power of God's Spirit we can and should fulfil its demands, but we cannot do it of ourselves. Before John's imprisonment the Lord taught Nicodemus, 'Ye must be born again'; but after his imprisonment He enunciated these precepts (see John 3:24 and Matt. 4:12). New birth must come first. Unregenerate man cannot comply with this Sermon; it can only condemn him. But not all regenerate persons obey it, and if we fail to do so, when the crises of life occur and life's storms are about us, we shall discover that what we have built will collapse.

Matthew 7:16ff teaches that it is not the talk of the lips but the doing of the word that counts with the Lord. Note the emphasis on the word 'do' in verses 21, 24, 26. Let us not seek to escape our obligation by getting under a false dispensational cloak; it will not help in the stormy day.

It has been necessary thus to deal with the matter in this general fashion so that we may get the laws of the kingdom in their right perspective. But we will go into a few details.

It is said that the so-called 'Lord's Prayer' found in this sermon is unsuitable for our days, but is that really so? Let us test the matter.

'Our Father which art in heaven' is not incompatible with the truth set out by Paul in his Ephesian letter. There he speaks of our being seated with Christ in the heavenly places; yet in that very epistle masters are reminded that they have a Lord in heaven (6:9). Moreover, the Lord spoke of His heavenly Father when He was on earth, and He possessed then as always the attribute of omnipresence.

'Thy kingdom come' is not unsuitable for our lips, seeing that Peter speaks of an abundant entrance into the kingdom of our Lord Jesus Christ, and Paul reminds the Thessalonians that God is calling them unto His own kingdom and glory (2 Pet. 1:11; 1 Thess. 2:12). It is proper that we respond to the Lord's word, 'Behold, I come quickly', by, 'Even so, come, Lord Jesus'; but surely we know that when He comes for us it will be the initial stages that will result in His taking to Himself His great power with the view of reigning (Rev. 11:17).

'Give us this day our daily bread.' What shall we say as to this, seeing that most are free to pray for daily bread were we in circumstances of need.

'Forgive us our debts, as we forgive our debtors.' Some say this is legal ground and that we stand on the ground of grace. But God never did forgive a person at any time on legal ground. If He forgave at all it was in sovereign grace, never otherwise. What chapter 6:12 means is that we cannot expect to have our Father's governmental forgiveness and live in the joy of His smile, whilst we are encouraging an unforgiving spirit against another. That would be living in sin, and how then could God forgive that?

It is freely granted that this prayer is so worded that it is both suited to our times and to those that will succeed the removal of the church. Of course, the use of it as a vain repetition is to be deprecated. It was never given for that purpose, but rather to give us guiding principles as to how we should pray. God and His interests should come first, our needs thereafter. Nor should there be any prolixity. Sincerity, subjection and definiteness are desirable in prayer as much as in other things.

Seeing then that this prayer is appropriate to us in our day, is not all the rest of the Sermon also? We should find most of the instruction of these chapters repeated in some form or other in the epistles which, without doubt, relate to us. We suffer an irreparable loss if we yield to that system of teaching which robs us of this tract of Holy Scripture. Those who do so are not logical. Are they willing to forfeit the comfort of the closing section of chapter 6? Would they exclude us altogether from this part? It is true that we are not under law but under grace. Yet we are 'in law' to Christ, and the imperative mood is by no means lacking in Paul's letters. He did not fear to tell the saints what they ought to do.

No, no, we bless God for the Lord's comforting words about the birds of the air and the lilies of the field, and the futility of worrying. We take courage from this, but it is dishonest to do that and yet to discount the rest of the Sermon.

The construction of this Sermon is very similar to the Mosaic law. That was given on a mountain; it had a Decalogue, then detailed applications, and ended with blessings and curses. So, too, this was given on a mountain; it had the beatitudes, then detailed applications, and finishes with our house standing or collapsing in the time of storm.

The Law-giver Himself is here speaking. He refers to the former law and then adds, 'But I say unto you'. He speaks with authority. He is not interpreting former statutes, but originating new ones. He is setting out His own laws which are in force in His kingdom, and when obeyed yield the very best out of one's life, making for security whatever changes may come.

We dare not go into details, but we must call attention to its two golden rules. The one is Godward: 'Seek ye first the kingdom of God, and His righteousness' (6:33); and the other manward: 'All things whatsoever ye would that men should do to you, do ye even so to them: for this is the law and the prophets' (7:12). By observing these two rules every other item will necessarily be fulfilled. Conversely, one cannot disobey any one point and fulfil the golden rules.

The present-day evangelist oftentimes uses the illustration of the broad and narrow ways to point out the way to eternal life in heaven, and the way to eternal perdition. Now while there is no harm in this application of the passage, it should be remembered that this does not appear to be its prime interpretation. The life mentioned in chapter 7:14 is that which is life indeed, enjoyed here and now. The destruction in verse 13 is ruination of this present life. The narrow way is that delineated by the precepts contained in this Sermon; the broad way is the path of uncontrolled self-will that will not brook being restricted by these kingdom laws.

The storm and floods and winds of verses 25 and 27 set forth those adverse circumstances of life which put to the test that which we have built. The standing or falling of such house pictures the manner in which we either stand up to such circumstances or collapse under them. The manner of our life will determine how we shall meet adversity.

There are many who would teach differently from what the Lord taught. They are false prophets (7:15) whose teaching may be judged not so much by what is said as by what kind of life the teachers live, and what kind of life their teaching produces. It is 'by their fruits ye shall know them'.

Before closing this chapter, two things call for special remark:

Divorce (5:32)

Seeing many godly men, after much thought, believe that the Lord sanctions divorce for adultery and permits the remarriage of the innocent party, it ill becomes any who think otherwise to dogmatise. However, it seems to the present writer that the Lord nowhere gives consent to divorce for adultery; but He permits putting away for fornication, which is not the same thing. A woman is bound to her husband so long as he liveth; but if he be dead, she is free to be joined to another (see Romans 7:2; 1 Cor. 7:39). This applies likewise to the husband. 'What God hath joined together, let not man put asunder' is the statement of the Lord Himself (Matt. 19:6).

There is a difference of opinion as to what is fornication; there being no doubt about adultery. Yet even that word 'adultery' has been given a wider meaning than would appear to be justified. Some believe that fornication relates to pre-marital sex; still others that it relates to prostitution for gain, whether the person is married or not: yet others regard it to refer to marriage within forbidden degrees. In any event, whatever it may mean, the following points should be borne in mind before reaching a definite conclusion:

a. Why in chapter 5:32 and chapter 19:9 does the Lord use the two words, fornication and adultery? To substitute the one for the other and regard them as synonymous would be to rob the statement of all good sense.

b. Why in the one category of sins are the two things mentioned separately? (See Matt. 15:19; Mark 7:21; 1 Cor. 6:9; Heb. 13:4.) If they were identical there would appear to be no good reason for mentioning both.

c. Why is it that there is no mention of the 'excepting clause' in any other part of Scripture save in Matthew? Had we not this Gospel, the question of divorce could never have been raised. The New Testament would have appeared to be absolute on the binding nature of marriage, 'until death do part'.

d. It would appear that the case of Joseph and Mary may be regarded as the classical test case. There was the appearance that fornication had taken place. The Lord did not disapprove of Joseph's intention of putting Mary away (that is, divorcing her; for the betrothal contract was as binding as marriage itself), but He explained the situation, which made it unnecessary for Joseph to continue with divorce proceedings.

e. If the tenor of the Lord's instruction was that, in certain circumstances, release from the married partner were permissible, why did the disciples say, 'If the case of the man be so with his wife, it is good not to marry'? (Matt. 19:10). That is, rather than run the risk of an unsatisfactory life union, it is better to remain a eunuch. If the Lord permitted release, this remark would appear to be pointless.

f. Some have pleaded unnatural hardship on the person who desires release but is not allowed to procure it. They have cited, 'It is better to marry than to burn' (1 Cor. 7:9). Altogether apart from unfaithfulness, circumstances do arise where such an unfortunate state must exist. For example, when one's partner falls seriously ill, either bodily or mentally.

Morality has fallen seriously in our day, and Christians should exercise the greatest care not to lower their moral standards. It can so readily result in lowered physical standards, with tragic consequences.

The literal interpretation of Scripture (5:39, 42)

Matthew 5:39 is an excellent example of a case where the literal interpretation of Scripture is untenable. Indeed, were this carried out literally it would be justly provocative to the offending party and incite further assault. As in so many instances, not only in the Sermon on the Mount but in Scripture generally, we have to ascertain the spirit that lies behind the words and not always be bound by the literal. It is a safe rule of interpretation that, where the literal yields good sense that must be regarded as the meaning, but if the literal interpretation leads one into an absurdity, as for example in the case of this passage, another meaning must be sought.

It is plain, for instance in chapter 5:42, that if one were to lend to all who would wish to borrow, it might be for harm and the ultimate serious embarrassment of the borrower, making his last state worse than the first. It might indeed be the inflicting of more injury upon him instead of doing him a kindness.

In interpreting any such passage we must bear in mind the whole of the context. For example, the verses here cited occur in a section where the Lord is correcting that hard, stickling legality which gives as good as is given. Instead of acting in this manner, we should show a merciful and generous spirit. The Lord surely is not here telling us to encourage every mendicant beggar, irrespective of the merits of the case. Apply the literal interpretation to chapter 7:6 and ask yourself: is this really what the Lord intended? Or to chapter 18:8-9. The inner meaning must be sought in such passages.

6. MESSIANIC MIRACLES (Chapter 8:1-9:35)

There remains one more question to be answered: Did Jesus

do the prescribed Messianic miracles? Did He 'bring the blind by a way that they knew not ... make darkness light before them'? Did 'the deaf hear', and did 'the eyes of the blind see out of obscurity, and out of darkness'? Did He 'bear our sicknesses and carry our sorrows'? Were 'the eyes of the blind opened and the ears of the deaf unstopped'? Did 'the lame leap as a hart'? Did 'the tongue of the dumb sing'? All these things Isaiah foreshadowed would be wrought by God's servant (see Isa. 29:18; 35:5-6; 42:7,16; 53:4). The answer to this enquiry is given in Matthew chapters 8 and 9. The leper was cleansed; the centurion's boy was healed; Peter's wife's mother was delivered from her fever; the tempest on the lake was stilled; the demon-possessed were liberated; the palsied man was made to walk; the ruler's daughter was restored; the woman who had been troubled by a long-standing haemorrhage was healed; the blind were given their sight, the dumb man was freed from the demon which troubled him, and he spoke.

Jesus had authority over things visible and invisible. Nothing was impossible to Him. He not only did all that the prophets had foreshadowed but much more. He forgave sins. This is not demonstrable to the eyes of men: so far as their senses are concerned it is limited to a verbal statement. The truth of that statement is tested by the accompanying miracle. If His word was effective in the physical sphere, contrary to all human precedents, it proves the effectiveness of His word in the spiritual sphere.

In chapters 8 and 9 we see the Son of Man with the crown of authority upon His head. He stands in a fallen creation, as Adam stood in an unfallen. Although Adam lost his crown of authority by sin, the Lord Jesus retains His because of His sinlessness. Hence His authority over things which are the consequent damage wrought by sin.

Guided by the Spirit of God, Matthew arranges his material in significant order. The Jewish leper is cleansed before the Gentile boy; the mother-in-law is healed when Jesus entered the house, and at eventide the crowd come to Him for healing. This depicts on a small scale in the physical realm what is being enacted on a worldwide scale in the spiritual since the Lord went back to heaven. The gospel went to the Jew first; then the Gentile was brought into blessing. When this day of grace is over the Lord will return to the 'house' of Israel and take up that people once more and, as a nation, they will be 'healed' (Isa. 53:5). And when that takes place the way will be open for universal millennial blessing of all. It is the same in the case of the ruler's daughter and the woman with the issue of blood: on His way to heal the child the woman pressed in and was healed. So the Lord came to bless Israel: but before they are healed the Gentiles press in and get a blessing earlier.

It is a useful key to the understanding of this Gospel to note that 'house' often symbolises [the house of] Israel. We shall have occasion to mention the Lord's leaving the house and returning to the house on sundry occasions as this exposition proceeds. His movements are symbolic of His ways with that earthly people Israel.

Matthew arranges his material not only dispensationally but also morally. Jairus's daughter is raised; the blind are made to see; the dumb to speak; and then the apostles are selected and commissioned. Note the order: life, sight, speech, service. Such is the moral order in the ways of God when saving and using anyone. The order is never varied. It could not be, for there must first be life and then sight before there can be speech and service.

These chapters are also full of evangelistic truth. Regeneration is hinted at in chapter 9:16ff: the mere patching up of that which is old is useless; there must be a fresh start. Old vessels cannot contain new wine. Judaism was not patched up, but a new thing which we now call Christianity was brought in. The flesh is irremediable; there must be a completely new start, and this is effected when new birth takes place. God never mends the old man, He displaces it by the new.

Man by reason of sin stands in a twofold state. He is under Satan's power, and subject to divine judgment. But the Lord Jesus is seen in these chapters to be able to deliver from both. In chapter 8:28ff we see demonstrated the first and in chapter 9:1ff we have a record of the second.

A few details call for remark:

Matthew 8:12

'The sons of the kingdom' do not represent those who are necessarily *bona fides* sons. This is a phrase indicative of what Israel was by religious profession. Believers today, as we have before remarked, are children of God in relationship; members of the body of Christ in privilege; and sons of the kingdom in responsibility. When John in his epistle writes on the subject of the children of God, he enumerates those inevitable marks which characterise genuine children. He realises, as a perusal of his letter will show, that the mere 'saying' that one is a child is insufficient: the verbal profession must be endorsed by the life's behaviour.

When Paul writes about membership in the body of Christ he does not contemplate mere profession, for real membership in that body and union with the head is only possible by the Spirit of God working in an individual. But the 'kingdom' is a sphere of profession, which profession may or may not be real. The 'sons of the kingdom' are those who profess to belong to it.

'The outer darkness' is not for the true child of God. It is an expression that occurs three times in Matthew's Gospel. Here in chapter 8:12 it has to do with the Christ-rejecting Jews. In chapter 22:13, it is the man who came in without a wedding garment, an outward title to be present. In chapter 25:30, it is the unprofitable servant. The Lord holds a man responsible for what he claims to be and acts accordingly. It is only a subterfuge to assert, as some do, that this 'outer darkness' is different from 'the blackness of darkness for ever' (Jude v. 13). The whole atmosphere of these three passages is one of finality. There is no hint that those outside are ultimately brought in. Such an idea is dangerously akin to the heresy of 'universalism' - at any rate, in principle.

Matthew 8:17

The quotation from Isaiah 53 is cited here, not in relation to the Atonement wrought by the Lord Jesus when He died, but rather relative to His sympathetic and miraculous working among the diseased of His day. That bodily healing in the present era is not a necessary sequel of the Atonement is shown in that: Paul had a thorn in the flesh which was not removed; he left Trophimus at Miletus sick; Epaphroditus was sick 'nigh unto death' and was not, apparently, miraculously healed. Besides, many godly saints since then have suffered bodily ills without relief until they departed to be with Christ, and who will dare to attribute this to their lack of faith?

Matthew 9:35

This closes the evidence which Matthew produces in support

of his opening words 'Jesus Christ'. He surely has proved his case to the satisfaction of all who are willing to be convinced. Of course, where the will is obdurate no amount of argument will succeed, so that it is not to be anticipated that the carnal man will acknowledge the claims of Jesus. The mind of the flesh is enmity to God. As we shall see, Israel deliberately stopped their ears and shut their eyes. They did not wish to acknowledge Him. Moreover, we shall also learn later from this Gospel that these things are hidden from the wise and prudent, but they are revealed to babes. Mere flesh and blood does not reveal who Jesus really is: the Father in heaven does that.

7. THE OFFER OF THE KINGDOM (Chapter 9:36-10:42)

In chapter 10 Matthew records the formal offer of the kingdom to the nation of Israel. This offer was to be given to the nation of Israel alone, hence twelve apostles were chosen as there were twelve tribes. These tribes were acknowledged by God even then, as a perusal of Luke chapters 1 and 2, and James 1:1 will show. Here they present a living Christ to the nation. In Acts 2, the apostolate having been made up to twelve, Judas having defaulted and Matthias having been appointed to take his place, a risen Christ is presented to the nation. It was in each case a genuine offer, notwithstanding that the Lord knew what the issue would be. The fact that He knows how things will turn out, and what other moves He will adopt in the new circumstances, does not prevent Him from making a genuine proposal to the nation. The members of the nation are thus put on the ground of responsibility and are liable if they fail to do what they should. Accordingly, the Lord appoints the twelve apostles and sends them forth with a restricted commission, limiting them to the lost sheep of the house of Israel (10:6). Neither the Samaritans nor the Gentiles come within the scope of His charge.

Matthew 10 is plainly no charter for modern missionary work. Not merely because of the aforesaid restriction, but because it supposes the presence of the King who would shortly follow them up. 'All nations' and 'all the world' is now the rule, not so then. This was not a long-term programme, for they are forbidden to take money or surplus clothing. The nation was to be tested by this mission. Would the messengers find open doors and willing recipients? Elijah in his day could not find any such open door in Israel; but he found the widow of Sarepta, outside the land, who was willing to receive him. Would they fare any better than he?

Although it is true that there are in this chapter certain principles which should be observed no matter in what age one lives, yet a careful reading of this chapter will make clear that its terms are strictly limited, temporal, and local. The message was, 'The kingdom of the heavens is at hand'; for the King Himself was there. If they had been willing to receive Him on His terms, He was willing to establish the kingdom. There was a time when they would have taken Him by force and made Him king, but they were in no proper condition to submit to His rule. All they then thought of was their material sustenance; more important matters did not weigh with them. We shall see how this mission fared when considering chapters 11 and 12.

As we have already observed, Scripture often brings together two events in one sentence which are separated by a long period of time. This is the case in verses 23. The beginning of the period is implied in the words, 'Ye shall not have gone over the cities of Israel', and the end of the period is covered by the phrase, 'until the Son of Man be come'. Between these two points lies the whole of the present era, beginning with Pentecost and terminating with the Rapture of the church. It is not mentioned; it is not considered, it is, indeed, not in view. (There are numerous cases where two such events are conjoined in one phrase but which are separated by a long period of time, e.g. Isa. 61:1-2; John 5:29.)

The conditions which obtained in the days when the Lord sent out these men were (a) an apostate Jewish nation in Palestine, (b) a dominant Roman power to whom they were subject, and (c) a godly remnant. These conditions do not exist today, whatever may be said about the present state of Israel and the land of Palestine as it is at present. But these very conditions will be resumed, not by the design of men but under the governmental ways of God, after the church has been taken away and before the Lord Himself returns to earth. For, be it carefully noted, we have nowhere in Matthew's Gospel the coming to the air of the Lord Jesus for His church. That was a mystery not contained in the synoptic Gospels.

The 'coming' of the verse under consideration is that of the Son of Man for judgment. Prior to that coming the special ministry here inaugurated, and the special message to be preached by the apostles at this time, will then be resumed by His Jewish servants. There will be troublous times of persecution but 'he that endureth to the end shall be saved'. This is not the message to be proclaimed to the sinner today, but it will be the hope of the godly in those times of persecution. 'The end' referred to is when the Son of Man comes back to earth to claim His throne by force. The 'salvation' mentioned is bodily salvation from the then existing troubles. The preachers will be believing Jews; the place of their preaching will be the land of Palestine.

In a word, what was begun in chapter 10 will be resumed after the church, which is the Body of Christ, has been removed from earth. The rejection by Israel of their true King caused God to break off His dealings with them for the time being, and to effect something new in the earth, namely the calling out of the nations a people for His name, thus forming the church. When this new interim work has been completed and taken away, then that which was started here in chapter 10, and suspended because of the guilt of Israel in putting to death their Messiah, will be resumed, and they will not have gone over the cities of Judah until the Son of Man actually returns.

Thus the apostles here at this time are a representative company of those who from the Jewish nation, wrought upon by the Spirit of God, will be witnesses of Christ: announcing His coming to earth to set up His kingdom. It is true, of course, that the apostles formed the nucleus of the church which was brought into being on the day of Pentecost when the Spirit of God was sent from heaven, but they are not viewed as such in this chapter. There is not a hint of that. They represent here another company.

It should further be remarked that verse 23 implies (though it does not go into details) that the Lord Jesus would be rejected and would depart from the earth and later come back. The implications of this are most important. Its true interpretation can only be ascertained by having regard to the general tenor of New Testament teaching touching the future of the Jew and his land. The Lord would go away, so the verse implies (though it does not categorically say so), and He would return as Son of Man - a title which is never used by Paul in regard to the church of which Christ is the Head. The title 'Son of Man' has to do with judgment; for all judgment has been given to the Son because He is Son of Man (John 5:27).

This chapter is a case wherein the principle applies that all

Scripture is for us, but it is not all about us. We may read this chapter 10 and glean important practical lessons. Such as, good works should attend our preaching; faith should mark His servants in regard to their recurring material needs; we should be wise as serpents and harmless as doves; we should not be surprised if we are opposed and persecuted, but be faithful until death. All these things have been wonderfully demonstrated throughout the whole of the time since the Lord ascended to the Father. But this does not affect the true interpretation of the chapter. As with all Scripture, the application of its principles is one thing: the interpretation of its meaning is altogether another.

The coming of the Lord Jesus to earth was the most important event in human history. Its effect has been worldwide. How has it affected men? Verse 34 will tell us. This verse does not state the purpose of His coming but rather the result that accrued from it. Christ is a dividing factor. Families are divided because of Him; nations are divided; mankind is divided. Those who ally themselves with Him necessarily find themselves opposed by the world and often by those nearest to them. It cannot be otherwise. He is the touchstone of mankind. This has been so ever since Bethlehem's manger received the Son of God. Simeon forecast this. He claims the first place with every one of us: His claims are greater than those of either parents or children. We should be prepared to follow Him though it entails bearing a cross and losing our life. After all, the salvation of the soul is at stake, and what can be more vital?

One remark more. The words of the Lord here do not relate to the domestic claims of those whom He was then commissioning, but to the domestic claims of those who heard their message. Its parallel today is when a heathen becomes a Christian and has, in consequence, to lose every earthly tie and friend. The passage has nothing to do with the sacrifices of those who go from other lands to work among them.

8. HOW WAS THE MESSAGE RECEIVED? (Chapter 11)

This chapter presents four kinds of persons, showing how the message reacted on them.

1. In the first instance John the Baptist comes before us (vv. 2-15). This may seem to be strange, but he represents a class. He himself had proclaimed the very same message, but was now in prison and he could not understand why the Lord Jesus did nothing to effect his release. He represents that class of person who may be described as *honest doubters*.

   Appearances seemed to contradict John's belief and his preaching. Among the messianic miracles was the 'opening of the prison to them that are bound'. Yet here was John, bound in prison, but the Lord did not open the doors and set him free. Had he been mistaken? He sends messengers to make enquiry. The Lord does not solve the mystery but calls attention to His positive actions. The answer which He gives to John's perplexity was designed not only to reassure him but to call for the further exercise of faith. There is no sternness or reproof for such doubting - how gracious the Lord is in such cases!

   This leads the Lord to speak to the multitude about John. He would not have him discredited in their eyes, despite the fact that his faith wavered. John was no self-indulgent man, wearing soft raiment; he lived in the wilderness, not a palace. Nor was he fickle, as a shaken reed. He was in fact 'the greatest ever born of women' (11:11). Oh, the immensity of such a statement! Yet in their midst was One who was greater than John.

'The lesser' (R.V. margin) in the kingdom of heaven is a covert allusion to the Lord Himself. Did He not go much lower than ever John did? True greatness is dependent on the depth of humility. John indeed was great, but the Lord was greater. Had the people been willing to receive it, John would have been that foreshadowed Elias that was to come prior to the King Himself (v. 14).

No doubt in those days there were many like John, who were honestly perplexed and found it impossible to reconcile things satisfactorily by their reasoning. But though reason has often to halt, faith goes on. John must still trust though there was no active intervention by the Lord to release him from prison.

2. The next class is spoken of as 'this generation' (vv. 16-19). The word 'generation' does not denote merely those living at one specific time, but rather those characterised by childish behaviour. They were like children playing in the market squares: neither the game of weddings nor the game of funerals would satisfy them. They did not know what they wanted. John was maligned as having a demon, and the Son of Man was contemptuously spoken of as a gluttonous man, and winebibber, a friend of publicans and sinners. Neither was accepted by the people although each was so different from the other. John stood for law, the Lord for grace. The people were pleased with neither. Even so, the issue proved the wisdom of His course - was not Matthew himself indebted to the Saviour? And he was a publican.

3. There was a third class, such as the inhabitants of Bethsaida, Chorazin and Capernaum (vv. 20-24). Perplexity did not

mark them, nor could they be said to be undecided. They were definitely unbelieving and unrepentant. Christ was rejected by them notwithstanding all the mighty works that He had wrought among them. Their privileges were immense; their penalty would be commensurate. We cannot stay to comment on all that is wrapped up in the words of the Lord to these cities, but it is evident that the earthly judgments which came upon Tyre and Sidon and Sodom did not annihilate their inhabitants; they will still have to appear in the day of judgment, though for them their judgment would be more tolerable than for the cities of the Lord's day, their privileges not having been so great. Those who deny a resurrection and believe in the annihilation of the being will find the Lord's words here to be an insuperable difficulty to their theories.

4. There was yet a fourth class (vv. 25-30). They are not the wise and prudent of this age but the babes. Children, though unsophisticated, are often more intelligent than their elders. They are often more quick witted, and being guileless they believe what they are told by those in whom intuitively they have confidence. It was so here.

Matthew's main contention is that Jesus is the Christ, but here he reports the words of the Lord Himself, which show Him to be much more. He is, in fact, incomprehensible to all but the Father. The Father may be known by those to whom the Son wishes to reveal Him, but not so the Son. None knows Him but the Father, and it is because of this that the Father has made Him the Universal Administrator of all His counsels: He has given all things into the hands of His Son.

This being so, who could hesitate to believe that He is able to meet the need of the labouring and heavy laden sinner? All the works of the law, in which man is either engaged himself or which were imposed upon him by others, could never give him rest. Only One could lift the burden from the shoulders and give relief from such bondage. He, therefore, says 'Come unto ME and I will give you rest' (v. 28). Incomprehensible though He be, we can trust Him and shall find Him true to His word.

Such was the response to the offer of the kingdom: only a handful were willing to accept Him. In view of such a meagre response, something far different from what we read in verse 25 might have been expected. Jonah's successful mission was followed by his despondency and complaint, but far from complaining, the Lord says, 'I thank Thee, Father, Lord of heaven and earth, that Thou hast hidden these things from the wise and prudent, and hast revealed them to babes. Even so, Father, for so it seemed good in Thy sight'.

All depended upon the revelation of the Father, for man by his searching cannot apprehend who Jesus is. Only the Father reveals the things of God to the soul and the reasonings of man in his supposed wisdom altogether fail.

9. THE REJECTION OF THE KING (Chapter 12)

As is so often the case, the attitude of the common people is determined by the agitation of their leaders. The Pharisees instil into their minds blasphemous notions concerning Christ. They complain against Him, they hold a council with the view of seeing how they could destroy Him, and they seek a sign from Him. In this chapter the Pharisees are the chief actors (vv. 2, 14, 24, 38).

Jesus was greater than the temple, which they regarded as

their greatest edifice. He was greater than Solomon, who was regarded as their greatest king. He was greater than Jonah, who was that mighty prophet that had the unique distinction of being sent to the Gentiles. But despite that greatness it was all too evident that Jesus was a rejected king, as David was in the days when he went into the house of God and ate shewbread, which it was not lawful for him and his followers to eat, but the priests only. The Lord does not deal with David's faults in this matter; He is merely concerned with the parallelism of the case.

If David infringed the law, why do they complain if His disciples pluck corn on the Sabbath day? A zeal for tradition at the expense of mercy is worthless. Besides He was the Son of Man, and as such He was Lord of the Sabbath. Man had not been made for the Sabbath but the Sabbath for man, but the Pharisees did not realise this any more than they knew Him. His acts of mercy performed on the Sabbath day were no infringement of the spirit of the Sabbath. Indeed He who desired His creatures to enjoy its rest, delighted to heal those who otherwise on the Sabbath day could have had no rest.

The trend of events was all too obvious. Although the people followed Him for the material benefits which they received (v. 15), yet the Lord charged them not to make Him known. He knew that the nation would reject Him and He intended to open the door to the Gentiles (vv. 18, 21), for they would trust Him. The time for that, however, had not yet come, but it was plain how things were developing. Like David, He too was in rejection with a handful of followers.

His miracle of healing the blind and dumb man was rightly regarded by the people as giving proof that He was David's Son, the long expected Messiah. But the Pharisees thought differently. They attributed His power to Beelzebub.[1] Nothing more wicked could have been uttered. This was sin against the Holy Ghost, for the Lord was working His miracles by the finger of God - that is, by the Spirit of God (v. 28), and to say that He was actuated by the prince of demons was to commit a sin for which in the nature of the case there could be no forgiveness in time or eternity. Besides, the charge was both illogical and stupid, as the Lord clearly shows. What they said assumed a divided kingdom and its certain fall (v. 25).

The Pharisees were determined to destroy Him; on no account would they receive Him. The only sign the Lord would give to them was that of Jonah, who, as a risen man after his experience of incarceration in the fish, went to the Gentiles and they heeded his message. So the Lord, after His death and resurrection, would go to the Gentiles. They indeed would receive Him; for did not the Queen of Sheba go to see the glory of Solomon, and she was a Gentile?[2]

---

[1]SIN AGAINST THE HOLY GHOST (12:31)
In addition to what we have said touching this matter, it should be made clear that the sin against the Holy Ghost in that day was attributing the power by which the Lord wrought His miracles to Beelzebub and not to the Holy Spirit. This particular phase of the sin cannot be repeated nowadays, seeing that the conditions which obtained then do not exist today. The Lord Jesus is not here on earth, but the principle abides; and should anyone in any instance affirm that what is being wrought by the Spirit of God is of Satan, there is sin against the Holy Ghost.

Clearly, in the nature of the case such a sin is beyond the possibility of forgiveness. For example, a man is born again by the Spirit of God. To say that that was the work of Satan is to make plain that the person who thus speaks is maligning beyond forgiveness the One by Whom alone he himself could have been born anew.

[2]DESCENT INTO HADES (12.40)
'So shall the Son of Man be three days and three nights in the heart of the earth' (Matt. 12:40). Based on this statement it has been affirmed that Hades is in the heart of the earth. But it is submitted that this is not what the Lord

The prospect for the house of Israel was dark indeed. The Lord had been to the house and by His presence had swept and garnished it. By His miracles, He was driving the unclean spirit out of the house. But the time will come when it will return to the house in a sevenfold more evil form, and their last state will be worse than the first. They will accept the Antichrist and worship the image of the Beast set up in their temple, and then this 'worse state' will be upon them. Jesus had come in His Father's name and they had rejected Him. Another, the Antichrist, will come in his own name; and him they will receive, to their eternal shame. Verse 45 envisages this time. The 'generation' spoken of there is the class of people. He is not speaking merely of those then living, nor their immediate successors: verse 45 goes on to the end-times.

---

intended, nor does it accord with the rest of Scripture teaching on the matter. The Creed says, 'He descended into hell', but is this correct? Only after a considerable struggle was this item allowed to be embodied in the Creed, and that is not surprising for it would appear that Scripture does not teach it.

Psalm 16:10 quoted by Peter in Acts 2:27 should read, as in the RSV, 'Thou will not leave My soul unto sheol (or hades) nor suffer Thy Holy One to see corruption'. The one part of the verse is as absolute as the other. The Lord's body did not see corruption; the Lord's soul was not abandoned to Hades. Soul and Spirit are distinguishable but not separable: where the one is the other is. The Lord said, 'Father, into Thy hands I commend My spirit', and where His spirit was there was His soul also.

1 Peter 3:18ff has been made to do duty to support the theory, but it is submitted that this passage has no bearing whatever on the matter. It relates, as appears indubitable to the present writer, to the days of Noah, when people were disobedient to his preaching and in consequence are now 'spirits in prison'. It is not the only place where departed persons are spoken of as spirits (see e.g. Heb. 12:23). The Spirit of Christ was speaking in Noah, as indeed the later prophets had the Spirit of Christ in them.

Ephesians 4:9 has been called in to support the idea of a transfer of Paradise from underneath the earth to heaven, but the marginal reading, 'a multitude of captives', is not correct. For a true understanding of the phrase 'He led captivity captive' we must consult Colossians 2:15. Moreover, 'the lower parts of the earth' would appear to mean 'the lower parts, that is, earth', in contrast to the heavens to which He ascended.

In all this, it is pleasing to note how the Lord Jesus behaved. He did not clamour for recognition, He did not enforce His rights. He did not cry, nor cause His voice to be heard in the street (Isa. 42:2). He knew He was the Chosen of God, the beloved in whom God was well pleased, and on whom He had put His Spirit. There was no need, therefore, to force the issue. He would wait for God. Victory was sure (v. 20).

It seems as if Matthew, taught by the Spirit, passes in quick review the many names and offices of the Lord Jesus. He is Son of Man; Lord of the Sabbath: My servant; My beloved; Son of David; greater than the temple; greater than Jonas; greater than Solomon. He does so in order to show the enormity of the sin of refusing to accept Him and accord Him His rights. Moreover, he delights to magnify his Saviour.

As we have seen, at His temptation the Lord had bound the strong man, Satan. He had shown Himself to be stronger and had entered his house and spoiled his goods. He had been robbing the devil of his captives. In this manner too, He had been sweeping the house and garnishing it. His activities had been limited to 'the house', but it has now been left and the nation set aside for the time being. The Lord has other work to do.

Up till now Matthew has written of Someone whose earthly lineage can be traced back to David and to Abraham; Someone who is entitled to rule over His earthly people and to sit on the throne. But, seeing that they will not have Him, all such natural ties are now renounced. Natural human relationships, even though as close as that of mother and brothers and sisters, are worthless. Those who are truly related to the Lord do the will of His Father which is in heaven (v. 50). He was doing that will, and if they did it they were giving evidence that they possessed the same nature, and were, therefore, His kindred. It was this that counted with Him. It was useless either to say, 'We have Abraham to our Father' (Matt. 3:9), or even Jesus for our brother.

We have now reached a crisis in Matthew's Gospel. It seems as if all is lost, and that the mission of Christ in regard to His own earthly people Israel has proved to be a complete failure. He came as Son of Man unto His own property, but His own people received Him not. Does this mean then, that man has triumphed; that sin has conquered and God has been defeated? We shall see.

10. AN UNEXPECTED MOVE (Chapter 13)

'The same day Jesus went out of the house and sat by the sea side' (v. 1). This action was significant, for He has now temporarily left the house of Israel and is about to embark on a wider ministry; not restricting Himself any longer to that nation but going to the Gentiles, who in prophecy are often symbolised as the 'sea'.

This chapter gives us the 'mysteries of the kingdom of heaven' (v. 11); that is to say, things hitherto kept secret are now revealed. It shows that, far from the Lord having been defeated and frustrated, the adverse circumstances reviewed in chapter 12 have but furnished the opportunity for Him to develop His hitherto unknown programme (v. 35). He will have a kingdom, but in many respects it will be of an unusual kind. It will be a kingdom without a visible king, without geographical limits, without national restrictions, and without an earthly capital. It will be spiritual.

The Lord adopts the method of teaching by parables. He does so because, despite the fact that Israel have seen His miracles with the natural eye, they have not seen with the inner eye the deeper truths (v. 13). They may have heard with their natural ears, but the lessons have penetrated no further. Those who deliberately shut their eyes must expect to be judicially blinded. So it was with that nation. Israel has failed. From that vine the Lord had expected good grapes, but it brought forth sour grapes despite all the attention given to it (Isa. 5). Of what use were they, for a vine is worthless and useless for anything unless it brings forth edible grapes. But so it was and, therefore, the Lord has for the time being to abandon them and start afresh. He must do something altogether new.

'The sower went out to sow' (v. 3). The Lord is the sower, and He commences what has developed into the mysteries of the kingdom of the heavens. We need not stay to consider how the seed fared, or the differences of this parable with the records in the other Synoptics, but we should ask how it is that things have developed so badly?

The kingdom of the heavens, here in mystery form, has become Christendom, in which are found all kinds of so-called Christian cults. Mixed up among the real are the false. Who has done this? The answer is, 'An enemy hath done this' (v. 28). Tares have been sown among the wheat and by imitation the whole has been at length adversely affected. The day of separation of the one from the other awaits the return of the Lord. That is to say, we must wait for the 'consummation of the age' (v. 39) - as the phrase 'the end of the world' should read. The consummation of the age is when the Lord returns and finishes off the age which He brought in by His ministry. It certainly is not the end of the world, which will not be till very much later. But when He returns He will judicially separate the wheat from the tares, and the righteous will shine in their true light, without mixture, in the kingdom of their Father (v. 43).

The Lord goes into no details here; they must be sought elsewhere in Scripture. He only speaks of the matter in bare outline, telling us of the doom of the tares and the glory of the wheat. It must never be forgotten that Matthew 13 is occupied with God's testimony on earth; the corruption which the enemy has wrought and the time soon to come when the Lord will come again to earth and effect a clearance and establish here that which will be for the glory of His Father and the vindication of His people.

'The kingdom of their Father' is not to be regarded as a different kingdom from that in which the Lord will be ruler. The phrase must be read in the light of 1 Corinthians 15:28. It is the Father's kingdom in which the Son rules, but as subject to the Father. This will be so at all times. Whether it is the inauguration of that kingdom or after the time when every enemy shall have been destroyed, and the kingdom is cleared from every possibility of revolt. 'Then also', as the two words in 1 Corinthians 15:28 should read, as at all other times the Son will still be subject.

The period covered by these parables is from the day that the Lord commenced His public ministry till the time that He establishes the kingdom on earth. We have already seen that believers of the present time are in the kingdom of the heavens. So too, by mere profession, is every so-called Christian community, no matter by what name they are called. But the believer today has a far higher privilege than those who passed away before the church was formed, or those who will yet live after it has been translated to heaven. It will produce the utmost confusion in the mind, a maze from which there is no escape, if we mix up Paul's special teaching of the Body of Christ with this chapter touching the kingdom. The reader is advised to consider again what has been said concerning the kingdom of the heavens in connection with the 'Laws of the kingdom', in order that he may better understand the teaching of this chapter. It must not be assumed that everyone in the kingdom of the heavens is genuine, whereas in the Body of Christ none but real believers have a place. In the kingdom there is a mixture.

Although some of the parables were spoken outside of the house, the interpretation was given when the Lord returned to the house (v. 36). That is to say, the full completion of the things signified by the parables will be when the Lord returns to the house of Israel. It will not be till then that He will sort out the wheat and tares, the good fish and the bad (v. 48).

This chapter gives the prophetic outline of Christendom, the sphere where Christ is genuinely or nominally acknowledged. Its degeneration is set forth in the parables of the leaven and the mustard seed. All kind of evil influences lodge in its branches and the whole of the professing mass has become permeated with evil doctrine. Christendom is a mighty power in the world, with its many branches all springing from one main trunk, affording a lodging place for all sorts of religious vagaries. Slowly but surely its original pure teaching has insidiously been vitiated by the leaven of evil teaching, till all has been leavened. The desire to jettison all distinctive Christian truth in the pursuit of unifying the divided factions of Christendom is going on before our own eyes.

Let us be clear about this. The leavening of the mass is not the progress of the gospel. Leaven in Scripture always denotes evil: a thing which may be readily verified by considering all the references to it. The birds of the air are not genuine believers who find a place of rest in the branches of the tree: they have better cover and greater security than that.

Notwithstanding all this, there is that which is good in this sphere of profession: the true among the false, the valuable among the worthless, the treasure and the pearl. In order to secure it, the Lord Himself as the merchantman sells all that He has. 'You know the grace of our Lord Jesus Christ, that, though He was rich, yet for your sakes He became poor, that ye through His poverty might be rich' (2 Cor. 8:9). He was cut off and had nothing (Dan. 9.26). He bought the field in order to secure the treasure. Whether land or sea, the price was paid, and that upon which His heart was set was purchased. This is not the case of a sinner giving up all for Christ. Though Paul speaks of his having suffered the loss of all things on account of Christ, he is not telling us that he abandoned all in order to obtain Christ, but that, having gained Him, he is now willing for His sake to abandon all.

The utmost care must be exercised in interpreting this chapter. We should guard against going beyond what is written or introducing into it truths that, while concurrent, are distinctive in nature. The mysteries of which Paul speaks are not to be found here. Paul's mysteries relate to a glorified Christ in heaven; to the church which is seated with Christ in the heavenlies; and to the rapture, which has to do with taking the church to the Father's house. There is nothing of any of this in this chapter. The sowing is on earth; the tree has its roots on earth; the treasure is in the world; the pearl is in the sea - everything in the chapter is earthbound. The two lines of truth must be kept apart. The utmost that can be said of them is that they are concurrent, though not co-extensive. The kingdom is larger than the church. For example, in verse 30 the tares are gathered first and bound into bundles, but the wheat is thereafter gathered into barns. Now it is just the reverse at the rapture. The redeemed are gathered first and they meet the Lord in the air; the rest are left on earth for judgment. These distinctions ought carefully to be observed.

Here are things new and old. The old things are those that speak of the kingdom and the new are those that relate to the mysteries of the kingdom.

11. PARADOXICAL EVENTS DURING THE KING'S ABSENCE (Chapter 14)

In chapter 14 we are told of paradoxical events which characterise the period during which the king is absent. They are given in historic-pictorial form.

a. Unchecked persecution (vv. 1-12)

This has marked the age ever since the Lord returned to heaven. His followers have suffered imprisonment and death and tortures of every kind, and the silence and apparent inactivity of God has perplexed the sufferers and their sympathisers. So it was with John, who was beheaded. The only recourse of the apostles was to bury his body and go and tell Jesus, unburdening their sad hearts to Him. What more could they do? He did not explain the problem to them; they left their difficulty with Him; He was silent.

It was here a case of the political power being dominated by a sinister unseen power behind the scenes. It was similar in the case of Balak and Balaam, Ahab and Jezebel, and later it will be so when the woman, scarlet clad and drunken, will ride the beast. Politics and religion characteristically combine to this present day to persecute the godly, yet heaven seems to be silent. Why?

b. Gentile blessing (vv. 13-21)

The Lord fed the multitude and there were twelve full baskets left over, telling of the present era when the Gentiles are receiving their portion, while later on Israel will have theirs. The Jew had judged himself unworthy of eternal life and so Paul turned to the Gentiles. He explains in his letter to the Romans chapters 9-11 why that nation is now set on one side, having been put on a level for the time being with the Gentile in respect of divine mercy, and how the gospel goes out to 'whosoever'. But he shows that later on Israel will be re-instated into their former place of privilege. The figure employed is different, but the truth is the same.

c. International strife (vv. 22-36)

This is set forth by the storm on the lake. Whilst the Lord is on high praying, His own are in the midst of the storm. But He manifests Himself and they find Him to be superior to the elements which so troubled them. He has not forgotten them; He comes to them. The waters cannot swallow them for they cannot swallow Him, and He becomes their protector. None need sink.

All these are paradoxes, for they are so contrary to what we might have expected, but 'the just shall live by faith'. He leaves His own here in such circumstances, all of which could have been avoided had Israel received Him when He first came to them.

An illustration may be used. If a machine has lost its kingpin the machine cannot possibly work properly. And if an integral part of the machine is in the wrong place, it will tend to make confusion worse-confounded. So it is with the nations of the world. The King is missing. He has been rejected and cast out. His earthly people too are in the wrong place, for they have been ejected from their land. A few are back in a very small portion of it, but the majority of the nation is away from the fatherland and the bulk of their proper territory is enemy-occupied. No wonder there is international confusion. Could it be otherwise? Man has created his own troubles, and Christ allows His own people to be in the midst of them so that they should exercise faith and be a testimony to Him.

12. THE KING'S LOYALISTS (Chapter 15:1-16:12)

This chapter naturally flows out of chapter 14. It gives pictorially those principles which should be observed by the loyalists of the King during the time of His absence. We need only make a few suggestions which will enable the reader to pursue the study for himself.

Chapter 15:1-8. The first principle mentioned is *freedom from tradition*. This has nothing to do with true apostolic traditions, which should never be abandoned. But this is human tradition, which can be both cruel and heartless. It displaces God's word and puts the commandments of men in its place. Constant vigilance must be exercised if we are not to be unwittingly bound by this subtle snare. Very few are free from bondage to human tradition in some way or another.

Chapter 15:21-28 demonstrates in a most remarkable way the second great principle, *faith*. The woman did not belong to the house of Israel, but she approached the Lord calling Him 'Son of David'. She had no national rights in David, she was a Gentile 'dog'. But there was faith, if not intelligence; and the better of these is faith. The Lord tested her, though He knew what He intended to do. The disciples were out of sympathy with her and failed to understand. She did not call after them, she knew better than that; she called to Him. She did not resent being called a dog and was willing to take the place even of a 'little dog' for whom crumbs fell from the table above him. After all, she thought she was only asking for a crumb and the Lord would not begrudge her that. No marvel the Lord said, 'O woman, great is thy faith'. She shames us.

Chapter 15:32-39. These verses emphasise the third great principle, *compassion* on the hungry multitude. He can multiply our small resources and make them go round.

Chapter 16:6-12. These verses enjoin upon His disciples *caution* against the leaven of the Pharisees and the Sadducees, ritualism and rationalism, a warning by no means superfluous today. These are pits into which we may easily fall. F. W. Newman was a professing Christian, yet he became a leading rationalist and apostatised from the faith he once avowed. His brother, John Henry Newman, once in the Church of England, seceded and became a Cardinal of the Roman Church, thus falling victim to extreme ritualism.

These are some of the principles which should be observed by the followers of the Lord. It is not enough merely to assent to the validity of the Messiahship of Jesus; such assent must be accompanied by conduct that reveals that the heart has been won. Where that is the case, there will be simple trust in the midst of all the paradoxes of life, and manifestation of loyalty despite all the opposition which we encounter.

The summit reached (Chapter 16:13-28)

We have now reached the summit, having climbed up from Bethlehem to Caesarea Philippi. We have reviewed the evidence in support of the claim of Matthew that Jesus is the Messiah. We have considered the offer of the kingdom He made to the nation and how they received it; the final decision which was made; His next move in revealing the mysteries of the kingdom; and the things that characterise the period of His absence.

Now the question is: What conclusion have you reached? What do the people think? The answer is that public opinion is divided. But Peter is bold and clear: 'Thou art the Christ, the Son of the living God'. This was not a deduction Peter had made from what he saw of the Lord as a man of flesh and blood, nor indeed was it a conclusion reached because of the persuasion of others, but it was a revelation given to him by the Father.

It is, indeed, an amazing confession, having regard to the then common expectation of a glorified and reigning Messiah. That Peter should have confessed such a humble and poor man whom he had accompanied to be that Messiah, grows in wonder the more it is pondered. His poverty and rejection were so contrary to the national expectation. 'We supposed it would have been He that should have redeemed Israel.' They expected a mighty deliverer, yet, notwithstanding that, Peter makes this fearless confession. In it he stands alone. Peter is at his best here.

In addition to what the Father has revealed to Peter, the Lord also has something to say. He speaks to him about His coming decease, the church He will build, and the coming that will result in His establishing His kingdom (v. 28).

'Upon this rock I will build My church' (v. 18). What is this rock? Much has been written touching this; much that is positively wrong and much which is at least thought-provoking. But the best commentary upon these words is Peter's own explanation in 1 Peter 2. The Lord Jesus is the living stone; believers are living stones. Christ is the foundation, not Peter. Peter says so, and he should know.

Admittedly Peter was given an important position. To him were given the keys of the kingdom, not the keys of the church (v. 19). By his preaching of the gospel he stated the terms on which God is willing either to remit and loose a person's sins, or else He must retain and bind them on him. The effect of what Peter preached is regarded as what Peter himself did. That effect was, of course, dependent on the manner in which the hearers treated his message.

From this point we commence our descent on the other side of the mountain and, as remarked before, we now meet allusions to His death. In verse 21 we are told that it is inevitable; the nation having rejected Him, this would be the outcome. Yet there was another cause why His death was inevitable. Apart from it, the church could not be built; sins could never be remitted; the kingdom could never be established. His death was the necessary foundation of all His future plans. For all in heaven and earth is to be established on resurrection ground.

That, however, does not reduce the criminal responsibility of the chief priests and elders and scribes; they would be held liable for having killed Him. Yet the Jews could not effect this without Gentile collaboration, and so in chapter 17:22 we are told that the Son of Man would be delivered into the hands of men, that is the Gentiles. Later He tells them that it is 'one of you', one of the little band of twelve men around Him that would commence the whole sad business. He referred to Judas. The clouds gather and thicken and the darkness grows until the whole tragedy is enacted. But we are anticipating.

Despite Peter's bold confession, the thought of the death of his Master was too much for him, and his repudiation of the Lord's words called forth the Lord's stern rebuke. But it was so natural for Peter to say what he did, for it ran counter to all their hopes. And more, the principle was so contrary to all natural feelings. The notion of saving one's life is by the avoidance of death, but the Lord shows that if the soul (or life) is really to be saved it must be by the denial of self and the acceptance of the cross. Life is to be gained through death.

Part 2

OUTLINE OF CHAPTERS 17-25

We have scaled one side of the mountain, from Bethlehem to Caesarea Philippi, and we now commence our descent to Calvary. But before doing this Matthew gives us a vivid picture of the King, resplendent in His glory, sitting enthroned in His kingdom surrounded by His subjects. It is a miniature of the coming power and presence of our Lord Jesus. This was no cunningly devised fable, three apostles having visually seen it and given an adequate testimony to its truth. We 'were eye witnesses of His majesty' (2 Pet. 1:16). Their eyes beheld Him, their ears heard the Father's testimony to Him, and the prophetic scriptures were thereby made more sure to them (see 2 Pet. 1:16-21).

After recording the Transfiguration, Matthew gives us a series of questions which are put to the Lord Jesus. This King is far wiser than Solomon, to whom the Queen of Sheba put her hard questions; what is more reasonable than Matthew should record the answers to the questions which were put to 'the Christ, the Son of the Living God'?

Interspersed with the answers to these questions he records certain parables which were spoken by the Lord and which had a bearing on the questions. So this second part has almost exclusively to do with the sayings of the Lord Jesus, not so much with His deeds, while all the time He is moving forward from place to place until at length He reaches Jerusalem and is found in the temple. It is plain that those who share Peter's avowed conviction are very few indeed. The mass of the people are against Him and their hatred gains strength the longer He abides among them, until, at length, it knows no restraint and chapters 26 and 27 record His trial and death.

13. THE TRANSFIGURATION (Chapter 17:1-13)

Jesus had said, 'The Son of man shall come in the glory of His Father with His angels; and then He shall reward every man according to his works' (16:27). He does not speak of it as in the distant future, but rather as near at hand. His words actually are, 'The Son of man is about to come'.

He has not come thus yet, but as we have noted He has given an assurance that He will do so. The Transfiguration scene was a foreshadowing; it was the kingdom in miniature. It is one of Matthew's seven mountain scenes, a position which connotes power and authority, speaking of the time when all will know that 'all authority has been given unto [Him]'. With Him are Moses and Elijah, the great Lawgiver and the great Prophet; each identifiable despite the fact that they had long left this life. Both are speaking with Him: what blessed communion!

They are representative men. The one had died and been buried, though now brought forward for the purpose of this appearance. It must not be supposed that he had his glorified resurrection body, for Christ is 'the first fruits of them that slept'. Therefore, before He arose none could have a glorified body. Elijah, however, had not died; he had been translated. So these two represent two companies of saints: those who have been raised from the dead, and those who 'living and remaining' shall be translated without dying when the Lord comes. But these are not the only ones there. The three privileged apostles represent the godly remnant of Israel.

Any interpretation of this scene must agree with the plain statements of Scripture given elsewhere. We must not intrude our ideas into it, making deductions which are untenable. It is so easy to allow our imagination to master us.

Matthew tells us it was 'after six days' that this took place. Luke, however, says 'it was about an eight days after'. There is no error here. The two phrases are in perfect accord with each other, but each is instructive. 'It was after six days' when this present dispensation will have run its course and God is about to bring in His millennial Sabbath rest. 'It was about eight days after' because everything will then be established on the principle of 'resurrection', or 'regeneration', of which we shall speak later. It will be a fresh start; the first day of the week being the eighth. Man as he now is cannot by any means attain to such a blessed state as is here portrayed.

Although Peter had made such a bold confession at Caesarea Philippi, yet now, as so often, he speaks when he should have been silent. Christ is all in all with God, and all others are His servants. It is unthinkable that they could be put on a parity with Him, yet Peter's suggestion looked in this direction. The only thing that can be said in its favour is that he did name Christ first, but in all other respects he put Him on a level with Moses and Elijah.

Peter was all confused, not knowing what he said. Why suggest tabernacles, if the state was so good? Why not erect permanent buildings? But how then could the kingdom be established, since the Lord had intimated beforehand that the Cross lay between Him and it? What too of the other apostles: why should they be shut out? And what of the people and the land? How narrow and self-centered was Peter's vision. No marvel that the Father gently reproved him by sending an overshadowing cloud, which caused them to see 'no man save Jesus only', and they are enjoined to 'hear Him'. Moses must be silent now; so too, Elijah; and, of course, Peter. The Lord alone must be heard.

He is the Father's beloved Son in whom the Father was delighted, not only in respect of His secret private life of thirty years spent in Nazareth, which He attested at His baptism, but in respect of His public work now moving on to its conclusion. He always did the things that pleased the Father.

The vision was to be kept close till the Son of Man was risen from the dead. The nation had given their verdict that they would not have Him, and they soon would be guilty of putting Him to death. It would be useless, therefore, to proclaim to them the kingdom now; His death and resurrection must ensue before the kingdom is established.

Is it not strange that, despite these plain words of the Lord, the apostles remained as blind as they did? When He died all their hopes died, and they seemed not to have expected Him to rise from the dead. His death to them appeared to be the end of all.

But this led to further questioning.

14. REPLIES TO QUESTIONS (Chapters 17-18)

'Why then say the scribes that Elias must first come?' (17:10)

Nothing was to be gained by the apostles now proclaiming the kingdom to Israel. But this raises a question in their mind. It was, they knew, common teaching that Elias had first to come before the establishing of the kingdom of God, in visible form, on earth, but they had just seen him on the mount and now he had disappeared from their view.

Were the scribes right? The Lord assures them that Elias indeed will come (He used the present tense in a future sense); he will restore all things and thus prepare the way for God's rightful king. 'As a matter of fact', says the Lord, 'he has already come, yet men have done to him what they would.' Although it was Herod who beheaded John, it but reflected the spiritual attitude towards that noble man. He was not known to be the Messiah's forerunner (v. 12), any more than the nation knew the Messiah Himself. Had they known, who can tell whether they would not have done to him as was done? Certainly it was so with Christ Himself (see 1 Cor. 2:8), for had they known Him they would not have crucified the Lord of glory.

This passage gives to us an important clue as to the interpretation of prophecy, i.e. that it may have two fulfilments, the one within the other. Had they received John, this prophecy would have been fulfilled, for he filled the role of Elias in whose spirit he came. But since they did not receive him, the prophecy still awaits its final fulfilment when Elijah will himself actually precede the Messiah before He brings in His millennial kingdom.

'Why could we not cast him out?' (17:19)

It was quite evident that the time for establishing the kingdom had not yet come, for when the Lord came down from the mountain there met Him the father of a lunatic son.

The three records of this miracle should be carefully pondered; all three evangelists tell us of it. It was not to be marvelled at that the scribes could do nothing for the father, but why could not the disciples cast out the demon? Were they not in close touch with their Lord and had they not been given power to cast out demons and to heal the sick (10:8)?

The generation to which the father belonged was faithless and perverse; that is, there was no faith to be found among them. That could not be said of the disciples, but they were of little faith (see v. 20 R.V.). It was not the total absence of faith but the smallness of their faith which rendered them totally unable to help the father and to heal the boy.

The potentialities of faith are immense, no less today than then. 'Nothing shall be impossible to you.' Do we really believe? Unbelief says, 'If Thou canst' (see Mark 9:23 R.V.) but faith says, 'He is able'.

'Doth not your master pay tribute?' (17:24)

The tribute here referred to is the half shekel of silver which had to be paid by every Israelite. It was the redemption money (Exod. 30:13; 38:26). When Peter was asked this question he inadvisedly said, 'Yes', prompted no doubt by love for his Master and a desire to show Him to be in all things a worthy person. But he said this, as on another occasion, not knowing what he said. The Lord Jesus, whom Peter knew to be the Christ, the Son of the living God, was under no obligation to pay this money. He needed no redemption, neither by silver nor by gold. He was, in fact, the Redeemer. It was only those who were slaves to sin and under divine judgment that needed to be redeemed. He was never such.

The kings of the earth take tribute and custom from strangers. They never do so from their own children, and was not He the Son of the Living God? Had not Peter confessed Him to be such? Had he not heard the Father acclaim Him thus at His transfiguration on the holy mount? How then could he have accepted this liability for the Lord?

However, the Lord knew that people generally would not understand if He claimed this privilege of exemption, for they did not know Him. Therefore, in order not to stumble them, He directed Peter to go to the sea and cast a hook. He did so, and there was a Stater in the fish's mouth, enough to meet Peter's proper obligation and to cover the Lord's willingly accepted but not obligatory payment. In this manner yet once more He identified Himself with His people: a thing which we have already seen Him do frequently in many ways.

'Who is greatest in the kingdom of heaven?' (18:1)

The context of this question should be noted. It is most important. 'At the same time' (lit. in that hour), that is, when the Lord Jesus had manifested the truth of His own words, 'I am meek and lowly in heart', by not insisting on His freedom from liability to pay the redemption money. He willingly paid it for Himself and for Peter; and it was at that same time the disciples put this question to the Lord. How unlike Him they were! True greatness belongs to those who are childlike in humility.

Self-assertion and self-importance are the twin evils which cause so much offence in the world. It is common to all, and only those who are converted and become as little children will enter the kingdom of heaven. Doubtless these twin evils secure a man's greatness before his fellows, as the weakest have to 'go to the wall' and the strong push ahead. Men praise them when they do well for themselves. But it is not so in the kingdom of heaven. The subjects of that kingdom are characterised by meekness. It is one of the laws of the kingdom, as we have already noted, and those who are not marked by it are not real subjects, whatever they may profess to be.

We should note how the whole section from chapter 17:27-18:14 has to do with 'offences'. The word occurs in chapter 17:27; 18:6, twice in verse 7 and in verses 8 and 9. The apostle Paul knew the importance of this and urged both the believers at Rome and those at Corinth not to forget it. There he is concerned with our proper liberty, but recognises that its abuse may lead to stumbling a brother. Here the Lord has in view the stumbling of 'one of these little ones which believe in Me'. 'It were better', says He, 'for him that a millstone were hanged about his neck, and that he were drowned in the depth of the sea' than he should do this. 'Take heed that ye despise not one of these little ones.' Their angels always behold the face of His Father who is in heaven, watching for indications as to what He wants them to do. And who can tell what action He will take through them in judgment on those who either stumble or despise such little ones? 'It is not the will of the Father which is in heaven that one of these little ones perish.'

'How oft shall my brother sin against me and I forgive him? Till seven times?' (18:21)

Peter is again the spokesman, and no doubt he thought he was very generous in proposing seven times, since the Rabbis limited the number of offences to four. He may also have had Amos 1 and 2 in mind, where 'three transgressions and four' are constantly repeated.

Moreover, in chapter 18:14 the Lord had spoken of 'your Father' and in verse 15 of 'thy brother'. Peter now takes up the same thought and speaks of 'my brother'.

From chapter 18:15 to the end of the chapter is one complete section, dealing with the matter of forgiving an offending brother. Although some would doubt the inclusion of the words 'against thee' in verse 15, and enlarge the subject to sin of any kind, yet the context seems to justify their inclusion. It is a sin which must first be discussed between the offender and the aggrieved party alone. Failing success then other means must be adopted to secure, if possible, a proper adjustment.

The word 'church' is used here of that local company of believers who meet together 'in My name' in any one place. So Matthew uses the word 'church' in only two senses. In chapter 16 it is that large invisible company of the redeemed which the Lord is building together, and which but for a very short space of time has never fully been on earth. Here in chapter 18 it is that small visible company located in one place, from which it is possible to excommunicate a person.

It is in this connection that Peter puts his question and the Lord replies by stating that the limit is not to be as Peter said, but 'until seventy times seven'. It is not to be supposed that this is to be interpreted literally and that the Lord set the limit at four hundred and ninety times, and justified the refusal to forgive the four hundred and ninety first offence. Peter apprehended the force of the Lord's words, for he wrote, 'Love covereth a multitude of sins' (1 Pet. 4:8). It is not difficult to imagine that an aggrieved party, long before he had reached this total, would think contemptuously of himself for including in his list some offences which time has caused to appear but trifling, indeed childish. He would never reach the total.

This gives rise to the parable of the unmerciful servant. We must be careful not to make a parable the basis of doctrine, nor to enforce every detail. It is the main picture which should engage our attention. Verse 34 seems to indicate that there is a possibility of our sins against God being again brought up against us, despite the fact that we supposed they had once been forgiven. Now we must not let this unclear verse upset those verses which are clear. God has pledged to 'remember our sins and iniquities no more'; 'He has cast them behind His back'; He has 'cast them into the depths of the sea'; 'He has blotted them out as with a thick cloud'. We have 'in Him redemption by His blood, even the forgiveness of sins'. All this is so clear and sure that we must not allow anything to upset that assurance.

Yet we must honestly face the teaching of this parable. It is quite plain that the king expected his forgiven subjects to show a like spirit to any that had offended against them. He expected them to make attempts to 'gain his brother', and failing that to make other endeavours to get matters put right. Most assuredly he did not expect any of them to 'lay hands' on the offender and 'take him by the throat', saying, 'Pay me that thou owest'. After all, what was such a small sum of indebtedness as compared with the enormous amount that the king had already forgiven him?

The lesson seems to be this: that it is doubtful whether the one who refuses to forgive his brother has himself had any true experience of God's forgiveness. It is expected that those who have been forgiven will be 'kind one to another, tender hearted, forgiving one another as God in Christ has forgiven them' (Eph. 4:32); that they will 'forbear one another, and forgive one another, if any man have a quarrel against any, even as

Christ forgave you, so also do ye' (Col. 3:13). Also this is an amplification of Matthew 6:12-15.

15. MORE QUESTIONS (Chapters 19-21)

'Is it lawful for a man to put away his wife for every cause?' (19:3)

The motive behind this question should not be overlooked. The Pharisees were the speakers. They saw the Lord Jesus being followed by great crowds and knew that He was healing them. This stirred them up with envy and they tested Him, with the view of possibly ensnaring Him in His words and thus discrediting Him before the people. They put this question, therefore, knowing that there were at least two different schools of thought touching the matter of divorce. One school sanctioned divorce for the most trifling cause; the other was not so liberal. Who was right? The Lord refers them to the Scripture, going back to the original divine institution as shown in Adam and Eve. His decision is unequivocal: 'Wherefore they are no more twain, but one flesh. What, therefore, God hath joined together, let not man put asunder.' Can any words be clearer? Can it be supposed that the Lord would contradict His own verdict?

It is true that Moses conceded divorce because of the hardness of their hearts, but God did not so purpose it for man. Only in one instance does the Lord sanction the putting away of one's wife (the word is actually 'woman', a very important thing to note when considering the subject in detail). The disciples, seeing clearly the force of the Lord's direction and the narrowness of the 'excepting clause', said, 'If the case of the man be so with his wife, it is not good to marry.'

It is a serious risk; a union for life which experience may prove has been very undesirable, but which the divine statute forbids to be cancelled. The reader is referred back to page 111 where we have discussed the matter of Divorce.

Children, the proper outcome of marriage, are next mentioned (19:13), wherein are the Lord's notable words, 'Suffer the little children to come unto Me, and forbid them not; for of such is the kingdom of heaven'.

'Good Master, what good thing shall I do, that I may have eternal life?' (19:16)

The section from chapter 19:16 to chapter 20:16 is a whole and should be considered as such. The parable of the labourers in the vineyard has a bearing upon this question. The questioner is told by the Lord to 'come and follow Me', and Peter says, 'Behold, we have forsaken all and followed Thee'. He asks the Lord, 'What shall we have therefore?' and in replying the Lord gives His parable, which opens with the word 'For'. Thus the whole section hangs together.

The law proposed life to the one that kept it. This man was satisfied that he qualified for the benefit, yet the Lord revealed to him that he did not do what he professed. He did not love his neighbour as himself, else he would have sold what he had and given to the poor. But he went away sorrowful; his possessions had too great a hold on him.

Peter thought that he was not like this rich man. After all, they had forsaken all and followed Jesus. Would they not get a reward? The Lord assures them that they certainly would be more than compensated for anything they had sacrificed for Him, and that indeed everyone that has done the like will receive an hundredfold and shall inherit eternal life - the very thing the enquirer was desirous of obtaining.

The 'regeneration' of verse 28 is that period when the Lord, having returned, will make all things new. When His will shall be done on earth as it is in heaven, and He will have established His kingdom and reigns in power. When the confession that Jesus is 'the Christ, the Son of the Living God' will not be that of one man only, but of the whole nation. Then Israel will be restored and the apostles will have their position of judicial authority in respect of them. The word 'regeneration' is found only again in Titus 3:5 where it has to do with the believer. Thus the Lord does now for the believer what He intends to do on a worldwide scale later.

In the parable that follows, the Lord deals with the motives that prompted both the enquirer and Peter. 'I am prepared to do to get,' said the one. Said the other, 'We have done, and now what shall we get?' It was very low ground to occupy. It was the ground of law, of works, of justice. There was higher ground, that of sovereignty and grace.

The ground Peter and the enquirer were taking was that of 'agreement' (see v. 2). They could be sure of justice (v. 4) but the householder's heart could not be thus restricted. He was 'good' (v. 15), and if he wished in sovereign grace (v. 14) to treat the latecomers as generously as the early workers, no one had cause for complaint: they received what they had agreed. The first received precisely the same as the last because they complied with the conditions, and the last because they depended on the justice and mercy of the one that had engaged them.

The lessons of the parable are many. A bargaining spirit in serving the Lord is unworthy of any, yet that is an overt principle in Christendom. So much spiritual work for so much pay. It does not display confidence in the Lord nor evidence delight in His service.

There may also be here a hint that the 'others' are the Gentiles who, brought in later than the Jew, are also granted eternal life (Acts 11:18), though that does not seem to be the surface meaning.

'What wilt thou?' (20:21)

The Lord Jesus makes a further statement touching His death at Jerusalem. He tells them how the Jews and the Gentiles will each work with the other in their cruel rejection of Him, though He again tells them of His resurrection which would follow. At this time, when He was preoccupied with that decease which He was to accomplish at Jerusalem, the laying down of His life on behalf of others, then came the mother of Zebedee's children. Having incited them with the same aspirations as were in her breast, she was desirous of asking something of Him. Discerning this, He said, 'What dost thou wish?'

She was thinking of the kingdom, He of the Cross. She was thinking of glory, He of suffering. She was ambitious, but He made Himself of no reputation. She wanted her two sons in the nearest, most prominent, conspicuous place of authority in the kingdom. But He, the Son of Man, had not come to be ministered unto, but to minister and to give His life a ransom for many (20:28). What a contrast! True greatness lies in a readiness to serve. The very indignation of the other ten indicated that the same spirit animated them. They inwardly thought that these two places of honour should be theirs. They could not be occupied by ten - no wonder there was strife. They all needed to learn that the path to greatness is the path of humility, the road to the throne is via the cross. They do not seem to have understood that the establishment of the visible kingdom on earth had been deferred.

In certain respects the baptism with which the Lord was to be baptised, and the cup which He was to drink, could not be shared by others, but there were aspects of it that could be shared. All too thoughtlessly James and John said they were able to experience these same things, and so the Lord assured them that they in their measure should have that honour, but the honour of sitting at the left or right hand in the kingdom was not His to bestow.

This sheds light on the inner relations of the Godhead. 'Times and seasons the Father hath put in His own authority' (Acts 1:7), and the allocation of places in the kingdom is prepared by the Father also. The Son says, 'It is not Mine to give'. How clearly this shows what we have noticed before, that the Son willingly occupies the subject place.

The principle of self-exaltation characterises the world. The princes of the Gentiles, the great ones of the earth, love to dominate others; but 'it shall not be so among you'. It ought never to be found amongst His disciples. He must be willing on behalf of others to go down and down, and not only to be their minister (v. 26) but their slave also (v. 27).

'What will ye that I shall do unto you?' (20:32)

It would seem that the similarity of the question which the Lord addressed to the mother and her two sons led Matthew to put beside it the question to the two blind men at Jericho. The other Synoptics tell us that there was one, but as Matthew

Henry said, 'If there were two there certainly was one'. It is no error. Matthew has a purpose in saying 'two', and maybe it is because the nation of Israel had for long been divided into two. The Lord's mercy extended to both sections. The day would come when they would be reunited and appoint over them One Head (Hos. 1:11).

Like those men the nation is blinded, and the veil is both on the book and on their eyes. But when they turn to the Lord and cry to Him for mercy, they will receive it and their eyes will be opened. The blind men did then what the nation will do later: they owned Him to be the Son of David and thus heir to His throne. They had inward sight. Moreover, had they known it, this would have been their last opportunity, for the Lord was going to Jerusalem where He would be crucified and thereafter be seen by none but His own followers.

As the greater than Solomon He knew the problems of these two and the overwhelming desire of their soul to tell Him. What compassion His question showed! How glad they were to tell Him their need.

'Who is this?' (21:10)

At His birth the question was asked, 'Where is He?' But now, as He is about to enter into the capital city - in order that (ἵνα) the prophecy might be fulfilled, 'Tell ye the daughter of Sion, "Behold, thy King cometh unto thee, meek and sitting upon an ass, and a colt the foal of an ass"' - the question is asked 'Who is He?' The same ignorance which we noted marked the people when the Lord was at Caesarea Philippi marks them still. They do not know Him, despite all the time He has been among them. His very works had not caused their message to enter their heart. He will not, therefore, enter Jerusalem riding a horse. These are days of disorder and, as in the time of Absalom, the true king is rejected. He, therefore, rides an ass. He will not force His claim; He comes in meekness. But He is the central figure in the throng that gathers. Some of the multitude go before and some follow. On their lips are goodly words, but soon other words are to be on those same lips. Instead of giving Him the throne of David, to which as his acknowledged Son He was entitled, they will cry for His blood. 'We will not have this man to reign over us'; 'We have no King but Caesar'; 'His blood be on us and on our children'.

At His birth Herod was troubled 'and all Jerusalem with Him'. Now, at His entry into that city, 'all the city was moved' and perplexed. The question is put, 'Who is this?' And the answer given is not that which Peter boldly gave, but, 'The prophet Jesus of Nazareth of Galilee'. Could any answer have betrayed greater unawareness of Who He really was? Was the word 'prophet' deliberately chosen in order to make confession to His obvious excellence, yet to deny Him His royal rights? Was the word 'Christ' intentionally omitted because they did not admit it? Was 'Nazareth' named because of its ill repute? Was 'Galilee' mentioned because of its insignificance? At any rate all was very ominous: it seemed to indicate a threatening storm.

He enters the temple. Not of course the sanctuary, the holy place, but rather the temple court, for it is evident from this Gospel that our Lord sprang out of Judah, as to which tribe Moses said nothing touching the priesthood. He acts with authority and holy indignation. His Father's house had become a place of merchandise, cheating, fraud, extortion and all that goes along with the commercialisation of the things of God.

He does in the temple what God designed it to be: He makes it a place of healing for the lame and blind. He did 'marvellous things' (v. 15). It is little wonder that the chief priests and scribes, who were so powerless to impart any good to the common people, should have been moved with indignation and envy. But the Lord is unmoved; His arrows are taken from the quiver of the Scriptures. He leaves them.

'He left them'; 'He went out of the city'. His movements were always pregnant with meaning. In the morning as He returned into the city He hungered, but finding nothing on the fig tree He speaks strange words which cause the tree to wither. Such miracles were only wrought on trees or animals, never on man. Yet it was the sin of man that was responsible for the fall of creation. Oh, the amazing mercy that has been shown to us!

The Lord again takes advantage to emphasise the necessity of faith. Listen to His golden words: 'Verily I say unto you, if ye have faith and doubt not, ye shall not only do this which is done to the fig tree, but also if ye shall say unto this mountain, Be thou removed, and be thou cast into the sea; it shall be done. And all things, whatsoever ye shall ask in prayer, believing, ye shall receive.' These words admit of no dispensational limitation. They are true and the Lord would say, 'Prove Me now'.

16. STILL MORE QUESTIONS (Chapters 22-23)

'By what authority doest Thou these things? and Who gave Thee this authority?' (21:23)

At times it is proper to answer a fool according to his folly and at other times it is proper not to do so (Prov. 26:4-5). On this occasion the Lord adopts the latter course, and He did not tell the source of authority by which He acted. His words are plain and call for no comment. 'We cannot tell' was a lie of the lips, their conscience meantime accusing them. Their own response to John's preaching was a condemnation of them, for publicans and sinners believed him and when they saw that they did not repent, despite all their protestations that they served God.

They were wicked husbandmen and belonged to a class that had a bad record. Jesus could see how things were developing and that these were the very people who would say concerning Him 'This is the heir; come let us kill Him, and let us seize on His inheritance.' Israel was the vineyard that had had such careful attention by the Householder (Isa. 5). The husbandmen were such as the scribes and chief priests; the servants who were sent at times to gather the fruit were the prophets. We must remember this is a parable, and while it seems to indicate that the Householder was surprised at the treatment given to his son, yet the Cross was no surprise to God. It was predetermined before the foundation of the world. But the Lord has in view the doom that awaits the Jewish people: their removal from the place of privilege, the breaking off of the natural branches, and the gospel going to the Gentiles. And God establishing by it another testimony in the earth, grafting wild olive branches into that tree of testimony. Romans 11 is the inspired commentary on verses 41-43 of this chapter.

'The kingdom of God' (v. 43) is that sphere in which God's rule is acknowledged, that 'holy nation' of which Peter writes (1 Pet. 2:9). Indeed, Peter's remarks there are a commentary upon the Lord's words here. Israel have fallen on the stone (and that Stone is Christ) and as a people are now broken. Putting the two passages together we discover that (a) one may build on that stone and never be ashamed, or (b) one may fall over it and be broken, or (c) it may fall on a person, in which case there is no remedy; it is utter disaster.

Such plain speaking led the Pharisees and chief priests to seek to arrest Jesus, though because the multitude held Him to be a prophet they feared to do so. What was His answer to all this?

Oh the wonderful grace of the Saviour! 'Jesus *answered* and spake' the parable of the marriage of the king's son and the invitations which were sent out. Matthew has still before him that Jesus is the Christ, the Son of the living God. The invitation of verse 3 has its parallel in the offer of the kingdom of chapter 10 of our Gospel. Verse 4 speaks of the preparation of the feast by death and of the benefits made available because of the Cross. Verse 4 also tells of the further offer made to the 'bidden'; that is to the specially privileged Jew, of which second offer we read in Acts 3. But the issue was that the servants were killed, as was Stephen of whom we read in Acts 7. That for the time being closes God's dealings with the Jews, save to allow them to reap the consequences of their evil deeds, which took place when Titus destroyed them and their city. Now the good news goes out to 'as many as ye shall find', to 'whosoever'.

The man who had not on a wedding garment is not a genuine Christian. This is a 'kingdom of heaven' parable, and here it is viewed as a sphere of profession. The man was in at the feast all right, but he had no true sense of what was due to the king or to his son. Nor did he come in by the appointed way. He was an intruder, a mere professor, who had not that which constituted a proper standing before the king. When the time of judgment comes he is appointed to his proper place, and has nothing to say in self defence. What could he say?

All of this has sprung out of the question, 'By what authority doest Thou these things, and who gave Thee this authority?' The answer is, 'I am the Son of the Householder; I am the King's Son. My Father has sent Me to claim My inheritance; He has arranged for Me a marriage. You who question Me are My Father's husbandmen, you are the specially invited guests. But see how wickedly you have behaved; you have destroyed My Father's servants and now you want to kill Me.'

'Is it lawful to give tribute unto Caesar, or not?' (22:17)

The Pharisees did not believe Jesus to be the 'Christ, the Son of the living God'. They, therefore, sought to ensnare Him, but they could not.

The Lord's words become sterner as the wickedness of the religious leaders becomes more open. 'Ye hypocrites', He calls them. He saw through their question. Had He said, 'Yes, give tribute', He would have appeared to be against the people. Had He said, 'No', it would have had the appearance of inciting rebellion. They desired to put the One who claimed to be the Ruler of God's kingdom at variance with the Ruler of Rome's kingdom. His answer is well known. If ever a word was fitly spoken, it was then. It was proper that they should 'render' (not δοῦναι but ἀπόδοτε - to pay a due), to Caesar his things, for their subjugation to him was the penalty of their sins in disobeying God. To have done otherwise would have been to have pulled the shoulder away from the yoke which God, in judgment, had put on them.

But there were also divine claims, and these must be met. They should have rendered the fruits of the vineyard, but they had defaulted. They should have come to the marriage feast, for they had been bidden so to do, but they did not wish to come. As to the things of Caesar, they knew if they did not render them trouble would have ensued. As to the things of God, blinded as they were by hypocrisy, they failed to see that they were not rendering these either. Did they think they would escape God's judgment?

'In the resurrection, whose wife shall she be?' (22:28)

Nor did the Sadducees believe Jesus to be 'the Christ, the Son of God.' They supposed they too could easily belittle Him before the people.

The Sadducees who put this question taught that there was no such thing as a resurrection, or angel, or spirit. On the other hand, the Pharisees taught that in the resurrection a woman who had married two or more husbands would be the wife of the first. The Lord by His answer repudiates both assertions and tells us the truth of the matter. The case envisaged was obviously an imaginary one but it touched principles of great importance. In the intermediate state all live unto God. Man has not ceased to be, despite death. The citation which the Lord makes from Exodus 3:6 proves that, for though the patriarchs had long since been dead, God was still their God.

Let scientists and philosophers say what they will regarding the impossibility, as they suppose, of the resurrection of all mankind; they know not the Scriptures nor the power of God. Who, in the first instance, called the whole into being? And if God could do that, is He powerless to recall those who seem to have passed out of being because they are out of sight? Moreover, as to human and earthly relationships, they do not exist as such for in heaven the redeemed are as the angels of God.

Note how this 'greater than Solomon' silences all His interrogators, and by His decisions reveals their inner thoughts.

'Which is the great commandment in the law?' (22:36)

The Pharisees return to the attack. One of them, a lawyer, puts this question, testing Him. If He is 'the Christ, the Son of the living God', He will surely manifest it by the answer He will give. Or will He? Matthew has recorded the 'laws of the Kingdom', showing their superiority to the Mosaic law. He now tells us how this question was answered.

The Lord replies by reciting the two great items of the law which summarise the duty of man to God and to his fellow. Mark records how this impressed a certain scribe, and the Lord remarked that he was not far from the kingdom. But it is amazing how far man can go in approval of the things of God and yet advance no further. With the mind there is approval, but another law operates which holds back.

'What think ye of Christ? whose son is He?' (22:42)

The Lord having silenced His questioners, and having as it were 'smitten three shepherds in one month' (Zech. 11:8), now Himself puts a question which not only they could not answer but which deterred them from asking Him any more questions.

The true answer to the question was the twofold nature of the Lord Jesus. As David's Lord He was God, and was prior to David. As David's Son He was man, and was subsequent to David. In Him were united two whole and perfect natures: He was very God and very Man. Eternal God had become Man by His virgin birth. He was both root and offspring of David. As root He was before David, as offspring He was after David.

Everything depended on their attitude toward Him and their thoughts of Him. Did they love to be called Rabbi? They should recognise that 'one is your Master (Teacher) even Christ'. Did they wish to be called Father? One alone is their Father, which is in heaven. Did they wish to be called Guides or Leaders? (23:10). One alone is Leader, that is Christ.

It could not but be that in the midst of such conditions His followers would, like Himself, be killed and crucified (23:34).

And for the persecutors there could be no possible escape from the damnation of hell. If they refused to accept Christ, how could they escape? Besides, His rejection would be calamitous for Jerusalem. He wept over the city. That city that had had such a remarkable past, whose history from the time of its heyday glory had been so chequered. The city that had been favoured above all others by the presence and workings of the Son of God was now to be left. Its glorious house was to be abandoned, the nation was temporarily to be given up. They would not see Him again till their whole attitude had altered, and they said with honesty, 'Blessed is He that cometh in the name of the Lord'. It will require a complete change of heart: they will have to be washed with clean water and a new spirit put within them. But that day will surely come. The Lord has sworn to do it.

'How can ye escape the damnation of hell?' (23:33)

In chapter 23 the Lord first addresses the multitude and then the scribes and Pharisees.

To the multitude He exposes the utter hypocrisy of those who posed as their religious guides. 'They say and do not.' Their precepts are all right, but their practice is a denial of their teaching. Therefore, what they bid them to do should be observed, but what they do should not be imitated.

They impose themselves in every sphere of life: at the 'feasts' socially; in the 'synagogues' religiously; and in the 'markets' commercially. They want men to take notice of them, and to give them laudatory titles, such as 'Rabbi', 'Father' and 'Teacher'. How far Christendom has wantonly disobeyed the Lord's plain prohibitions is manifest to all. The rule in the kingdom of God is the very opposite to this. 'He that is greatest among you shall be your servant. And whosoever shall exalt himself shall be abased; and he that shall humble himself shall be exalted' (vv. 11-12).

The Lord Jesus Himself was the great exemplar of this principle. 'He humbled Himself'; 'Wherefore God also hath highly exalted Him' (Phil. 2:8, 9). He therefore should be owned as the only One who is entitled to take the place of leadership among His people: 'One is your master.'

This causes the Lord to utter some of His strangest words. 'Strangest' because 'judgment is His strange work': it gives Him no pleasure. 'Woe' tolls out in this chapter as the sounding of a death knell, and indeed it was that for both Israel and Jerusalem until the time comes for their national resurrection. This section must not be read as expressing the wish of the Lord regarding His enemies, but rather as a forecast of the inevitable doom that awaits them on account of the course they have taken. It could only lead to the 'judgment of Gehenna', from which the only possible escape was to abandon their hypocrisy and opposition to Him, and wholeheartedly accept Him and all His claims. Apart from that there could be no escape from eternal doom.

But they were not prepared to do this. They loved outward show far too much, and they would on no account abandon their religious power that held the common people in its unmerciful grip. They were hypocrites - play actors, desirous of creating an impression on others that they were what they, in their conscience, knew they were not. They were 'whited sepulchres' with an ornate exterior but corruption within. They debased Divine institutions so that they became the means of their own enrichment, to the further impoverishment of the poor. They prayed long prayers 'for a pretence'. 'Outwardly' they 'appear righteous unto men', but 'within' they are 'full of hypocrisy and iniquity'. It is all too plain that they are 'the children of them which killed the prophets', for the Lord knew that they were intent on putting Him to death.

We have already seen that when the Lord entered Jerusalem 'the multitudes that went before, and that followed, cried, saying, "Hosanna to the son of David: blessed is He that cometh in the name of the Lord; Hosanna in the highest"' (21:9). But that only excited the envy and hatred of the chief priests and the scribes (21:15), and the very same people, led by such blind guides, were soon heard crying, 'Let Him be crucified'. The chief priests and elders had persuaded the multitude to do this and to ask for the release of Barabbas (27:20).

The shadows of the Cross are over the whole of chapter 23. Jerusalem would soon be stained with the blood of the Christ of God. That 'prophet like unto Moses' would shortly be put to death and that 'city' and its notorious 'house' would be left to its inevitable doom. God's Christ would not return to it until there was a radical change of heart in the people and they were willing to say again, 'Blessed is He that cometh in the name of the Lord'.

'How often would I have gathered thy children together, even as a hen gathereth her chickens under her wings, but ye would not', He exclaims. He knew that the 'fox' would now get them and the damage that would be wrought (see Luke 13:32). Thank God, the day of 'gathering' is only deferred; it is not cancelled altogether (see 24:31).

The practical lessons of this chapter are immense for all who in these days take the lead in the things of God. For the sins here condemned are not those of one people only, or merely of one era; they are common to Christendom as much as to Israel of old.

How often is exterior show preferred to inward reality and the letter of the law to the weightier matters such as judgment, mercy and faith! The gnat is strained at, but the camel is swallowed! There is protestation against past national crimes but the prosecution of even worse crimes of a like sort! What hypocrisy! Yet who cannot see that all this exists in our world, and who of God's servants does not feel at times the very principles asserting themselves within him today? Only as the 'mind of Christ' is in us can these evils be put to death.

17. WHEN SHALL THESE THINGS BE, AND WHAT SHALL BE THE SIGN OF THY COMING? (Chapters 24-25)

Chapter 24 of our Gospel is a classical prophetic chapter. The question is a most important one. So many have foolishly given dates for the coming of the Lord, and those dates have come and gone and the prognosticators have belittled themselves in the eyes of their fellows. Such errors would have been avoided had more attention been paid to this chapter. The question asked is, 'When', and the answer given is, 'Not yet' (v. 6); 'the beginning' (v. 8); 'then' (vv. 9-10, 14, 16, 21, 23, 30 (twice), 40; 25:1); 'When' (vv. 15, 32-33); 'immediately after' (v. 29). It is clear that the Lord is answering this question throughout the whole of the chapter.

Note the question: 'When shall these things be?' - that is, the utter destruction of the temple buildings, 'and what shall be the sign of Thy coming [*parousia*]?' The *parousia* of the Lord is His presence, and the context of the uses of this word must determine where that presence is. A reference to the R.V. will show that the word 'coming' may alternatively be read 'presence'. Actually *parousia* means a coming of someone who has been absent, his arrival, and his stay. It is used of the coming of a king to his capital and in other senses. In Matthew 24 we shall see that it has to do with His coming to and His presence on earth, whereas elsewhere it relates to His presence with His people after they have met Him in the air. This is its significance in the two Thessalonian letters. Confusion of thought is bound to result if this simple rule of determining the scope of a word by its context is ignored.

The question is differently framed in Luke 21:7. There it reads, 'But when shall these things be? and what sign will there be when these things come to pass?' The Spirit of God caused these two writers to record the question thus differently, for in Matthew He will take us on to the end-times, while in Luke He is more occupied with the things that occur in the meantime before the end comes, though He does not exclude the end.

Matthew speaks of the 'end of the world', which we have before remarked is a most unfortunate reading. It should read 'the consummation of the age', that is, the winding up of the present state of things and bringing in a new era.

Deception (especially of a religious kind), wars and rumours of wars there must be. We should not be panicky when such are occurring. It is the inevitable consequence of rejecting the Prince of Peace. Indeed, they are but the beginning of sorrows, or as the word is 'birth pangs'. They augur the incoming of a new life, but as always it can only be through pain and sorrow: 'The whole creation groaneth and travaileth together in pain until now.' It will continue to do so for a little yet, until the Lord Himself has come as the true Benjamin after the hard labour of Rachel.

The Lord passes over in quick survey all that will mark the time of His absence, getting swiftly to the end times. He is speaking to the disciples who are Jews: godly Jews, loyalists of the rejected King, however weak and faltering they may be. They will be afflicted, betrayed, killed: many will be stumbled and betray one another and hate one another. Many false prophets will arise and deceive many; lawlessness will abound and in consequence the love of the most will wax cold. Surely this is evident all around us today.

But, he that shall endure to the end shall be saved. Now while it is always true that continuance proves genuineness, even at the present time (Col. 1:23) and that apostasy would reveal that those who so apostatised were not really what they professed to be, yet today we preach the good news concerning the grace of God available to all sinners. We do not make verse 13 our gospel-text. Later on, however, the good news of verse 13 will be preached, for it relates to bodily salvation from the sore troubles which will then prevail by the advent to earth of the Son of Man. Indeed, the troubles will be so severe that unless the days were shortened 'no flesh would be saved'. Observe this phrase: it is a question of saving the body, it is not here a question of saving the spirit. One may ask, will not those who thus 'endure' be born again - will not their spirit be saved? The answer is of course that it will, but that is not in the chapter and we must not introduce what is not there. It tends to confusion of thought.

This is 'the gospel of the kingdom': the good news that the kingdom will very soon be established, and that will put an end to all the earthly troubles spoken of. It is to be feared that the phrase 'the gospel of the kingdom' has been beclouded with ideas which mix up things that differ. Quite plainly the good news which God has for man differs from age to age. Thus good news was preached to the Israelites who left Egypt and were on their way to Canaan. It was good news, it was a gospel, but its terms differ from that which we preach today as gospel.

Any good news is a gospel. The words appended to the word 'gospel' define its nature and scope. Things relating to its foundation, or the basis on which it is founded, must be looked for in other parts of Scripture. Thus we read of the 'gospel of Jesus Christ' denoting the Person who is its subject; 'the gospel of God' who is its author; 'the gospel of the grace of God' which is its theme; similarly 'the gospel of His Son'; 'the gospel of Christ'; 'the gospel of the glory of Christ'; 'the gospel of the Uncircumcision' (signifying the special sphere where Paul was to preach it); 'the gospel of your salvation' (denoting the benefit to be received from it); 'the gospel of peace'; 'the gospel of our Lord Jesus Christ'; 'the gospel of the glory of the Blessed God'; 'the everlasting gospel'. Each phrase is employed consistent with its context and appropriate to the time in view.

The time in view in our chapter is 'the consummation of the

age' when the Lord will come to earth and set up His kingdom. The message then to men immediately prior to that time is called 'the gospel of the kingdom'.

Verse 14 needs careful attention. It does not teach that the gospel of the grace of God will be preached to all the world before the Lord returns. Indeed, it has nothing to do with that phase of the gospel. The 'world' here is the habitable earth, an almost technical New Testament word for the then Roman world, and prophetically it relates to what is commonly called 'the revived Roman empire'. We must not be diverted into a discussion of how and when this empire will be revived and whether, in fact, it will be. But a perusal of Daniel 2 and 7, to say nothing of Revelation 17, ought to satisfy everyone that there is to be a resuscitation of that empire under one head, the Man of Sin, who will have his partner, the False Prophet, with his seat in Jerusalem.

So verse 14 envisages the preaching of the good news relative to the then soon-to-be established kingdom in that particular sphere and to all the nations that comprise it, for it will comprise ten such nations ruled by ten kings. This is parallel with chapter 10:23, which we have already examined, though in that verse the preaching is in the land of Palestine and here it is in the revived Roman empire. When this has been done then the way is clear for the end to be brought in.

Verse 15 introduces the 'abomination of desolation' identifying it as that which was 'spoken of by Daniel the prophet'. This surely should dispel all notions that that abomination has had its complete fulfilment in Antiochus Epiphanes. He was an adumbration of it, there is no doubt, but more than that we cannot say. Nor could it be said to relate to anything that occurred in Palestine before the city was destroyed by Titus, else the terms of verse 14 would not then have been fulfilled. It clearly relates to days yet to come, when the Jews will be back in their land, when the temple will have been rebuilt, and when this abomination has been set up in the Holy Place. That this abomination is the image which the False Prophet makes, which is capable of speaking, and to which all are expected to bow down and worship the beast, seems reasonably clear and certain (Rev. 13:15).

This will be a time signal for flight, directions concerning which are given by the Lord in verses 17ff. Whatever guidance may have been obtained from these verses for believers in the days of Titus, we are bound to say that the verses relate to later times than even our present. God is able to use His word by application no matter the time or persons concerned, but we are interested in the interpretation of the passage and what we believe to be its proper meaning.

Verse 21 speaks of the great tribulation spoken of again in Revelation 7:14; there called 'the tribulation, the great one'. It is unequalled. Jeremiah 30:7, Joel 2:2 and Daniel 12:1 refer also to such times. Now it is plain that not more than one period could be spoken of in this way. There could not be more than one period 'the like of which would never have been before, nor will be after it'. It stands unequalled and therefore unique, and any passage that speaks in this manner must obviously refer to the same period. The time will be so severe that, indeed, 'unless the days were shortened' (Scripture shows elsewhere that they have been limited to 1260 days) 'no flesh would be saved'. But this limitation of the times is 'for the elect's sake'.

Here is another word, the meaning and scope of which must

be determined according to its context. All the children of God are 'elect', but not all the children of God are in view here. There is no mention whatever made of 'the church, which is the Body of Christ', although indubitably they are the elect. In this chapter these are the elect who are on the earth at the end-times.

It would take us far from the exposition of this chapter to show that the church, which is His Body, will have been translated to heaven before ever these times come on earth. The reader has but to peruse 1 and 2 Thessalonians to be assured of this. Especially does the second chapter of the second epistle make clear that neither the Man of Sin nor the False Prophet can be manifested until the hinderer and the hindrance have been removed from earth. What that is we do not stay to discuss here, save to say that that chapter was written specially with the view of making clear the distinctive position and timing of the *parousia* of the Lord Jesus and the gathering together of the saints of the present calling to Him in the air, as shown in 1 Thessalonians 4:17. (See the author's book, '*Will the Church Go Through The Great Tribulation?*')

But there is nothing of this whatsoever in the chapter now before us, for the reason that that was a secret communicated by a special word from the Lord to Paul, and formally communicated by him to the saints in his letters. We shall get greatly confused if we endeavour to introduce these things into this chapter.

Note verse 27: 'As the lightning cometh out of the east and shineth even unto the west, so shall also the *parousia* of the Son of Man be'. The title is significant. Believers today are awaiting a Saviour from heaven, even our Lord Jesus Christ (Phil. 3:20).

They are awaiting God's Son (1 Thess. 1:10). But the title 'Son of Man' has to do with judgment, and relates to His coming to earth for that purpose.

He will come to judge the world in righteousness. His earthly people, guilty of the murder of their true Messiah, will be as the carcass; the eagles, His agencies of judgment, will be gathered together. This forecasts those dreadful days when the armies of the world will be gathered together in the valley of Jehoshaphat of which Joel 3 speaks, called in Revelation the battle of Armageddon (see Rev. 16:16).

Immediately after these terrible times there will be signs in the heaven. In Acts 2 these signs are mentioned as coming *before* that 'great and notable day of the Lord'. Here they are said to occur 'immediately *after* the tribulation of those days'. The day of the Lord is a protracted period, but the 'great and notable day of the Lord' is a special point in that period. That special day comes *after* the heavenly signs, but those heavenly signs come immediately after the tribulation. Thus the Lord is very clearly answering the specific question which has been put to Him.

When this has occurred, then shall the sign, which is the Son of Man, appear in heaven. (They had asked what would be the sign of His *parousia*.) This will produce mourning on the part of all the 'tribes of the land', for they will then have the most convincing of all evidence that Jesus, who gave such clear credentials to accredit His claims, is really their Messiah. He will come then not as at the first, in lowly guise, but in power and great glory. Then He will send His angels with the great sound of a trumpet to gather His elect from the four winds: from one end of heaven to the other. All this is so different from

1 Thessalonians 4:17ff. There the Lord Himself comes; He does not gather by angels or any other agency; He comes personally.

We must guard against confusing the trumpets of Scripture. This trumpet here has nothing to do with the series of seven in the Apocalypse, nor has it anything to do with that of 1 Thessalonians 4:16 or 1 Corinthians 15:52. It occurs after them all.

There may be indicators that these things are about to come to pass. When the fig tree shows signs of life, then we know that summer is near, and 'when ye see *all* these things, know that it (or He) is near, even at the doors'. Israel in the past has been likened in Scripture to a vine and her present position to that of branches broken off from an olive tree, but when her future is in view she is likened to a fig tree. No one who has eyes to see can doubt that the wheels of God are beginning to revolve towards the goal He has in view, though it would be too much to say that the prophetic scriptures touching Israel and their land are yet being accomplished. That cannot be until the hinderer and the hindrance has been removed (2 Thess 2:7). The present writer believes this to be the Spirit in the church.

It is utterly impossible to be precise as to the day and hour. A mere general outline is all that is given, for no one save the Father knows the precise moment. Not even the Son, whose territory it was not; for 'times and seasons the Father hath put in His own authority' (Acts 1:7). We may expect the world to go on its own perverse way, following its ordinary routine of life, all oblivious of the fact that the day of its calamity is fast approaching. But come it will, and then judgment will sweep the earth and take away the tares, the bad fish, all that are hostile to God and His Christ.

Verses 41 and 42 are the very reverse of what will obtain at the Rapture. Then one will be taken away for blessing and the other will be left behind for judgment. Here the one is taken away in judgment and the other left on earth for millennial blessing.

When the Lord comes to earth He will do so much as a thief breaks into a house (v. 43). He will spring a surprise and rob men of that which they prize. It will be no act of injustice; it will be the day of vengeance of our God. He does not come in that manner for His people, He comes as the Bridegroom; and who would fear? He is the morning star shining in the heavens in the darkness. Later He will appear as the sun of righteousness on the horizon of earth, for the relief of His godly brethren and for the judgment of His and their enemies.

In this chapter we have again what we have already seen in other parts of the Gospel: the beginning of things and the end-times spoken of as if there were no interim period. There is nothing here incongruous with that interim period, but if we do not bear it in mind we shall find that we appear to have contradictory statements, and that the teaching of the Lord is not in accord with that of His apostles. But if we allow for this period, all becomes plain.

There are practical lessons common to the whole period. We should be 'faithful and wise servants'; we should 'watch', for certainly we do not know what day our Lord will come; we should be ready. We, too, may console our hearts with the thought that faithfulness here will be acknowledged by added responsibility and privilege of service in the kingdom.

Chapter 25 is a continuation of chapter 24 and it is a pity

there is a break. The parable of the ten virgins teaches the importance of watching, i.e., keeping awake (see 24:42); and of readiness (24:44). While the bridegroom tarried they all slumbered and slept, but when the bridegroom came it was those that were ready who went in with him to the marriage. As we have seen, the kingdom of the heavens is a sphere of profession in which there is a mixture of the true and the false. So here, there are five wise and five foolish. All ten have much in common. They were all virgins, professedly loyal to the bridegroom; they all had lamps; they all went forth to meet the bridegroom; they all slumbered and slept; they all arose and trimmed their lamps - but there was a vital difference, for some had oil and others had not. Professedly they all appeared at the beginning to be alike but ultimately the difference became obvious. So it was with the wheat and the darnel.

The parable must not be pressed beyond the bare outline which it gives. Its main principles apply throughout the whole of the period from the time the Lord returned to heaven till the time He comes back again to earth. Its principles apply to us of the present calling and its principles will also apply to the godly after the Church has been taken away.

There is only one thing that will keep alight our lamp of testimony in the darkness of this age, and that is the oil - a type of the Spirit of God. 'If any man have not the Spirit of Christ, he is none of His.' Whatever he may have professed or appeared to be to others, it will all come out at the end.

The Lord gives the parable of the talents, which, though similar to that of the pounds recorded in Luke's Gospel, is very different in detail.

We have three parables touching work for the Lord. That of the pounds speaks of a common responsibility, for all ten servants had one pound each committed to their trust. Ten is a numeral of responsibility and the one pound was common to all. The parable of the talents, however, speaks of differing capacities, for the talents were given not equally but according to each man's ability. The trust was superimposed upon the natural ability. In the parable of the workers in the vineyard we are reminded of unequal opportunities, for there were some who, not having been called earlier, had a very limited opportunity to work. Yet they suffered no consequential loss.

It was 'after a long time' that the lord of the servants returned, though we must not suppose that that suggests that the Lord will be away for a prolonged period. What, after all, is two millennia to Him, with whom a thousand years is as one day? But though it was after a long time, he came back in the lifetime of those servants, so it was not so long after all. The disciples had been warned against saying, 'My Lord delayeth His coming' and falling into all kinds of reprehensible conduct. It may seem that He 'tarries' (25:5), but He does not wait till the morning sun has arisen. He comes at midnight.

Though the trust differed in quantity, yet the ratio of return was the same, and therefore the commendation and reward is the same. But in the case of the one who buried his talent in the earth (a thing so easily done, allowing mundane things to swamp our responsibility to the Lord), the Lord takes him on the ground of his profession and utterances. He did not really know his Lord though he professed to do so. It was ever Paul's aim to know Him (Phil. 3:10), a goal which he ultimately reached (2 Tim. 1:12). But this man revealed his own ignorance and the wickedness of his heart. Really he objected to working for another: he had no room for such a capitalist. He admits that he was afraid, which showed that there was no love, for there is no fear in love. Had there been love there would have been devotion and zeal. Instead of that, the talent is handed back, but without any gain. He did not even allow anyone else to use it so that it might have yielded gain. As a result, the lord deprives him of the trust and he is cast into the outer darkness. We have already remarked (see 6. Messianic miracles, page 113) that no true believer will ever go to the outer darkness. This man signifies a mere professor who takes the place of being a servant, as many in Christendom do today, but he does not know Christ and has no love for Him.

The Lord has still in mind the question put to Him, 'When shall these things be? and what shall be the sign of Thy coming?' Now He tells them that when the Son of Man shall come in His glory, and all the holy angels with Him, then He will judge the nations. It will be a dividing time; to which we have before noted several allusions. This is the winnowing floor and the wheat and chaff will be separated: the wheat and the tares; the good fish and the bad: the sheep and the goats. This is the consummation of the age. It is the great goal to which things are moving: the return to earth of Jesus as the Son of Man to rule the nations with a rod of iron (Psa. 2). He will come as King and His rights will then be accorded Him. No longer will He be hunted, as Herod once hunted Him; no longer will He be rejected, as once the Jews rejected and disowned Him; no longer will He be usurped, as the wilful king (who is accepted by the apostate Jew) will usurp Him. He will sit upon the throne of His glory; His rule will be universal; and before Him shall be gathered all nations.

This is not the judgment of the Great White Throne, which

will not take place till after the end of the Millennium. This is at its beginning and is a judgment on earth. It is clear that the Judge will not deal with nations, but with individuals of all nations. It could not be said of nations that they did not 'visit Him' in sickness and the like; but such charges are applicable to individuals. All then will have to do with Him. He shall judge the world in righteousness. God has appointed that day, in which He will judge the world by that Man whom He hath ordained, whereof He hath given assurance in that He raised Him from the dead. The verdict is determined by their attitude to the King's brethren, and these are they who have been doing the will of the Father, as we noted when considering chapter 12:50. One can readily understand how, in the stern days that will precede His advent to earth, those who have been seeking to do His will and proclaiming the soon coming Kingdom would suffer hunger, thirst, nakedness, imprisonment and the like.

Their sufferings would be for His sake and in sympathy He, who had been despised and rejected of men and shamefully crucified, regarded their sufferings as an extension of His own. Consequently, those who helped to relieve them in their time of distress will be welcomed into that earthly kingdom. Those who refused to do so would go away into everlasting punishment. This is not salvation by works but salvation by the only faith that saves: namely faith that works. Those who enter the kingdom are those who had faith in the coming King.

Part 3

18. THE TRIAL AND DEATH OF JESUS CHRIST (Chapters 26-28)

The record of the trial, death and resurrection of the Lord Jesus is given by all four Evangelists, though they differ in detail one from the other. Matthew says nothing about the ascension of the Lord; Mark, however, mentions it, and His continuation of service at the right hand of God in heaven; Luke, whose narrative is continued in the Acts, tells not only of the ascension but of His promised return; and John's record is a pictorial outline of the dispensational ways of God consequent on the resurrection of Christ. His appearances are recorded by him, first, to the individual, Mary; then among the apostles met together, representing the church; then to restored Israel, set forth by Thomas; and thereafter among the Gentiles, where the vast number of fish are gathered (see John 20-21).

Matthew began his Gospel with the assertion that Jesus is Christ. He finishes it by recording how the Lord Jesus declared that all authority in heaven and earth had been given unto Him. Matthew tells how God has vindicated His Son, Jesus, though His claims were rejected by men generally and acknowledged by but a very few. God proves them to be valid in that He raised Him from the dead.

There is the clearest possible evidence through Matthew's Gospel that he was inspired of God, for he selects those details which are consonant with his main theme. For example, he tells how Mary anointed the head of the Lord as if she were anointing a king (26:7); the title 'Son of Man' is frequently used (26:24, 45, 64); he mentions the Father's kingdom (v. 29); he tells how the heavenly hosts could have been put at the disposal of the Lord for His deliverance, had He so requested (v. 53); notwithstanding His remarkable silence, Matthew tells us how He spoke when He was adjured to say if He were 'Christ the Son of God', which as we have seen Peter had declared Him to be; he tells also how He answered when asked if He were the 'King of the Jews' (27:11). He records that the choice is offered to the people of either Barabbas or Jesus which is called Christ (27:17); 'What then shall I do with Jesus which is called Christ?' asks Pilate (v. 22). He tells of the scarlet robe and the crown of thorns and the reed put into His right hand, thereby cruelly mocking His claim; of the wicked taunt, 'Hail, King of the Jews'; of the superscription declaring the same thing, 'This is Jesus, the King of the Jews'; 'If He be the King of Israel, let Him now come down from the Cross, and we will believe Him' (v. 42).

Matthew selects all that was relevant to his opening words 'Jesus Christ'. The fight is on and, despite the meekness and lowliness of Jesus, the people are determined (led of course by their religious leaders) to repudiate His rights in order to get rid of Him. Even the Father's claim (3:17) is rejected; 'If Thou be the Son of God, come down from the Cross' (v. 40); 'He trusted in God; let Him deliver Him now if He will have Him, for He said, "I am the Son of God"' (v. 43). Elias too is mentioned: he was supposed to come as Messiah's forerunner - 'Let be, let us see whether Elias will come to save Him' (v. 49).

Matthew tells us, moreover, how He was given a royal burial by Joseph of Arimathea, similar to that of King Asa long ago, and how the sepulchre was guarded, much as sentries stand at royal tombs. But the grave could not hold Him. He arose and, exercising those rights which pertained to Him as Christ, the Son of the living God, He tells the apostles of His investiture with all authority in heaven and earth. He charges His own to do His bidding and teach His doctrines, assuring them of His presence even unto the end of that age, the consummation of which we have already spoken of. The issue can leave no doubt in the reader's mind that Matthew is right, and Jesus is the Christ. Peter, solitary as he was in his confession, was right. Matthew's record is all relevant to the subject he has in view.

Of course there is much which is common to all the evangelists, but it is the distinctive features which are of special interest, and Matthew arranges his material with meticulous care. The devotion of Mary is immediately preceded by the subtlety of the chief priests, scribes and elders, who, as if they were endeavouring to catch a noisome pest, determined to lay a trap in order to kill Him.

It is also succeeded by the treachery of Judas, who went to that very body of men to bargain for and endeavour to secure the highest figure to satisfy their own hatred. The highest bid he could get, however, was the price of a slave, and he was willing to accept it. What a framework for such a picture of Mary's love, devotion and worship. It is as bright colours on a dark background; the shining of a brilliant star between the clouds of a stormy night.

Another writer tells us that Judas had been there when Mary anointed the Lord and had complained of the waste; a complaint in which the others sympathised. But see the contrast. She gave liberally of her substance to Him; Judas wanted to make as much as he could out of Him. Unlike others, she declared what she thought of her Beloved whilst He was alive; most wait until they are dead. She anointed Him for His burial, for she saw clearly that men were bent on securing His death and she had no certainty that she could have done anything then, for it was doubtful if He would have a grave. They would, she feared, 'appoint His grave with the wicked'. At this time, she had no idea that He would be 'with the rich in His death'. But that death of His was to be the Good News for all mankind, and wherever that gospel was to be preached in all the world (26:13) - here it is *kosmos,* and not limited to a particular part of the world - what she did is to be told for a memorial of her. As a result, we have heard of it.

The plot has been laid, but Judas is still in the company. The Lord reveals that He is aware of all that is about to transpire and how the plot will be started among that small number of men. Heart-burnings and enquiries follow, Judas posing as concerned and innocent as the rest. It will always be a moot point whether or not Judas was at the institution of the Lord's Supper. Had we only the three synoptic Gospels, Matthew, Mark and Luke, we should have no doubt whatever that he was there. It is only when we read the later Gospel of John that doubts arise in our mind. But it is certain that if he was not there then, he has in his moral successors been there since.

The Lord recognised that what was taking place was the fulfilment of Scripture. We have already seen how the circumstances of His birth agreed with the prophetic foreshadowings; now we are to see it was so also in the circumstances attending His death. His death had been foreshadowed: one who had posed as His familiar friend had lifted up his heel against Him (Psa. 41:9). The Lord never at any time put His trust in Judas (as David once trusted Ahithophel); and so was not surprised at this time that he did what he did. Again, it had been written, 'I will smite the shepherd and the sheep of the flock shall be scattered abroad' (v. 31). Now the great mystery was to be enacted, and the sword of divine justice was to be unsheathed and plunged into the great Shepherd of Israel.

Indeed, all was done 'that the scriptures of the prophets might be fulfilled' (a general title by which the prophetic section of these Scriptures was known). Jeremiah had foretold the price of thirty pieces of silver, and Zechariah, the purchase of the potter's field (Jer. 32:6-9; Zech. 11:13). Now the purchasers of that field were all unwittingly fulfilling what had been written. With the price of blood, they bought the potter's field to be a cemetery for strangers. Further, the very disposition of His garments had been prophesied (Psa. 22:18); as also the taunts of the crowd (v. 43; Psa. 22:8); and the cry of the Lord Himself (Ps. 22:1). Matthew does not cite all the passages from the Old Testament Scriptures that were then being fulfilled, but writing by the Spirit - and no doubt as the result of the post-resurrection instruction of the Lord, who opened their understanding that they might understand the Scriptures (Luke 24:45) - he made his selection and wrote of those things concerning Him.

The Lord Jesus is the touchstone of all. Everyone is tried by Him and revealed in their true colours. By Him hypocrisy is exposed, weakness discovered, self-confidence is brought to light, human wisdom is turned to folly, unprincipled expediency is seen to be cruel injustice.

Moreover, the Lord is revealed in the excellence of His moral glories. Though a rejected King, He presses on submissive to His Father's will, for He is His obedient Son. Though the Divine equal (and His replies to His judges declare that), He is the Good Shepherd who, not only lays down His life for the sheep, but will even yet go before them into Galilee (26:32). As the sacrificial victim He is led to the place of slaughter, yet He is also the sinner's substitute and takes the place of Barabbas. Man is seen here at his worst, but we dare not say that Jesus is seen at His best, for there was no 'best' in Him. All about Him was perfect. He is here seen to be what He truly was, 'altogether lovely'. We ourselves were once like Israel and 'saw no beauty in Him that we should desire Him', for He was so maltreated that His external appearance was 'marred more than any man' (Isa. 52:14). But it was at that time that His moral glories shone out the brightest, and God has, in mercy, opened our eyes to see them.

It was the time of the Passover and the type was now to have its fulfilment. A greater redemption was about to be wrought, a greater deliverance by far than from Egypt's bondage. A new covenant was about to be brought in, not repeating the onerous 'Thou shalt' but declaring the Divine 'I will'. Yet at what a cost, and through what bitterness of soul, this covenant was to be inaugurated. The vine, speaking of Israel, which had had so much care bestowed on it, was now bringing forth its sour and bitter grapes. The Lord from now on would have nothing more to do with that vine, until the day that He drinks its wine 'new' in His Father's kingdom (26:29). Then Israel will be different. They will welcome Him and gladly own Him as their king.

His heart will then be filled with joy, but it is all so different now. It was a bitter cup of unequalled sorrow that had to be drunk. 'Behold, and see if there be any sorrow like unto My sorrow' (Lam. 1:12) said He prophetically. No wonder He prayed that if there could be a way out it might be adopted, yet He was ever willing to do the Father's will. Had He not undertaken to do so before He came (Psa. 40:6-8 and Heb. 10:9)? Why then pray? Because prayer is the submissive expression of a real wish. It does the heart good to unburden its grief to the Father. The Lord did not fear death. He was not less than the greatest hero among men who has bravely faced death, but this was to be no ordinary death. There were features about it that made the Holy Son of God shrink from it.

It is quite apparent that the Lord knew what the Scriptures foreshadowed and that the Cross was inevitable. But we must not conclude, therefore, that His prayer in Gethsemane, thrice repeated, was inconsistent with that knowledge. We should ever remember that the Person and history of our Lord are unfathomable mysteries to us. They are full of antimonies; we must give full weight to all that we read, and not attempt to reconcile that which appears to be incongruous.

As we have seen, Peter's bold confession is the highest point of the Gospel. He has also frequently appeared in a far less brilliant light, and this is so in these chapters. His self-confident boast and denial is a matter of common knowledge. No doubt, on reflection it was his precipitous defence of the Lord by the sword that caused him to urge those to whom he later wrote, to add to their faith self-control (2 Pet. 1:6). He made a grave error in using the sword, for he was a fisherman not a trained swordsman, and to wield a sword near to a man's head was to risk becoming a murderer. He was prompted by love and devotion, but it would have been better had he not done this. Many a hasty deed has inflicted damage, which no one but the

Lord can remedy. Why did he defend the Lord? Would not the Father have done so, had it been His will? If He had prayed for such defence, would not that prayer have been instantly answered? If He took no steps to defend Himself, it was useless for others to take the matter in hand (26:51-54).

Moses had a Joshua; Gideon a Phurah; David a Jonathan; Jeremiah a Baruch; Peter a Mark; and Paul a Luke. But the Lord was left alone and forsaken by all. Indeed, God also forsook Him. Here we are in impenetrable darkness; we have no light on such a mystery, and words would only ensnare us. 'Jehovah heaped upon Him the iniquity of us all.' We can only wonder, for the mystery of all this is made greater in view of the fact that Judas admitted that he had betrayed innocent blood (27:4). Pilate three times averred that he could find no fault in Him; both he and his wife called Him a 'just man' (27:19, 24); the Council were driven to make do with false witnesses. If this was the verdict of men, what shall we say of God Who never more delighted in His Son than at this moment?

It was not as if only part of the nation concurred in His death. They had all been swayed by their religious leaders, and they all said, 'His blood be on us and on our children' (27:25). They were not content merely to accept liability for themselves, but to transmit the consequences to their posterity, the bitterness of which has been reaped through two millennia and is being reaped today. 'They all say' - note the word 'all' - 'Let Him be crucified'. 'All the people' were as one in their cry (vv. 22, 25).

For three hours, from the third to the sixth, their cruelties went on, but from the sixth to the ninth there was darkness. The Lamb of God was on the altar and the upper part of the grating could be seen, but the underneath (for it was halfway down) was altogether out of view (see Exod. 27:5 R.V.). His end was not that of a soul irresistibly expiring, but the triumphant exit of a Victor on whose lips was the victorious cry (27:50).

The effects were amazing. The veil of the temple was rent in twain from top to bottom. An invisible hand of the invisible God had opened the way into the holiest. At one and the same time the emptiness and uselessness of earthly ritual were exposed and all that hindered the believing sinner from approaching God was removed. 'The earth did quake and the rocks were rent.' That was a kingdom that could be shaken, for hanging on the Cross had been one who was King of a kingdom that could not be shaken (Heb. 12:28). Death had been conquered, the graves were opened, and the bodies of the saints which slept arose and came out of the grave after His resurrection. We are told no more about these saints and speculation is futile.

But the effects were also seen among living men. The centurion seeing these things admitted that Jesus was the Son of God, despite all that had been said to the contrary. So Peter was right when he spoke at Caesarea Philippi to the same effect. Many women were there beholding the whole tragic scene, wondering and confused. It baffled them: it was all so contrary to their thoughts and destructive of their long cherished hopes. Joseph of Arimathaea, for some time a secret disciple, can no longer remain silent and secret. He must come out now and own his true convictions. Boldly he approaches Pilate and begs the body of Jesus, so that it is not disposed of as would be the bodies of the two malefactors. It is granted, and he wraps it in clean linen and lays it in his new tomb. There can be no doubt who came out of that tomb, for none other had ever lain there.

What does the mother of the two sons of Zebedee think now?

What are the thoughts of her two sons, who had been nearest to Him in Gethsemane's garden and now see their Master put to death? Are they still ambitious to be associated with Him, or do they think a kingdom and a throne and high honours now at all likely? What does Simon the Cyrenian make of it all? He had confronted Christ bearing His Cross; he had been turned about, and bearing that Cross he followed Jesus. Will he continue to follow in a spiritual sense, as he had been made to do in the material?

This, therefore, was not only 'the trial of Jesus Christ', it was also the 'trial' of all who came into contact with Him then. His 'trial' revealed His wonderful moral glories and graces; their 'trial' revealed the true state of their hearts. Those who figure in the scenes of chapters 26-27 are shown up in their real colours, as they come within range of Him Who was the light of the world and He shone His light on all men.

The chief priests, the scribes and the elders of the people are there besetting Him like 'bulls of Bashan'. The high priest Caiaphas is there, glad to be 'consulted' by them as to how they could 'take' Jesus and 'kill Him'.

Mary comes into the scene; not as one who is plotting His death, but as one who acknowledges His royal rights and she anoints His head. Her heart is revealed.

Judas Iscariot is there. He is seen now in his true character; not in the midst of the other apostles, before whom he posed as innocent as all the rest, but in consort with the chief priests. He was prepared to cooperate with them.

The good man of the house in which the last Passover was held, and in which the Lord's Supper was instituted, comes into the picture. His heart too is made bare; he is willing to open his doors to this hunted King.

The disciples are there; each searching his heart as to whether or not the Lord was referring to any one of them as the one who should perpetrate this, the darkest and foulest crime of history.

Peter, in particular, is a conspicuous figure on this canvas. He does not know his own heart and cannot measure his own weakness. The Lord reveals his heart to him, but he does not heed the warning.

The two sons of Zebedee are also selected for special mention. Their hearts are now searched, for it seems as if their cherished aspirations, which had received such a rebuke from the Lord, were now not at all likely to be achieved. Not for them, nor anyone else for that matter. Their hearts must have been troubled.

The whole council is in the picture. They join in the search for false witnesses, for they knew it would be useless to search for true witnesses. Such could only have testified in a manner that would have failed to produce any evidence of a capital offence.

Many false witnesses are there also, but they are worthless for the accomplishment of the cruel intention. At last two false witnesses come forward and they distort the words of the Christ of God, taking words which He spoke concerning Himself and construing them in relation to their great temple. The frivolousness of such testimony was evidently felt, for it was not followed up. His judges were preoccupied with the claims which the Lord made for Himself, not with the threats that it was alleged He made concerning the temple.

In the morning Pontius Pilate, the Roman governor, is brought into the picture. He acts in a double role. When he is spoken of as 'Pilate', he is seen in his personal capacity. When referred to as 'governor', he is seen in his official capacity. His inner thoughts are revealed and he seeks to free himself from such an awkward 'case'. He does not want to upset the people; nor does he want on any account to give any occasion for what might seem to be a charge of treason against Rome. He is anxious also to keep his hands 'clean' and not to participate in the guilt of the death of an innocent party. He has a way out. At the feast it was customary to release to the Jews a prisoner.

Barabbas now comes on the canvas. He was a notable prisoner who, we are told elsewhere, was an insurrectionist and murderer. The people clamour for his release and the condemnation of Jesus, and so it came to pass. What must have been the thoughts of this released criminal, as later he would look on the Man on the central Cross? He could only have admitted, 'He was given up for my offences' (as in Rom. 4:25). Did he ever say, 'He loved me and gave Himself up for me'? (see Gal. 2:20.)

Pilate's wife is also affected by the events of that day. She counsels her husband to have nothing to do with the case. She knows that the central figure is a 'just man', and should never have been arrested or put on trial.

The soldiers are there also and now they come out in all their cruelty, roughness, ribaldry and evil. He is stripped of His own garment and arrayed with a scarlet robe, thus mocking His royal claims. They are not prepared to stand beside Peter and say, 'Thou art the Christ, the Son of the living God'; rather they mock that claim with a scarlet robe and a crown of thorns, with reed and bowed knee. Unless in God's day of grace they later bowed the knee to Him in sincerity, they will yet have to do so because of the divine decree that 'in the name of Jesus every knee shall bow' (Phil. 2:10).

Man seems to be at his worst and grossest here. They spat upon Him; they wrenched the reed from Him and smote Him on the head with it. They would never do what Mary did: they would not anoint His head. They mock Him, strip Him of the scarlet robe, they replace His own garments and lead Him away to crucify Him.

Another is brought on to the canvas. Simon the Cyrenian is impressed by Roman custom to bear the load of the Cross, under which the Saviour of sinners was showing physical exhaustion. Other evangelists tell us of this man: his coming out of the country, suddenly confronting Christ, taking His Cross, turning around and following Him - all so clearly depicting what happens spiritually to a man who leaves the world and is willing to 'take up his cross and follow Him'. This is true conversion. Simon had two sons, Alexander and Rufus; to whom there may be references in Romans 16:13, 1 Timothy 1:20; 2 Timothy 4:14. If these are in fact his two sons, how different each one is from the other.

The picture is not yet complete. Two robbers are brought into it, one crucified on the left hand of the Lord and one on the right. As in all else, Jesus was 'in the midst:' the central place is always His. Matthew tells us nothing about the repentance and confession of one of these; it is left to Luke to do that. But Matthew does record how the crowd laid emphasis on the notion of salvation: 'Save Thyself'; 'He saved others, Himself

He cannot save'. How true were these words in one sense; yet how false in another. If He were to save sinners, then He could not save Himself.

'If Thou be the Son of God ...' (27:40). This sounds strangely like the devil's voice, who had said the same at His temptation. They cried: 'If He be the king of Israel' (even should the word 'if' be omitted, as some suggest, the sense remains the same), 'let Him now come down from the Cross and we will believe Him' (v. 42). But would they? Though He was raised from the dead, they did not as a people accept Him as their king. The day is yet to come when they will do so.

In common with Mark, Matthew records only one cry from the Cross: 'My God, My God, why didst Thou forsake Me?' The emphasis should be placed on each pronoun: why Thou, and why Me? The mystery of the three dark hours and what took place then will never be fully known to any but 'Thou' and 'Me'. It was the mystery of a thrice-holy God forsaking His equally holy Son (Ps. 22:1-3). Yet there were depths in this that raise it infinitely far above the level of what would appear to be callous and immoral in a merely human setting. But of that we cannot speak particularly now.

> *Upon the cross of Jesus*
> *Mine eye at times can see*
> *The very dying form of One*
> *Who suffered there for me;*
> *And from my smitten heart, with tears,*
> *Two wonders I confess,*
> *The wonders of His glorious love*
> *And my own worthlessness.*

19. THE RESURRECTION AND ITS SEQUEL (Chapter 28)

It is remarkable that the chief priests and Pharisees should have remembered that Jesus had said, 'After three days I will rise again'. It shows they must have given more heed to His words than many supposed. It is astonishing that those words did not weigh more with the apostles, but grief seems to have swamped them and banished every hope. However, the religious leaders, boiling over with hatred, take steps to ensure that His words do not come to pass. How strange! No watch like that had been set to any other tomb. Surely they had not given sufficient thought to their plans. What could a small band of weak disciples do against their enemies? However, the watch was set.

The 'end of the Sabbath' had come. The old dispensation was about to pass and an altogether new dispensation was about to 'dawn' (28:1). It had been through a woman that sin had been brought into the world, for Eve transgressed and gave to her husband, who shared her fall. It is now through a woman that the good news of the resurrection of the sin-removing Saviour is brought to the world, and she communicates it to the men. The Lord God was at work: He had sent His angel, who had rolled away the stone and was sitting on it. The good news is made known to those sad hearts. 'The keepers shake for fear', but there is no need for these godly women to do so - 'Fear not ye'. Oh, the magnificence of the news: He is not here, He is risen. He said He would and He has. And what is more, as the Great Shepherd of the sheep, 'He goeth before you into Galilee'. Tell His disciples, 'There shall ye see Him'. Light after darkness; calm after storm; hope after despair; joy after grief.

The news was bound to leak out and the council learned

of it. A tale was concocted to try and prevent this thing from spreading. But what a tale! If the disciples actually did steal His body, why not arrest them for theft? If they were asleep when the body was taken, how did they know who took it? It might have been anyone other than the disciples. Why indeed did they sleep, since to do so on duty was to incur a court martial and its stern penalty? Besides, how were they not awakened by the inevitable noise of the proceedings in removing the body? Could that seal have been broken silently? Who broke it? Was it likely that a band of fishermen would risk breaking through an armed guard?

And again: the tale was most unlikely, for the disciples apparently did not expect Him to be raised from the dead, though He had plainly told them He would. It was not to be expected that they would spread such a false rumour, but if they did go about saying that He was raised, the likelihood is that He actually was alive. In addition to all this, there was a very easy way of exploding the rumour. Make them produce the body. If they had stolen it, it would have been somewhere. Bring pressure to bear on them and demand the production of the body.

But they did none of these things. Rather, they bribed the soldiers and made up their story, and the Jews, not desiring Jesus to be their king, took it in.

The Jewish people and Jerusalem is now temporarily set aside. The disciples go to Galilee; there they meet the Lord and seeing Him they worship. Even so, some doubted, but Matthew does not go into that. His great theme is the Person of Christ and His claims, not the weaknesses of His followers. Others will write about those doubts and how they were dispelled. It is not Matthew's province.

He is showing the King triumphant, heralding His Great Programme for the age that He has now brought in. 'Go, make disciples, baptise and teach' is the charge He gives. No longer are they to limit themselves to the house of Israel; they are to go to all nations. No longer are they to be followers of One who, in the days of His flesh, appeared as all others in fashion as a man, and poor at that. They are representing One to Whom all authority in heaven and earth has been given. They may count on His presence everywhere and at all times. No longer will they have experiences when He is absent, like being alone on the stormy lake. He will never leave them. The commission is to be in force from the time of its issue till the consummation of the age - that is, till He returns.

Ultra-dispensationalists have taught that it is not for the present interim period when the Church is being called out, but it has to do with the period that is to follow the translation of the Church to heaven. But it would appear to be strange that such a Commission should be applicable to so short a period, as that which will elapse between the Rapture and the Coming to earth of the Lord. For, whatever its length, it surely cannot be as long as the two millennia that have almost run out now.

The words 'disciple all nations' do not mean that there is to be a Nationalised Christianity throughout the world. The word 'make disciples' occurs only in one other place (Acts 14:21), and there it clearly means making disciples of individuals. Here the same sense must apply, though the individuals are stated to be those of any and every nation. As we say, 'canvassing a constituency', or 'fishing a lake', so too, 'discipling all nations'.

Besides, it would seem that baptism relates in a peculiar way to the present era. This is not the place to give a dissertation on baptism, but suffice to say that the words 'in the name of the Father, the Son and the Holy Spirit' are in perfect accord with all Pauline teaching. This is not a formula to be recited parrot-like at a baptism; it is a statement of fact that the person immersed is in relation to God as child to a Father, to the Son as one of His 'brethren', and to the Holy Spirit who indwells him. It appears to the present writer that there is no formula given in Scripture to be recited at a baptism.

'Teaching them to observe all things whatsoever I have commanded you' is not contrary to Christian doctrine. The 'whatsoever' does not relate to the restrictive duties given to the apostles, such as those given in chapter 10 of our Gospel, but all non-restrictive duties, such as the laws of the kingdom, which have been considered.

Matthew has completed his task. He has given to his readers the record of the life and work of 'Jesus Christ', beginning with His lowly birth at Bethlehem and ending with His triumphant declaration, 'All authority in heaven and earth is given unto Me'. We are left in no doubt whatever that his opening words are true. 'Jesus Christ' was all He claimed to be, and what Matthew believed Him to be. He was, as the Father had revealed to Peter, 'The Christ, the Son of the living God'.

When the Apostles saw Him in resurrection, a resurrection which vindicated all that He had said, they worshipped Him. Can we do otherwise?

The Epistle to the Ephesians

- **Part 1**   The Purpose of God
- **Part 2**   Paul's Prayer
- **Part 3**   What a Change!
- **Part 4**   The Jew and the Gentile
- **Part 5**   The Mystery
- **Part 6**   Ministry in the Church
- **Part 7**   Gathered Threads
- **Part 8**   Some Practical Lessons

Part 1

The Purpose of God

This epistle has rightly been described as the Mount Everest of the Bible. It gives the highest truth. Its near rival is that to the Colossians with which it has much in common. The student should compare each to discover what is common to both and how that common material is differently presented. In Ephesians, the believer is regarded as "in Christ", whereas, in Colossians, Christ is in him. In Ephesians, the believer is seated in the heavenlies, whereas, in Colossians, he is on earth. In Ephesians, there is no mention of the coming back of the Lord Jesus, but there is in Colossians.

Both letters were written, as it would seem, from Rome when Paul was a prisoner, as was also, presumably, its companion letter to the Philippians; see Ephesians 3:1; Phillippians 1:7; Colossians 4:18.

It also appears that the letter to the Ephesians was of an encyclical kind, and it may well be that this is the letter which was sent to Laodicea and which ultimately went to Colossae, Colossians 4:16. The words "in Ephesus" in Ephesians 1:1 are of doubtful authority. The place may have been left vacant, and available for the insertion of any desired name. This seems all the more likely since there are no names of individuals mentioned in the letter, not even at its close. At any rate we do know that "all the word of God is for all the people of God" and that this letter is, perhaps, amongst their most valuable treasures.

Its human penman was Paul, once known as Saul of Tarsus, the erstwhile inquisitor who terrified the early Christians, but now their ardent and authorised apostle. While, at times, he magnifies his office, yet at other times he is very conscious of his personal unworthiness for such an honour. In fact, in this letter he calls himself "less than the least of all saints", chapter 3:8. He is now learning by experience "how great things he must suffer" for the name of the Lord Jesus, yet instead of bemoaning his lot, and pitying himself, his eye is on Christ in glory, and his heart is towards the well-being of his many converts to whom he writes as he thinks of, and prays for them.

> *"Two men looked through prison bars;*
> *The one saw mud, the other stars."*

It all depended on the way they looked. Paul looked up and saw Him whom God had set "far above all", chapter 1:21. Faith's penetrating eye knew no limits.

We shall adopt the following analysis for our detailed studies of the Epistle.

1:1-2: Introductory Apostolic Greetings.
1:3-14: The Purpose of God, which
    covers all time,
    embraces all parties,
    engages all three Persons of the Holy Trinity,
    defines an ordered plan,
    imparts permanent benefits,
    declares the nature of God.

1:15-23: Paul's Prayer,
>"what is the hope of His calling",
>"what the riches of the glory of His inheritance in the saints",
>"the exceeding greatness of His power to us-ward".
>The metaphor, the body of Christ.

2:1-10: What a Change!,
>what they were,
>what they had become,
>what they should be.

2:11-22: An Illustration.
>The position of the Jew and Gentile prior to the effective operation of God's grace towards them.
>
>The offer which was made to the Jew first and then to the Gentile later.
>
>The position in the case of those who have accepted the offer. The foundation of this new place.

3:1-21: The Mystery.
>Paul's prayer

4:1-16: Ministry in the Church
>Walking worthily of the calling.
>The unity detailed.
>The diversity existent in the church.

4:17-5:20: Gathered Threads
>"In Christ." Saints.
>Grace. The Spirit of promise.
>Enlightenment. Walk.
>"New man." One body.

5:21-6:24: Some Practical Lessons
>   Wives and husbands.
>   Children and parents.
>   Servants and masters.
>   Christian warfare.
>   Concluding words.

Introductory Apostolic Greetings, Chapter 1:1-2

The writer speaks of himself as "Paul, an apostle of Christ Jesus through the will of God". (1:1 R.V.) There were other apostles with their own specific spheres of service. He was the apostle to the Gentiles. He was not such by personal choice or by self-assertive appointment: he was such "by the will of God". When writing to Timothy he says that he is an apostle by the "commandment (*epitage*) of God" (1 Tim. 1:1). He was thus assured that he was both in line with the "will of God" and authorised by sovereign divine appointment.

For the most part he speaks of the Lord as "Christ Jesus", a title that denotes His present risen glory, and he describes his addressees as "*the saints* that are at Ephesus and to the *faithful* in Christ Jesus". Their original belief is manifest in their continued faithfulness. The title "*saints*" signifies the wonderful state of holiness which is theirs consequent upon the cleansing work of Christ, while the word "*faithful*" indicates their present character.

His greeting in verse 2 is couched in such words as would appeal both to Gentile and Jewish converts. "*Grace*" would be understood by the Gentiles, while "*peace*" (Heb. *Shalom*) would be well understood by the Jewish believer. "Grace" is the source of the "peace" that flows from it, and both have their spring in God our Father and the Lord Jesus Christ. The one preposition "from" (*apo*) governs the two names, God and Lord, thus stressing the absolute equality of the two Persons.

The Purpose of God, Chapter 1:3-14

This constitutes one of the longest unbroken sentences in the Scriptures, (see R.V.). It is, perhaps, the most comprehensive statement of the purpose of God, its every word being weighted down with a volume of truth. It relates to a purpose which:

Covers all time. Perhaps we should say, it goes from eternity to eternity. It looks back to the remote past and affirms that the believer was "chosen" in Christ before the foundation of the world. The age of this earth on which we sojourn is one of those things which the scientific investigations of man has not yet finalised. It may be doubted whether or not it is exactly discoverable. Maybe it is one of those "secret things" which belong to the Lord. But whensoever the world was founded (the word *katabole* has nothing to do with an overthrow), *before* then God chose "us in Him" with the view to our being "holy and without blemish before Him" (1:4 R.V.), a purpose which will ultimately be achieved (5:27). We cannot here enter into a discussion on election, but suffice it to say that God did not choose us as a class, but rather as individuals known beforehand by Him. Nor did He choose us because He knew that we would believe, but rather we believed because He chose us.

The ultimate accomplishment of this purpose will be when "the dispensation of the fulness of the times" has come, when all things are headed up in Christ (1:10 R.V.). This appears to refer to a time beyond the millennium, for that is but one of the "times" (or "seasons" – periods characterised by something special), at the end of which man, under Satan, will rebel against the best King he has ever had. But in this eternal future, when everything is headed up in Christ, it will involve both the heavens and the earth. Its present disharmony will then have been abolished. Then all earth's "times" will have run their complete course, and after God has worked out His eternal purpose throughout such "seasons", He will bring everything to its designed climax, and Christ will be its Supreme Head. In it we believers will have our part, as verses 2 and 12 show, (R.V.).

Thus God's eternal purpose had its roots in what we call a past eternity, and will have its ultimate fruit in a yet future eternity, both of which are dissected by the central event of the cross (v. 7: "His blood"). To it all God's past activities pointed; they had it in view, and from it all His further activities have flown and are consequential upon it. This purpose, moreover:

Embraces all Parties, both Jew and Gentile. The pronouns in this section, as everywhere, should be carefully noted. The "we" of verse 12 refers to believing Jews, who nationally hoped beforehand in a coming Messiah (see Luke 24:21). The "ye" of verse 13 refers to the Gentiles, who, having heard the word of truth, the gospel concerning their salvation, had trusted in that same Messiah and were thereupon "sealed with the Holy Spirit of promise", R.V. Their believing and sealing were synchronous: no lapse of time intervened between the one and the other (1:13 R.V.). The incident of the twelve Ephesians recorded in Acts 19 is of a special nature into which we cannot go now.

The "we" of verse 12 and the "ye" of verse 13, that is the believing Jews and the believing Gentiles are comprehended in the further pronoun "us" of verse 3 as also the pronoun "our" of verse 14. The all-embracive nature of the purpose of God is further developed in chapter 2 which we shall discuss later. Further, this purpose of God:

Engages all Three Persons of the Holy Trinity. The Unity of the Godhead and the Trinity of its Persons is a truth which the intellect of man cannot explain but which faith accepts. Each Person has His own peculiar territory of activity; hence it is the Father who elects, verse 4, the Son who redeems, verse 7, and the Spirit who seals, verse 13. Not that these are independent actions: Each works in perfect harmony with the Other, Each doing that which is essential to the achievement of the "purpose of the ages" (3:11 R.V. marg.), This harmonious co-operative action of the Persons of the Godhead is implied in the three parables of Luke 15, 1 Peter 1:1-2, 2 Thessalonians 2:13-14 and elsewhere. How marvellous that God, in the fulness of His being, has been throughout the ages and is now actively engaged in bringing about the eternal well-being of such unmeritorious creatures as we had become! And at such a cost!

It will be found in reading this wonderful section that it:

Defines an Ordered Plan. Note the words which are used: "love", verse 4, "will", verse 9, "good pleasure" or delight, verse 9, "purposed", verse 9, "counsel", verse 11, and "worketh", verse 11. The spring of all this wonderful plan lies in the love of God, which caused Him to have a "will" (or better "wish"), a wish such that He being so delighted with His One Son, desired to have heaven filled with "many sons" like Him. The thought of such a thing gave Him "good pleasure" (or better, "delight"). The very idea well-pleased His heart. He therefore and thereupon "purposed" that it should be so. He would take steps to achieve what His love had conceived, what was His delightful wish. There was however an obstacle in the way. Man was enslaved to self, and sin, and Satan. He needed to be released from his bonds; yet if this were to be done, the stern requirements of justice must be met. Hence there followed the divine "*counsel*" as to how to overcome the obstacles and how to meet the requirements. The solution of the problem was by the cross – redemption through the blood, and after that had been accomplished, operations have been set afoot by Him who is now working everything "according to plan".

Most of us have built our castles in the air, and it has given us great pleasure in their contemplation. The young man who espouses his bride-to-be because he *loves* her, wishes to settle down in a home with her: that *wish* gives him much *delight* in thinking over it. He, therefore, *purposes* to have his own home, though difficulties have to be met, for "the coat must be cut according to the cloth". But financial and other things having been arranged, building *operations* take place and he has the joy of seeing the home going up day by day. One day the happy time arrives when both settle down therein, their love having reached its goal, the wish having been obtained, the purpose having been achieved, the difficulties having been overcome, and the heart is satisfied. This purpose of God:

Imparts Permanent Benefits. There is "forgiveness", verse 7, sonship, verse 5 R.V., and "redemption", verse 7. Forgiveness settles the past; redemption secures the future; and sonship secures the present (as well as the future). It is not possible here fully to examine these benefits; that would unduly enlarge our pages. But the reader should do this for himself. It will be seen that in them God has provided for every conceivable contingency. The words here used are without any restriction and should be interpreted in the largest possible manner. Finally we may observe that this purpose:

Declares the Nature of God. It is "to the praise of His glory", (1:12). Glory is "displayed excellence" and this display evokes praise. That glory will be displayed in us, so that "we should be to the praise of His glory". But we are brought in by sovereign grace; hence it is "to the praise of the glory of His grace wherewith He freely bestowed on (graced) us in the Beloved", verse 6 R.V. marg.; see also verses 12, 14. God has declared what He Himself is, and this in turn has resulted in His showing grace to us, while that in turn results in a paean of praise to Him which eternity will not exhaust.

Part 2

Paul's Prayer

Everything touching the present position of the believer is different from that which obtained with Israel in their heyday. The old economy is far inferior to the present "purpose of God". Israel was then blessed in Abraham with sundry earthly blessings in Canaan. We are blessed with every spiritual blessing in the heavenlies in Christ. The disclosure of this was not made until the basis for its accomplishment had been laid, in the death, resurrection and glorification of Christ, and until the Holy Spirit had been sent as the present earnest or pledge of what we are yet to inherit in Christ. The "purpose" remained a "mystery", that is, an undisclosed secret, until the appropriate time had arrived for it to be revealed. It was the first to be conceived and will be the first to be consummated, yet it was the last to be revealed.

Paul had pioneered the gospel at Ephesus, Acts 19, and had later counselled the elders of the church which had there been formed, Acts 20. Now, some years later, his heart is rejoiced as he hears of their "faith in the Lord Jesus ... and love unto all the saints" (1:15). Their faith was genuine: their love proved it. Their love was not selective but comprehensive, it extended to *all* the saints. This revealed that their once darkened hearts had been enlightened. No wonder Paul was full of thanks and instant in prayer for them. His desire was that they might have such a full knowledge of "the God of our Lord Jesus Christ, the Father of glory" that three things might be wrought:

a) That they might be wise touching what lies ahead of them,

b) That they might be wise touching what lies ahead for God,

c) That they might know what is the power that will ensure the attainment of *(a)* and *(b)*.

Paul's desire was that they might know:

(a) *"what is the hope of His calling"*, chapter 1:18. He calls it the "one hope of your calling" in chapter 4:4. It is not yet manifest or realised, for "what a man seeth, why doth he yet hope for?", Romans 8:24. But it is set out in chapter 1:10 and 11. In Christ we have obtained an inheritance, the earnest of which we have already been given in the person of the Holy Spirit. As Rebekah's jewels and the modern engagement ring are pledges of what is yet to be possessed and enjoyed, so it is with the believer now. The Holy Spirit, who was promised by the Lord Jesus, has come as the "earnest of our inheritance", chapter 1:14, which we shall enter upon when we experience "the redemption of our body", Romans 8:23.

Then he desired that they might know:

(b) "what are the riches of the glory of His inheritance in the saints", chapter 1:18. There seems to be little doubt that both the A.V. and R.V. are possible translations of the Greek of verse 11: "We have obtained an inheritance" and "we were made a heritage". The latter phrase is explained by Deuteronomy 4:20 and 32:9 which affirm that Israel was God's heritage. On the other hand we have, doubtless, obtained an inheritance by reason of our identification

with Christ. Surely, the two ideas are in verse 14: "the earnest of our inheritance" tells us of what we are yet to have, whilst the words "the redemption of God's own possession", verse 14 R.V., declares what God is yet to have in His people. This latter is the second item of Paul's prayer, that the saints might know "what are the riches of the glory (the displayed excellence) of His (i.e., God's) inheritance in the saints". It is, it seems, an innate weakness with all God's people to think primarily of what they will possess later on, giving little heed to what God will possess in His redeemed people. But Paul would that the saints were intelligent as to both aspects of one thing – God's side and ours: what He will have, and what we shall have. "The riches of the glory of His inheritance in the saints" will be displayed "when He shall come to be glorified in His saints and to be marvelled at in all them that believed", 2 Thessalonians 1:10 R.V. Paul further desires that we might be intelligent as to:

(c) "the exceeding greatness of His power to us-ward", chapter 1:19, power which is able to effect His designs. No greater power toward us could have been exercised than that which He wrought in Christ when He raised Him from the dead. It was the display of the "exceeding greatness of His power" for there was no comparable event hitherto or since. It was not merely resurrection, it was exaltation to the highest point of honour in heaven, far above every visible and invisible authority or power, either present or future. Indeed that which had been lost by the first Adam has been more than abundantly restored by the Last Adam, and the whole universe has been put in subjection under His feet.

Yet this was the display of the "exceeding greatness of His power *to us-ward*" as well as *to Christ* – to us who have believed, for we are now vitally and inseparably linked with

Him as body to Head, and spiritually we have experienced already what He fully experienced, He who was "quickened by the Spirit", 1 Peter 3:18.

One has but to use little imagination to enter into the thrill that charmed the heart of the apostle as he lay in prison. His body might be incarcerated but nothing could imprison his spirit as he contemplated what God had wrought in Christ, taking Him from the lowest depths of shame to the highest heights of glory, and in that very act establishing a principle which was to be true of all who believed in Him. This Paul expands in chapter 2.

It may be retorted that it does not yet appear to be the case that everything in the universe is subject to Christ, but 1 Corinthians 15:20-28 declares that it will assuredly yet be seen to be the case. Potentially it is so now: in actuality and manifestation it will be so later: "we walk by faith, not by appearance", 2 Corinthians 5:7 R.V. marg.

The Metaphor, the Body of Christ

The notion of the "body of Christ" is peculiar to the apostle Paul. No other writer used this metaphor. Doubtless he learned the fact when arrested on the Damascus road. The question, "Why persecutest thou Me?" revealed to him that to touch the Christian was to touch the Lord Himself: to touch them was as touching a member of a body, and its pain was felt instantly by the Head. "He is touched with the feeling" which affects His members.

The "body" is the "church", the called-out and elect company, whose birthday was the Pentecostal day of Acts 2. They are the excellent of the earth, God's elite: a unity with infinite diversity: each member interdependent upon the other: each differing from the other: yet, "There is one body", Ephesians 4:4. It is the "fulness of Him who fills all in all" (1:23). That is to say, the Church is the complement of Christ as the body is the complement of the Head. A head without a body is a misnomer: a body without a head is a mere torso. The Church is not a lifeless organization, it is a living organism, indissolubly linked with the Head in heaven.

No higher position could be given to redeemed sinners than this. The Head of the Church is He who fills all in all – "who fills the Universe in all its parts", N.E.B. marg., and the church is His fulness – His complement.

How amazing it is that the ultimate purpose of God could not be achieved apart from His being associated with the Church, and that this Church – this company of redeemed sinners from all tribes and nations and peoples and tongues – is to share the manifested glory of Him who has been placed far above all principalities and powers, be they hostile to God or otherwise!

Part 3

What a Change!

Someone has said, "I am not what I should be, but by the grace of God I am what I am, and that at least is not what I was". Likely enough this was based on Paul's remark in 1 Corinthians 15:10. At any rate, the section now before us deals with these three things, for in verses 1-3 Paul reminds the saints what they once were, in verses 4-7 he tells them what the grace of God has wrought in them, while in the remaining part of the section he emphasises what they should be.

Twice he remarks, "By grace have ye been saved" verses 5, 8 R.V. He uses the perfect tense, denoting that what took place in the history of each believer has abiding and unalterable effects. He is for ever saved. Moreover it is not only by "grace" on God's part but "through faith" on the individual's part, chapter 2:8. Not that there was any merit in "faith". Man's original sin was his not believing and trusting God and, if the damage of sin is to be undone, man must go back on that action and believe and trust God. The words "grace" and "faith" are in the feminine gender in Greek but the pronoun "that" in verse 8 is neuter, thus showing that it is not faith which is the gift of God, but the salvation wrought by the initial work of God in grace on the one part, and which has become effective through faith exercised on the other's part. The capacity to believe and trust is an attribute of human nature. No one can truly say he cannot believe God, else how could God upbraid man for his unbelief? Hence the phrase, "it is the gift of God" must not be restricted to one thing; it covers the whole work of salvation by grace through faith. That this is so is shown by the next sentence, "not of works, that no man should glory", chapter 2:9 R.V.

Thus Paul assures the saints by this repeated statement, "by grace have ye been saved" of their eternal security, a thing for which they will eternally give praise, and as to which they can claim no credit.

What They Were
Verses 1-3 describe their former state. The pronouns "ye" and "we" relate to Gentiles and Jews respectively. The verses may be summarized as follows:

(a) They were *dead spiritually* – alienated from the life of God, consequent upon their trespasses and sins. (Note *"through"* instead of *"in"* in R.V.) Their wrongful commissions and omissions brought about this state.

(b) They were *dominated physically*: "walked" denotes their way of life, their general conduct, which, though they might have claimed to be free, was governed by the time state (age) of this cosmos, this world, of which Satan is the "prince", John 14:30. They lived for time and sense. The "course of this world" means the time-state of this world of matter, so that man in his fallen state, instead of knowing the freedom of eternity, is restricted by temporal and material considerations.

(c) They were *disobedient morally*: "the spirit that now worketh in the sons of disobedience", R.V. "Sons" has to do with character; "disobedience" is a word that signifies the obstinate refusal of man to be persuaded by the will of God.

(d) They were *selfish mentally* – "lusts of our flesh, doing the desires of the flesh and of the mind" (2:3). This marked the Jews as much as the Gentiles; "we also" says Paul. It marked the Gentiles but it also marked the Jew. Neither loved the Lord with all their heart, soul or mind: rather, they loved self.

(e) They were *condemned judicially:* they were "children of wrath, even as the rest," chapter 2:3 R.V., that is, even as the Gentiles. The wrath of God abode upon them. Moreover it lay before them as an awful destiny yet to be experienced.

Sin and its effects had invaded every department of their being, spirit, soul and body. Their position was altogether the antithesis of what God desired: they were earth-bound, time-restricted, Satanically-ruled, impervious to divine things for they were dead, and resistant to the divine rule, for they were "disobedient". What a state! What material on which God had to work! Yet, as we have said, verses 4 to 7 tell us:

What They Had Become
What they had become "by the grace of God"! The old things had passed away and everything had become new.

We may use an illustration to help us to understand these verses. Every (or almost every) river commences with a spring; it flows on into the river; it goes on to the estuary and thenceforward into the limitless ocean. Let us discover these four things in this section:

The Spring. This is defined in verse 4, "for His great love wherewith He loved us". We might substitute "on account of" for the word "for". Therein lies the source of all that God has done for us. He does not use the word *phileo*, but rather the stronger word of John 3:16 and 1 Corinthians 13 – *agape*.

> *Could we with ink the ocean fill,*
> *And were the skies of parchment made,*
> *Were every blade of grass a quill,*
> *And every man a scribe by trade;*
> *To write the love of God abroad*
> *Would drain the ocean dry,*
> *Nor could the scroll contain the whole*
> *Though spread from sky to sky.*

Hence we must resist the temptation to dilate on this tempting theme of the "everlasting love" of God. But it accounts for all that follows.

The River, "but God, being rich in mercy", chapter 2:4 R.V. The timeless participle "being" reveals that God has always shown mercy, and that He still does, and ever will, where it is called for. God does not show mercy in abridging punishment; He cancels it altogether. The cases of David and Manasseh in the Old Testament show that this is the case. One has but to read Psalms 32, 51 and 2 Chronicles 33:12, 13 to appreciate that, where there is real confession of sin, God's heart of mercy goes out to the delinquent. "God be merciful to me the sinner" cried the publican and it was he, not the Pharisee, who went down to his house justified, Luke 18:13-14. Saul of Tarsus, the erstwhile blasphemer, persecutor and injurious, declares, "but I obtained mercy", 1 Timothy 1:13. And though we could multiply cases such as these almost *ad infinitum*, God is so rich in mercy that He still has plenty for whoever needs it.

> *His mercy flows on like a river*
> *His grace is unbounded and free:*
> *His love is for ever sufficient,*
> *It reaches and saves even me.*

"Children of wrath" though we may be, due to His mercy "we shall be saved from wrath" through Christ, Romans 5:9. That mercy went out toward us "even when we were dead through our trespasses", Ephesians 2:5 R.V. Truth would have condemned us; justice would have doomed us; but mercy has saved us.

The Estuary. This is something wider, deeper and larger in every way than the river. And so it is here. Note the words used: "the exceeding riches of His grace in His kindness towards us through Christ Jesus", chapter 2:7.

> *Amazing grace, how sweet the sound,*
> *That saved a wretch like me.*
> *I once was lost, but now am found,*
> *Was bound but now am free.*

These were the words of that deeply-dyed sinner John Newton, so marvellously saved by the sovereign grace of God. Note "the exceeding riches of His grace"; not merely that God is rich in such an attribute, but that when He shows grace He confers wealth untold such as is called, "the unsearchable riches of Christ". Grace is unmerited favour, for there is nothing in the object of it which is worthy of such favour. Moreover, note the word "kindness" – such as meets our need in our distress, and does for us what is utterly impossible for us to do for ourselves.

Love, mercy, grace and kindness exceed all displays of these in times past; they are all now shown to us in Christ Jesus. The word "exceeding" does not mean merely the comparative nature of these qualities; it denotes their superlative quality. What God has done in and through Christ Jesus, His Beloved Son, chapter 1:6, finds no equal in any of the activities of God whether prior to or since the cross.

The Ocean. In the oncoming ages of eternity He will show what He has wrought, and the vast sphere into which He has brought the redeemed. He "quickened us together with Christ". The Lord Jesus became dead through trespasses and sins, but not His own; He did so substitutionarily for His people so that they might be redeemed. He came down to where we were, that He might bring us up to where He is now. As we all shared in the one action of disobedience of our earthly Federal Head, Adam, so all believers now share in what God has wrought in the case of our Federal Head, the Lord Jesus. When He was quickened in death, so were they. The fact that they did not then have being should cause no difficulties, for all were present in the mind and purpose of God at the time. Further, "He raised us up with Him", chapter 2:6 R.V., so that we share His life. Moreover, He made us to "sit with Him in the heavenly places, in Christ Jesus", chapter 2:6 R.V. His being there is the sure guarantee of our ultimate presence there sharing His glory and kingdom. But meanwhile, God reckons it as true of the believer now. This is further developed at the end of chapter 3, which will be examined later. But as the ocean is immeasurable, so we may ask who can measure the depths to which Christ went, and the heights to which we have been taken, or the length of the love that wrought and even planned it, or the breadth of its embraciveness? Let us now deal with the third item:

What They Should Be

We have seen what the grace of God has made us, and have reviewed what we were prior to our experiencing it. But are we, in practice, what we should be?

The word *hina*, which means "in order that", occurs three times in verses 7 to 10. It is first found in verse 7, "*that* in the ages to come He might show the exceeding riches of His grace". While this, of course, primarily relates to the millennial age and beyond, surely the present age cannot be excluded. Time would fail to tell of those conspicuous displays of "the exceeding riches of His (God's) grace in His kindness toward" some noted sinners such as Saul of Tarsus, John Newton, Ned Wright and many another known in their own special sphere, monumental testimonies to what God has done for them and can do for others. See particularly in this connection 1 Timothy 1:12-17.

The second occurrence of the word *hina* (in order that) is in verse 9 R.V., "not of works, *that* (in order that) no man should glory". God has rather so wrought that he that boasteth must do so only in the Lord, 1 Corinthians 1:31. "All things" pertaining to our salvation "are of God", 2 Corinthians 5:18, leaving no ground whatsoever for anyone to glory in himself. This cuts from under our feet all credit as to moral, educational, national or any other advantage as Paul well knew, see Philippians 3.

The third occurrence of *hina* is in verse 10 R.V., "For we are His workmanship, created in Christ Jesus for good works, which God afore prepared *that* we should walk in them". Good works are not a necessary precursor to salvation: they are, however, a necessary sequel to it. Our daily "walk" (cf. v. 2) should now be characterised by them. Instead of the erstwhile selfishness which characterised us, and instead of the formal ritualistic observances which characterised the Jewish religion, God has now prepared aforehand a life designed to be "full of good works", Acts 9:36; such was the life of Dorcas.

In all these things it must surely be obvious that there are defects with us; how imperfect is the display of God's kindness in us through our inconsistencies and the like! How liable we all are to boast in our own status and achievements! How liable we are to endeavour to avoid opportunities for doing good instead of walking in such a path where we know we shall find them! There is certainly room for improvement in these respects.

What I *was* in my old Adam-state is a matter of the past. What I *am* by the grace of God is unalterably perfect. But what I *should be* calls for constant occupation with the Lord of glory so that there may be a continuous transformation into His likeness, 2 Corinthians 3:18.

Part 4

The Jew and the Gentile

This section commences with the words, "Wherefore remember", and at its close are the words, "Now therefore ye are no more", verse 19. The whole paragraph, therefore, has to do with the extraordinary change which has occurred in the ways of God with men, so that the position once occupied by them has been abandoned for a new position which believers now occupy. Between these two statements the means by which this has been achieved is explained.

An Illustration. In order that we may be able to understand the matter, we will use an illustration. Imagine a double-storeyed house, in which there are occupants in both the upper and lower apartments. The upper is to be preferred to the lower; it is better in every way. Unfortunately, the occupants are at enmity one with the other, and on only one point are they agreed; they both hate the landlord. In an endeavour to secure the peace of the house, he has erected a barrier designed to keep the two parties separate from one another. This, however, had the opposite effect; it but engendered more enmity than ever. What, then, was to be done? The landlord demolishes the barrier thereby putting all the tenants on the same level, and depriving those who lived in the upper storey of their special advantages. Moreover, to them all he makes an offer that they may, on complying with his terms which are very generous, leave their present house and take up their abode in a new place which he has had built. This new place has no upper and lower apartments, for it is a bungalow, and every room is on the same floor. All that is requisite for the change of residence is the acceptance of the gratuitous and unmerited offer. Some of the upper storey occupants accept, but many more from the lower ground floor accept.

Let us use this illustration in examining the section of the Ephesian Epistle now before us. We will first consider:

The Position of the Jew and the Gentile prior to the effective operation of God's grace towards them. The position of each is defined as "in the flesh", verse 11, and "in the world", verse 12, the "flesh" being their standing as connected with the first Adam who fell, and "the world" being that system of which Satan is the "prince", John 14:30. Those who occupied the upper storey are the Jews, for they had many privileges over the Gentiles. They had the *physical right* of circumcision which was the external seal of the promise given to their fathers. *Religiously* they were "near" to God, in that He had given them a ritualistic and typical system which gave them a right of approach to Him which the Gentiles lacked. Contemptuously they called the Gentiles the "uncircumcision", verse 11, failing to see that this was but one of several carnal ordinances which were imposed until the time of reformation, Hebrews 9:10. Their *moral state* is as stated in Ephesians 2:3 which we have already examined.

Those who occupied the lower storey were the Gentiles, the uncircumcision. They were "without Christ" for "salvation is of the Jews", and the Messiah was not to come through

Gentile stock. Therefore, they were "without hope", this hope being that which was entertained by Israel: "we hoped that it was He which should redeem Israel", Luke 24:21 R.V. They were "alienated from the commonwealth of Israel", chapter 2:12 R.V. They had no rights in their national privileges. They were "strangers from the covenants of the promise", chapter 2:12 R.V. - that is, all the detailed covenants made later by God amplifying the one great generic promise made to Abram, Genesis 15:18-22, had no application to them. In fact, they were "without God", for their goddess Diana was no real god. *Bodily*, they lacked the national sign of circumcision. *Politically*, they were outside of Israel's commonwealth. *Spiritually*, they were hopeless, godless and lifeless. In fact, they were "far off", outside. There was a legal barrier which kept them apart. Just as at Jerusalem the balustrade kept Jew and Gentile apart and no Gentile might enter the temple precincts under the penalty of death (as all well knew, Acts 21:28-29), so in the larger sphere the Gentiles had no share in the special privileges of the Jews. Moreover, their *moral state* was as given in chapter 2:1-2, which we have already examined.

The barrier which was erected was "the middle wall of partition", chapter 2:14. It was "the law of commandments contained in ordinances" or, as Paul calls it in Colossians, "the handwriting of ordinances that was against us, which was contrary to us", Colossians 2:14. To it Israel had, as it were, put their signature before witnesses. They had agreed to comply with its terms, not knowing that, because of their fallen nature, it was contrary to their leanings and against their best interests. It brought death, not life. Indeed, it provoked even greater enmity than already existed between them and God, and between them and the Gentiles. Israel's legal code which contained enactments both civil and ritualistic only aggravated the position, and created more bitterness. Nothing but its destruction and the commencement of something altogether new could meet the case, and produce peace. Therefore, the Lord Jesus came being born "under the law". He "magnified the law and made it honourable", ultimately dying under its curse which He had not personally merited, but which was borne substitutionarily for those who believed. Thus He fulfilled its obligations and paid its extreme penalty. By that death He "broke down" the barrier; He "abolished" the whole divinely given legal system. He "took it out of the way, nailing it to His cross", Colossians 2:14. The Epistle to the Romans should be carefully studied in this connection, specially chapters 7 and 8. Ephesians 2 is illuminated by those chapters, as well as by the whole Epistle to the Galatians, and the parallel Colossian passage.

That the moral requirements of the Mosaic law are evidenced in those who walk after the Spirit is approved by all (see Romans 8:4). They are not a means of approach to God nor a ground of righteous standing before Him, but the essential product of His life within, producing such evidence as His righteousness required. Now let us look at:

The Offer which was made "to the Jew" first and then to the Gentile later. It was made to all, both those who were in the upper and lower storeys. As verse 17 shows, the offer of "peace" between the two parties, and between both God and man, was made to both of them - "to you that were far off" (the Gentiles) and "them that were nigh" (the Jews), R.V. His design was to reconcile them both in one body to God. That work of reconciliation was effected "by the cross". Paul amplifies this in 2 Corinthians 5:18ff. As an Emperor may make a proclamation of peace to them with whom he has been at war, so the Risen

Christ was the first to make the proclamation, Hebrews 2:3, and He thereafter sent His Spirit to enable His apostles and others to further that proclamation. He "came and preached peace to you that were far off, and peace to them that were nigh", chapter 2:17 R.V. The word "preached" is that for evangelising - proclaiming good news. It certainly was good news to be told that both parties might have access to the Father; none need remain at a distance, but all may come within the ambit of the family if so be they will, and may know God as their Father. We will finally examine:

The Position in the case of those who have accepted the offer. They have an altogether new position. He "made both one" - that is, they both occupy not differing positions as hitherto but one and the same. The word "one" is neuter and has to do with their position. They are no longer "in the flesh" nor are they regarded as "in the world", but they are "in Christ Jesus", a phrase characteristic of Paul's doctrine. They are in association with and in identification with Him whom God hath made "both Lord and Christ", Acts 2:36. That identification we have already seen in chapter 2:1-10. They have been quickened, raised, and seated with Christ in the heavenly places. Their position is altogether different from that which they once held.

They are, as it were, now resident in a new bungalow which has no upper and lower storeys, for all are on the same level. None has privileges above the other. There is no middle wall separating one party from the other, but they are at "peace" and have been reconciled both to each other and all to God. They are made nigh "by the blood of Christ", not by the symbolic blood of an animal sacrifice. Out of the "twain", that is, out from among the Jews and the Gentiles, God has created in Himself "one new man", verse 15. He has made "both one", in that they occupy a common position, verse 14. He has reconciled them "in one body" so that they all are vitally and harmoniously linked with the Head and with each member, verse 16. Both have access in one Spirit to the Father, verse 18. There is no separating balustrade. "So then ye are no more strangers and sojourners, but ye are fellow-citizens with the saints", verse 19 R.V. Note the variety of words Paul uses: fellow-citizens of one common heavenly Jerusalem which is the metropolitan city of us all, Galatians 4:26; "of the household of God", having been put among the children and been given the privileges of sonship. We are part of a "holy temple" in which God dwells. The Ephesians were over zealous concerning the temple of Diana, in which the image of the goddess resided. Demetrius was there, the silversmith, making silver shrines, miniature figures of the temple, but those who had become believers in the Lord Jesus were inbuilt into the vast divine temple, wherein God dwelt, and their local church was a holy temple in which the Spirit dwelt, 1 Corinthians 3:16. The Greek word translated "temple" does not relate to the outer buildings or the court, but is that which denotes the "most holy place", the inner sanctuary wherein was the ark of the covenant, between the cherubim of which God's presence was to be seen.

Paul's use of the metaphor of a "body" is peculiar to him. No other New Testament writer employs it. It did not exist in Old Testament times nor in the days when the Lord Jesus was here on earth. Its birthday was the Pentecostal day of Acts 2. It is a "new man", an altogether new departure in the ways of God. It was not revealed in Old Testament times, and although there are types of the church there, there is no type of a body. There is the type of Solomon's temple, and there are the types of brides such as Joseph's wife Asenath, Moses' wife Zipporah, and David's wife Abigail. But there is no type of the body.

In this section, Paul clusters them all together - "one new man"; "one body"; "fellow-citizens"; "of the household of God"; a "holy sanctuary", R.V. margin. "One new man" stresses its newness not only of date but of character. "One body" stresses the notion of harmonious unity, each diverse member doing that which contributes to the good of the whole. "Fellow-citizens" emphasises the equality of privileges. "Of the household of God" signifies that all have a common Father and a common nature. A "holy sanctuary" denotes the fact that holiness becomes God's house for ever, Psalm 93:5.

There is no doubt that there is here an intended allusion not only to the Ephesian temple but to that of Solomon, which latter had its sundry chambers. So, too, this Universal Church has its many local churches. We believe that verse 21 envisages that the various local churches constitute the whole Universal Church, but verse 22 refers to the local church itself wherever the letter went. While the notion of God dwelling among His people was not unknown in Old Testament times, it was altogether new that God should dwell among the Gentiles, but this is so now since Christ is risen and glorified. The pronoun "ye" denotes this. Finally, let us look at:

The Foundation of this new place. It is "built upon the foundation of the apostles and prophets, Jesus Christ Himself being the chief corner stone", Ephesians 2:20. The prophets alluded to are the New Testament prophets, not the Old. When the Old Testament prophets are intended, they precede "apostles".

This "holy sanctuary" is well founded. The Lord Jesus is the chief corner stone, binding both Jew and Gentile securely together. The apostles and prophets were not only chronologically in the foundation, but by their ministry they "laid the foundation" (see 1 Corinthians 3:10).

What unity and harmony God has wrought! Yet what havoc, discord and worse have been wrought by those who should have learned better. They certainly had not "so learned Christ".

Part 5

The Mystery

Verse 1 of this chapter is broken off suddenly (not uncommon in Paul's writings) and is resumed in verse 14 where we are given his great second prayer for the saints, (cf. 1:15ff).

He speaks of himself as, "I Paul, the prisoner of Christ Jesus in behalf of you Gentiles", chapter 3:1 R.V. He is not only a bondservant, and an apostle, but a prisoner of Christ Jesus. He knew the real cause for which he had been imprisoned. He had been divinely commissioned to go to the Gentiles and proclaim to them the Gospel of God's grace. This antagonised the Jews, for Paul insisted that God's salvation was by grace through faith, and in no way of works, not even the works of the Jewish religion. The Jews, therefore, stirred up opposition against him, because it seemed as if he were forming a new sect around a new religion, which was not only repugnant to them but illegal in the eyes of the Roman authorities. In chapter 4:1 R.V. he speaks of himself as "the prisoner in the Lord", or, as it might be expanded, "in the Lord's service". His eye is ever on Christ as supremely above all the circumstances of earth, be they never so grim under the regime of Nero. He regarded this as a great honour; indeed, in this section he speaks three times of the grace of God that had been conferred upon him, writing that he had been entrusted with "the dispensation (or stewardship) of the grace of God which was given me to you-ward", chapter 3:2 R.V. Again, in verse 7, R.V., "according to the gift of that grace of God which was given me" and again in verse 8 R.V., "Unto me, who am less than the least of all saints, was this grace given". He pioneered this evangelistic work among the Gentiles. Though it were against his natural bent, yet the grace of God that had been shown to him when yet in his sins now caused him to delight to proclaim the Gospel to the Gentiles, since he had been specially commissioned to do so.

A special revelation had been given to him. It related to what he calls:

"The Mystery". This is not something which is mysterious; rather it is that which has hitherto been kept secret, but is now revealed to the "perfect", 1 Corinthians 2:6. Just as certain societies in Paul's day had their mysteries which were disclosed only to the initiated, so the "mystery" of the Gospel is known only by those who are illumined by God's Spirit. It had been communicated to Paul by "divine revelation", and is the subject matter of chapters 1 and 2 which we have examined. This is, apparently, what he alludes to when he says, "As I wrote afore in a few words", verse 3, and the saints would see that Paul had a clear understanding of the mystery after they had read thus far in his letter. It is "the mystery of Christ", (see Col. 4:3), and it is defined in Colossians 1:27 as "Christ in you, the hope of glory".

That the Gentiles were to be blessed was clearly envisaged in the Old Testament writings. Paul quotes the relevant passages when writing to the Romans – see Romans 9:25-26; 10:19-20; 15:9-12,21, - but the idea that they should be blessed on equal terms with the Jews, and without the necessity of their becoming Jews, was altogether new. In fact it had not been made known to mankind until it was revealed to the apostles and prophets of New Testament times subsequent to the great Pentecostal outpouring of the Spirit. The Gentile believers were to be fellow-heirs, fellow members of the body, and fellow-partakers of the promise in Christ, Ephesians 3:6. This was the Gospel which Paul had preached, and which elsewhere he calls, "my gospel", for its peculiarity lay in the fact that Jew and Gentiles were brought to the one level, subjected to the same conditions, and afforded the same privileges each equally with the other. Nothing like this is to be found in the Old Testament Scriptures, and it is therefore an utter mistake to interpret the Old Testament as relating to the Church, which is the body of Christ.

A reference to the parallel passage in Colossians 1:26 will show that the word "as" in verse 5 of our chapter does not have the force of comparison, inferring that it was partially revealed but not fully revealed "as it hath now been revealed". Rather both passages affirm the total concealment of the matter till its revelation to Paul and others. In fact, nothing can be clearer than verse 9 which affirms that this mystery has been hid in God from all ages. It was, indeed, an "eternal purpose", or, as the margin of the R.V. renders it, "the purpose of the ages", chapter 3:11.

Paul thus equates this "mystery" with God's eternal "purpose". That purpose centred in, and revolved around Christ. It embraced all who had put their "faith in Him", verse 12 R.V. What a motley crowd of persons they were – how varied their characteristics, dispositions, records, status, and much else; yet God in His manifold (many coloured) wisdom could handle successfully such a variety of persons, bringing them all on to one level, to one common faith in His Son, and incorporating them all into the one Body, making them all co-heirs with Christ, and co-partakers of the promise. God designed that at the present time, and not in the future only (see 2:7), the invisible spiritual powers in the heavenly places should learn by the Church what the consummate wisdom of God had wrought, chapter 3:10.

Instead of being "afar off", and God being a God at a far distance, we now have freedom of speech (boldness) and access to Him in unwavering confidence, chapter 3:12. None need have an Esther-like fear in approaching God (see Est. 4:16); all may draw near with boldness.

Thus Paul defines the "mystery"; stresses its prior concealment but present revelation and entrustment to him as the favoured depository; defines its scope as reaching to the Gentiles; affirms that this was his specific ministry or service; and declares that the present objective in view is the manifestation of God's many-hued wisdom to the spirit-beings by the Church.

Why then should the saints lose heart because of Paul's tribulations? If he could rejoice in them, Colossians 1:24, should they not be able to glory in them?, Ephesians 3:13.

Paul traces everything back to its true source, to God. He recognizes that in his labours in the Gospel it has been "according to the working of His mighty power". He also knows that before the original creation (for it was God who created all things, v. 9) there lay an eternal purpose, and Paul regarded it as a high honour not only to be allowed to spread the good news of it, but also to partake in the sufferings that were thereby incurred.

Paul's Prayer. Paul now resumes in verse 14 his broken sentence of verse 1. In humble dependence upon God, he bows his knees to the Father of whom every fatherhood in heaven and on earth is named, as some translations read, but the A.V. has "the whole family". Scholars are divided on the point.

His prayer envisages what we saw in chapter 1, namely that the three Persons of the Blessed Trinity actively participate in the working out of the counsel of God. Hence here, the *Father* is addressed; it is the *Spirit* who imparts strength to the inner man, and the prayer is that *Christ* may take up His abode in their hearts through faith. That is to say, he desires that Christ may make His permanent dwelling place in their hearts, and that they may have the conscious experimental knowledge of this as their faith lays hold upon, and appropriates the fact that Christ is "in you, the hope of glory", Colossians 1:27. He does not desire a spasmodic experience; he prays that it may be an accomplished and complete decision – the tense of "may dwell" in verse 17 is aorist.

This is not a mere matter of academic or mental apprehension; we need to be strengthened by God's Spirit in the inner man for this, cf. 2 Corinthians 4:16. As individuals we must be "rooted" in His love, and as a company we must be "grounded" or "founded" on the same, verse 17. Thereby, and indeed consequential upon this (as the Greek word translated "able" implies), we may be "able to comprehend with all saints" what are the dimensions of the mystery which has been brought about by the operation of His love. Without going into the technicalities of the difference between *te* and *kai*, it is perhaps too much to say that verse 18 relates to the mystery, and verse 19 to the love. Both are inseparable. Some think we come to apprehend the dimensions of the sphere in which the divine counsel finds its fulfilment, and then we come to know the love which occupies it. The bridal home prepared by the bridegroom cannot be separated from the love which occupies it, and so it is here. Vast as the "mystery" is, and this we considered when studying chapter 2:1-10, the love is equally vast. Consider its dimensions: to what *depths* did the love of Christ take Him?

None of the ransomed ever knew
How deep were the waters crossed,
Nor how dark was the night that the Lord passed through,
Ere He found the sheep that was lost.

Consider the *heights* to which it has taken us. Read again the closing verse of chapter 1. Ponder its *breadth* and all-embraciveness, and forget not its *length*, which has its source in a past eternity and goes on into the endless future. It is an everlasting love.

The "love of Christ" is that which is stated to surpass all knowledge. Here is a science (knowledge) which exceeds all other sciences, no matter to what they relate. It is the paradox of knowing what exceeds all knowledge. The ultimate goal of all this is in order "that ye may be filled unto (into) all the fulness of God", R.V. We cannot be filled with that fulness for the finite cannot contain the infinite, but much as an empty bottle is in the ocean, and the ocean is in the bottle, or as we are in the air and the air is in us, so we may be in "all the fulness of God" (all that He is), and it may be in us. It is that for which the Lord Jesus prayed: "that they all may be one: as Thou, Father, art in Me, and I in Thee, that they also may be one in Us", John 17:21.

Verse 20 relates to the prayer which we have just been considering. God is able to do exceeding abundantly above all that Paul is here asking or even thinking, according to the power which is energising in him, cf. chapter 1:20. His doxology of praise is appropriate to all that has gone before, "glory in the church" and glory "in Christ Jesus unto all generations of the age of the ages. Amen", R.V. marg.

The expression "glory in the church" shows that the Church will have a distinctive place in the eternal ages. Whatever God may do in regard to other "families" of the redeemed, verse 15, the Church will ever hold its special place as that upon which Christ set His love and for which He died.

Part 6

Ministry in the Church

Paul's method is always first to state the doctrine and thereafter to show its practical implications; neither should be divorced from the other. In this Epistle, Paul applies previously developed doctrine in three directions – among the saints, chapter 4:1-16, in human society, chapter 4:17 to 5:21, and in regard to special relationships, chapter 5:22 to 6:9. In verses 1 to 3, the Ephesians are exhorted to:

"**walk worthy of the vocation** wherewith ye are called", that is *personal* and individual; to show "lowliness and meekness (which marked the Lord Jesus, Matt. 11:29), with long-suffering, forbearing one another in love", that is *relative*, having to do with others; "endeavouring to keep the unity of the Spirit in the (uniting) bond of peace", that is *corporate* relating to the whole body.

As the Prince of Wales is destined to be King of the United Kingdom, and his behaviour must be consonant therewith, so now we must individually act suitably to our high destiny as defined in the earlier chapters.

Nor must we forget that whatever defects we find in our brethren, and however much they may try our patience, they have similar feelings towards us. Hence Paul's exhortation that we must be Christ-like, not self-assertive, but marked by "meekness", which is strength under control, for meekness is not weakness; there must be forbearance.

Corporately we are enjoined to give diligence "to keep the unity of the Spirit in the bond of peace". We are not called upon to make this unity: that has already been effected as we have seen in previous chapters. But we are to give diligence in seeing that its manifestation is preserved by living peaceably with our brethren. The invisible unity remains intact, but its visible expression has been sadly lacking. In verses 4, 5 and 6 we have:

The Unity Detailed. Verse 4 indicates the *vital* unity; verse 5 the *professional* unity; and verse 6 the *governmental* unity.

There is one body, cf. chapter 2:15 – one new man. There is one Spirit, chapter 2:18, and there is one hope, chapter 1:18. These are inviolable.

There is one Lord whom each believer has confessed, Romans 10:9. There is one faith, to which each subscribes, Jude 3, - that once for all delivered to the saints: the objective faith committed to them. There is one baptism. This would seem to be water baptism, since Spirit-baptism, 1 Corinthians 12:13, is implied in the "one body". In the early Christian days of the Ephesians, the believers had been acquainted with John's baptism but that was now superseded, as were all Old Testament "washings", Acts 19:3. We call these "professional unities" because all Christians subscribe to them, yet the fact that there has been serious departure from the original simplicity of these things cannot be gainsaid.

There is "one God and Father of all" (i.e. of His children), who pervades the whole and to whom all are responsible.

This sevenfold unity is not expressed by any visible headquarters on earth. The saints' oneness stands in their common link with the glorified Christ in heaven. In verses 7 to 16 the apostle deals with:

The Diversity Existent in the Church, which indeed characterises all the works of God, no matter in what direction we look. "But unto *each* one of us was the grace given", verse 7 R.V., and maturity will be reached "according to the working in due measure of *each* several part", verse 16 R.V. Paul clearly points out in 1 Corinthians 12, as also our experience confirms, that in the body each particular part has its own particular function, and failure of any one part adversely affects the whole body. Since our function is a "gift" given by the Risen Christ, we have neither ground of boasting nor murmuring, 1 Corinthians 4:7. Prominent or otherwise, large or small, each is necessary to, and interdependent on, the other.

Paul quotes from Psalm 68:18. The picture is that of a returning victorious warrior, who has received many gifts from those whom He has conquered and who distributes many gifts on His return to His own people. The parallel and explanatory passages of verse 8 are found in Colossians 2:15 and Hebrews 2:15.

While it is true that the Lord Jesus came to earth, and here died and was buried, yet Paul does not enter here into those details. Another rendering seems to have assessed the meaning of his words: "Now the word ascended implies that He also descended to the lowest level, down to the very earth", verse 9. It is the Jesus of history who is the Christ of glory, the One who went to the lowest depths of shame is He who has been exalted to the highest pinnacle of honour.

In the verses before us, Paul enumerates the gifts, and states their aim, their duration, their object and the process by which they operate.

The gifts enumerated here differ from those of 1 Corinthians 12 which are more numerous. The reason seems to be that 1 Corinthians is chiefly concerned with the local church, whereas the Ephesian Epistle concentrates specially on the Church universal. Moreover the Corinthian Epistle had in view, in part, the early days of Christianity, whereas this Ephesian Epistle is not so limited. The "apostles" in their primary sense are no longer with us today; neither are "prophets". The essential credential for an apostle must be that he has seen with his own eyes the Risen Christ personally; see 1 Corinthians 9:1. The essential credential for a New Testament prophet is that he has received revelation of divine truth apart from the written Scriptures, (see 1 Corinthians 14:6 where "revelation" and "prophesying" go together, and "knowledge" and "teaching" go together). These are foundation gifts, Ephesians 2:20. The "evangelists" are such as Philip, whose evangelistic work is well indicated in Acts 8. "Pastors and teachers" seem both to refer to the one individual who instructs the minds of the saints by teaching the Word, and cares for their well-being as a shepherd cares for the sheep. These are elsewhere called "elders" and "overseers", and one requisite qualification for their recognition in a church is that they must be "apt to teach", 1 Timothy 3:2. If they fail here, how can they safeguard the flock? Acts 20:28-31.

The aim which God had in view in giving these gifts was "for the perfecting of the saints, unto the work of ministering, unto the building up of the body of Christ" (see R.V. reading of verse 12). The Scriptures do not recognize a specialized religious order of "the ministry", though they do acknowledge those who are specially called to spiritual work. The Revisers have done well in altering the words "the ministry" to "ministering", for that word denotes service, and, in its context, service amongst the saints. These gifts are given for fitting out the saints, with a view to the work of serving among them, and with the ultimate view of the building up of the body of Christ. Thus there is secured a continuity of operation *"until we all attain* unto the unity of the faith, and of the knowledge of the Son of God, unto a full-grown man, unto the measure of the stature of the fulness of Christ", verse 13 R.V. Thus adequate provision has been made until the time arrives when the purpose of God has achieved its goal. We may be sure that the Head will not at any time neglect the body; nor will the shepherd neglect the sheep, so that there will always be provided those who will teach and tend the flock of God.

The object in view is stated in verses 14 and 15. God does not want us to remain in babyhood; He desires us to "grow up". It is children who are caught by the subtleties and cunning craft and sleight of hand of tricksters. Who has not seen the open-eyed and open-mouthed children who are watching with amazement the "Punch and Judy show", little knowing that hidden inside the screen is one who is controlling the "show"?

We should note the words "we all" in verse 13, for this maturity not only has to do with each individual, but also with the whole community that constitutes the "body". That is the ultimate goal, but meanwhile the gifts are given so that the individual believer may not remain in spiritual infancy but may grow up. "The wiles of error", verse 14 R.V., are calculated to unsettle the believer and to carry him away as with a strong wind. These are the false doctrines of men who by trickery mishandle God's Word (see 2 Tim. 2:17-18), which must be resisted in a spirit of love. Lastly we notice:

The Process by which the Gifts Operate. Observe the prepositions in verse 16 R.V.: "from", "through", "according to", "unto". The body, being "fitly framed and knit together", as one symmetrical and stable whole, is firmly held together by its joints and ligaments, through which its various other parts are supplied with that which is requisite for their healthy functioning. Each part has its duty, and failure in any one member adversely affects the whole. All the supply comes "from" the Head "through" the joints (the gifts above named), and thereby makes the increase of the body. It is a mutual operation; it builds itself up in love, cf. Jude 20. Where there is discord between the members of our human body, there is general unhealthiness and disease. Paul deals with the various things that militate against the wellbeing of the body of Christ in later passages.

Part 7

Gathered Threads

EPHESIANS 4:17 - 5:20

In this section Paul appears to catch hold of threads which he had inserted into the fabric of his letter and pulls them through, thus binding together the earlier doctrinal part with the later practical section, forming thereby a united whole. We will trace some of these threads.

"In Christ." This is a phrase specially characteristic of the writings of Paul (see, e.g., 1:3 *et al*). It denotes the position of the believer before God, but it has its practical implications. Our state should agree with our standing. Our condition should be in accordance with our position.

There is a difference between "in Christ", and "in Jesus", chapter 4:21. The latter refers to the days of His flesh and the manner of His life on earth. "In Christ" refers to the believer's association with Him in His risen and glorified life in heaven. But there is more. Believers should model their lives now after the manner of the life of Jesus when He was here. It is assumed that they have heard Him as all the sheep hear the shepherd's voice ("if so be", 4:21, does not imply doubt, but assumes the case to be so) and that He has become the "object lesson" for their daily behaviour. We are given more than ethics or morals;

Christianity is not a philosophy. We are given a Person and His life for our imitation.

This is the very antithesis of the behaviour that characterised the society to which we once belonged. Paul's description of that conduct in verses 17-22 is very similar to what he wrote to the Romans touching those who are in the gutter of sin, Romans 1:20-32. But having now been taken out of that dire position, we should "walk, even as He walked". As our position is "no more" what it once was (see Eph. 2:19), so our walk should "no longer" be what it used to be, chapter 4:17 R.V.

Saints. This noun and its cognate adjective "holy" are of frequent occurrence in this letter (see 1:1,4,15,18; 2:19,21; 3:5,8,18; 4:12; 5:3,27; 6:18). The avowed purpose of God, that we should be "holy and without blemish", will ultimately be achieved, chapter 5:27. In the meantime Paul stresses that holiness of conduct should mark God's children. The "uncleaness" which marks the world should not be present with us. Note the words used: uncleanness; corrupt; deceitful lusts; corrupt communication out of the mouth; fornication; filthiness; foolish talking; jesting (jokes with double meanings); whoremongery. What a list! No wonder the wrath of God comes upon these sons of disobedience, chapter 5:6. It is a shame even to speak of these things which are done of them in secret, but which are all seen by the eye of the All-seeing God, chapter 5:12-13. The believer is indwelt by God's Holy Spirit; his life, therefore, should be holy. The fact that we have been taken out of the gutter of *sin*, and put into the holy temple of God's presence, requires that His people should tread in clean paths.

Grace. He has graced us in the beloved, chapter 1:6. The Greek word used here occurs elsewhere only in Luke 1:28. It implies not merely that we have been made the objects of His grace, but that this grace has been freely bestowed upon us, or "wherewith He endued us", Ephesians 1:6 R.V. marg. How appropriate, then, that we should be exhorted to be "kind one to another, tenderhearted, forgiving (showing grace to) each other, even as God also in Christ forgave (showed grace to) you", chapter 4:32 R.V. How much grace God has shown toward us! We have read of "the glory of His grace", chapter 1:6, "the riches of His grace", chapter 1:7, saved "by grace", chapter 2:5, 8, "the grace of God", chapter 2:7, "this grace", chapter 3:8, "grace given", chapter 4:7, "give grace", verse 29, "grace be with all", chapter 6:24. God's forgiveness sprang from His sovereign grace. The parable of the Lord recorded in Matthew 18:21-35 should be considered in this connection. His kindness toward us, Ephesians 2:7, should find a practical response in our forgiving kindness towards our fellows.

The Spirit of Promise. The believer has been sealed with the Spirit of God. He is thereby marked out as His own special possession, secured unto the day of redemption, chapter 1:13. (Redemption is regarded both as a present possession, 1:7, and a future prospect, Rom. 8:23.) We, therefore, should not grieve Him, Ephesians 4:30. The context of this verse will indicate in what manner we may grieve Him. Dishonesty, impure speech, bitterness, wrath, anger, clamour, railing, and all malice cause the Spirit pain. He is not insensitive to the conduct of the one in whose body He resides.

Moreover, we should "be filled with the Spirit", chapter 5:18. He should not be regarded as a guest in the house of our body, limited to certain apartments, but He should be regarded as the owner, and given access to the whole life. He should be shut out from nothing. A corresponding passage occurs in Colossians 3:16 and it would seem (if we regard the word "spirit" in Ephesians

5:18 as alluding to the spiritual part of our being as quickened by God's Spirit) that the manner in which we may be "filled" is by allowing "the word of Christ" to dwell in us richly.

Instead of that exuberance and uncontrolled excitement which accompanies the intoxication of wine, there will be the joyful expression of the lips by psalms, hymns (praises) and spiritual songs, the psalms we feel being compositions addressed to God and the "songs" or "odes" being that which is addressed to men. (It is better to insert a semi-colon after the word "yourselves" in 5:19 A.V. and to delete the comma after "songs".)

Enlightenment. The eyes of the heart of the believer have been *enlightened*, chapter 1:18 R.V., so that he is no longer in darkness. They once were like the Gentiles "being darkened in their understanding" on account of the ignorance that is in them because of the hardening of their heart, chapter 4:18. But things are different now, and these saints have been *enlightened*, and as we saw when considering Paul's prayer in chapter 1, they are capable of "knowing" the details of the divine counsel and working. Once they were "darkness" but now they are "*light* in the Lord", chapter 5:8. They, therefore, should walk as children of *light*, or, changing the metaphor, they should bear fruit in practical goodness and righteousness, and truth. There should be no participation in the unfruitful works of darkness. "What fruit had ye then in those things whereof ye are now ashamed?", Romans 6:21. Having been made "fellow-partakers of the promise", Ephesians 3:6 R.V., they should not be fellow "partakers" with these ungodly persons, chapter 5:7, nor should they have "fellowship" with their works, chapter 5:11. There must be no neutrality, no compromise, in this matter. Their shameful deeds should be exposed by the light – that is by the reproof which can be administered both by the Christian's life and lips.

Men love darkness rather than light because their deeds are evil. They do them "in secret", but when they are reproved they are seen in their true colours. Christians who keep silence in regard to such things are guilty of treachery; the enemy thrives on it. For they are much like others on a battlefield where there are both dead and sleeping soldiers, looking no different the one from the other. These should "awake, ... and arise from (among) the dead", chapter 5:14. They will then become aware of the warmth and light of the presence of Christ. Paul does not seem to quote from any specific scriptures in 5:14, but rather he gathers up the general sense from such passages as Isaiah 60:1; 26:19; 9:2.

Walk. This is yet another thread in the fabric of this letter. He has used this verb in chapter 2:2,10; 4:1,17; 5:2,8,15. "Walk" denotes behaviour, and that of the saints should now no longer be as hitherto, nor should it conform to that of the unregenerate world. They should "*walk* worthily of the calling", and specially should they "*walk* in love". Their Exemplar is Christ, who loved them and manifested that love in giving "Himself up for us, an offering (in life) and a sacrifice (in death) to God for an odour of a sweet smell", chapter 5:1 R.V. The benefit accruing from this is our "forgiveness". We, therefore, should be imitators of God as dear children, and we should "walk ... as Christ" walked.

Again we should "*walk* as children of light", chapter 5:8. Paul deals also with this in 1 Thessalonians 5:6-8. Sleep and drunkenness characterise those who are of the night. Watchfulness and sobriety should mark the believer who is of the day.

Furthermore, we should "look therefore carefully how ye *walk*, not as unwise, but as wise, buying up the opportunity, because the days are evil", chapter 5:15-16 R.V. marg. As prudent merchantmen we should corner the market, and make the maximum spiritual gain possible. The word translated "carefully" R.V., and "circumspectly" A.V., is better rendered "accurately", and suggests a rule given by which our walk may be regulated. That rule is, of course, the Scriptures, which indicate the path to be taken and the pitfalls to be avoided.

"**New Man**". To this Paul refers in chapter 2:15, and gathers up the thread in chapter 4:24. The first has to do with our position; the second with our behaviour. The "old man" is our former manner of life, which should be discarded as Elisha discarded his garments and donned those of Elijah, 2 Kings 2:12-13. These are the garments of "righteousness and holiness of truth", Ephesians 4:24 R.V. Therefore lying should be abandoned; theft should be given up. There should be honest labour not merely with the view of preserving a healthy independence of others, 1 Thessalonians 4:11-12, but also in order to have wherewith we may help the needy, Ephesians 4:28.

One Body. This, too, Paul has mentioned in chapter 2:16. Now in chapter 4:25 he reminds them that they are *members* one of another, and therefore there should be a total absence of falsehood, and each should speak truth with his neighbour. It is inconceivable that in a healthy human body one member should act falsely to another, but it is so in a diseased body.

How remarkable it is that, in the letter which gives to us the highest New Testament doctrine, there are such practical, simple and ordinary exhortations as to daily living. Yet how easy it is for us to be adept in doctrine and careless in practice. That is why the Spirit of God, through Paul, gives such well-balanced directions both for the mind and for the feet.

Part 8

Some Practical Lessons

EPHESIANS 5:21 - 6:24

Paul now embarks upon what someone has called the matter of "earthly relationships in the heavenly family", prefacing the whole with the injunction, "subjecting yourselves one to another in the fear of Christ", Ephesians 5:21. He says this because what he writes is not his own private exhortation; it has the authority of the Lord and, therefore, disobedience thereto is a very grave matter.

He speaks of wives and husbands, children and parents, servants and masters. The order is significant: first, those who are to be subject and, secondly, those to whom the subjection is to be rendered. This is not the advocacy of tyranny, but rather of that which makes for a healthy society. Firstly he considers:

Wives and Husbands

Wives are to be subject to their own husbands as unto the Lord. They will have read in this letter of the Headship of Christ in relation to the Church, and from this they may learn of the headship of the husband to the wife. As, therefore, the Church should be subject to Christ in all things, so the wife to her husband. This is, of course, the ideal, and does not suppose obligations imposed by the husband which are infringements of the divine duties. Rather, Christ is the Saviour (preserver, protector) of the body; thus should the husband be also of his wife.

On the other side, the husband is called upon to love his wife, and he has for his example Christ's devotion to the Church. He loved it; He gave Himself up (to the cross) for it; with the object in view that He might sanctify it (make it holy), having cleansed it by the washing of water with the word (a spoken word), chapter 5:25-26. As the laver of old was designed to provide means whereby the priests could wash themselves thereat, so the Word of God is provided today for the same purpose (see John 15:3; 17:17).

The whole range of time, from the beginning of the history of the Church till its final consummation, is envisaged here. In the *past,* there is Christ's love and self-sacrifice. In the *present,* there is its cleansing with the object of making it holy, and in *the future* there is to be the presentation of it to Himself, without defect or sign of old age. God's purpose will then have been ultimately achieved (cf. 1:4 with 5:27). Christ and the Church are as Head and the body; they are, therefore, one. This pertains to husband and wife also, confirmed as it is by their physical union. Each are complementary parts to a unity. No other party should, therefore, come between. On the part of the husband there should be a single-eyed devoted love, and on the part of the wife there should be submissive fear, not in the sense of terror, but rather in her recognition of his proper position as head. This is contrary to the ideas current in our present time, when the equality of the woman with the man is insisted on. But these directives are not inconsistent with equality. If the head of Christ is God (this does not imply inequality, but it denotes submission and dependency), so it should be with the wife and her husband.

It is difficult to understand how any should have misgivings as to the Church being likened to a bride, in view of the passage now before us. The whole is a tale of "love, courtship and marriage", the love being mentioned in verse 25, the devoted care, interest, feeding and comforting her in verse 29, and preparing her for the nuptial day is noted in verse 26, all with the view of her presentation to the Bridegroom (here *by* Himself) on the soon-to-be-wedding day, cf. Revelation 19:7-8.

It has been suggested that the "washing" is baptism, and that the spoken word is the interrogation and response thereat. But in view of Titus 3:5 it would seem that it is the "washing of regeneration" that is here meant.

Paul cites Genesis 2:23-24, showing that in the original institution of marriage God had in mind a secret which is now revealed, a divine mystery, of Christ and the Church. Next come:

Children and Parents
As with husbands and wives, where wives are first addressed though originally the husband was first, so here children are first addressed though manifestly the parents had priority. Parents can only expect obedience from their children if their commands are in agreement with the will of the Lord; the obedience is "in the Lord". The phrase does not mean "parents in the Lord". If parents are to be honoured, they must merit the honour. That there are mysterious exceptions to the fulfilment of the promise attached to the fifth commandment is recognised (see 6:2), the explanation of which is hidden from us, yet the general rule is according to it.

The parents' duty is both negative and positive. They should not be provocative, but they should discipline the children in regard to their conduct, and instruct them in things which they need to be taught. Never more than today was this direction to both children and parents needed. Next come:

Servants and Masters

This letter was written in days of slavery, and though neither the Lord nor His apostles attacked the system, yet they taught in such a manner that an atmosphere was created which was inimical to its survival. In our days of bargained employment, the principles still hold good. The Christian employee should have his eye ever on the Lord. He should "fear" Him and "tremble" at His word. His eye should be single, and his service should be rendered to Christ. To reduce such work to the level of merely pleasing men is unworthy of our high calling.

It must never be forgotten that our actions are like boomerangs, and they will come back, and leave their mark on our character. Whether it be "good" as in chapter 6:8, or whether it be evil as in Colossians 3:25, whatever kind it be, 2 Corinthians 5:10, all will receive again the thing done in the body. In this there is no partiality; it applies to all alike, whether they be slaves or freemen, servants or masters. Paul then deals with the matter of:

Christian Warfare, Chapter 6:10-20

The panoply (whole armour) is provided by God. We are not called upon to "make" it, but to "take" it up, and to "put (it) on". The armour is the objective provision of God, to which, in our putting it on, we subjectively give expression. There is a subtle enemy with whom we are bound to be engaged in close-at-hand wrestling. He adopts "wiles", chapter 6:11, and failing their success he becomes more violent and uses "fiery darts". This is not a physical contest, but with one experienced in the realm of spirits who would seek to rob us of the realisation of our true place in the heavenlies in Christ. We dare not enter the fray in our own strength, but clad with this divine armour we may gain the victory, though having done so we should then stand ready for the next assault, chapter 6:13.

All the armour is defensive save the "sword of the Spirit", verse 17, which is God's spoken word (the appropriate word for the occasion). It was this that the Lord Jesus Himself used to dramatic effect in the wilderness temptation. There is no armour for the back – God does not provide for runaways.

But how easily can the enemy gain an advantage if there is lack of truth and righteousness in the life of the believer, verse 14. How easily will his agents propagate their false philosophies and theories if the child of God is not ready to go and preach peace by Jesus Christ, verse 15; Romans 10:15. How safe is the believer if he is wearing the large body-shield of "faith", which unreservedly accepts and applies to himself all that is embodied in "the faith". Twice he has told "by grace have ye been saved" and through faith, Ephesians 2:5, 8 R.V.; now he must wear "the helmet of salvation" which will protect the mind against all uncertainty and misgivings. In 1 Thessalonians, the helmet is "the hope of salvation" from the coming wrath, chapter 5:8, a thing yet to be experienced. But in the passage before us is a present fact to be appropriated and enjoyed by faith. And as an overall covering there is to be prayer and supplication, constant and Spirit-led, all embracive and specific, Ephesians 6:18-19.

These are instructions, given not to a section of the church, but to all alike, husbands and wives, parents and children, masters and servants. They are in God's camp and provided with God's armour, because there is the enemy's camp, not superior in power or might, but none the less crafty, subtle and violent. It is the common lot of all the saints everywhere. There is nothing local or parochial here.

Paul describes himself as "an ambassador in chains", verse 20 R.V., but if chained in body his lips cannot be silenced. The saints should pray on his behalf that utterance may be given to him in opening his mouth that he may make known with boldness (freedom of speech) the mystery of the gospel. What that "mystery" is we have seen in his earlier chapters. For "the gospel" is not a limited thing, restricted to the elementary features of the Christian faith but is inclusive of "all the counsel of God", Acts 20:27. "As I ought to speak" are words Paul must speak, for he recognised a solemn binding duty upon him which led him elsewhere to say, "Woe is unto me, if I preach not the gospel"; "necessity is laid upon me". 1 Corinthians 9:16.

Concluding Words

There are a few concluding words touching Tychicus who was to bear this letter and its precious contents to the saints. He was "beloved" by the saints, and "faithful" to the Lord. He would personally inform them of Paul's state and thus comfort their hearts. What an insight into the sympathetic feelings that they had for their apostle to whom, under God, they owed their existence as believers and as a church. And how Paul felt for them and desired their comfort! Was he not in need of the same also?

"Peace", Ephesians 6:23, was the usual Jewish salutation, and "grace" the Gentile one. Here Paul mentions both, but not in close juxtaposition, verses 23 and 24. He had already warned their elders that from among them ones would arise speaking "perverse things" and "grievous wolves" would come into their midst, Acts 20:29-30, but he is assured that there are those who "love our Lord Jesus Christ in uncorruptness", Ephesians 6:24 R.V., and to these he expresses his good wishes of peace, love, faith and grace.

Paul's Pastoral Epistles - Introduction

Paul's thirteen letters may readily be divided into three groups: (1) those written during the history covered by the book of the Acts, viz. Romans, 1 and 2 Corinthians, Galatians, and 1 and 2 Thessalonians; (2) those written during the imprisonment alluded to at the end of the book of the Acts, viz. Ephesians, Philippians, Colossians and Philemon; (3) those written after his release therefrom and prior to his martyrdom, viz. 1 and 2 Timothy and Titus. We say nothing about the Epistle to the Hebrews; that may or may not have been written by Paul, we do not know. These letters are not arranged chronologically in our Bible, but, it would appear, they are arranged according to size, the longest being put before the shortest.

The letters to Timothy and Titus are commonly known as *Pastoral Letters* because they give to those two apostolic delegates guidance as to how the interests of the local church, and of believers in general, should be cared for. Manifestly there are no apostolic delegates with us today (the false claims of men notwithstanding), but we do have "overseers and servants" (unfortunately translated as "bishops and deacons", these being but anglicised Greek words which, if translated, would be shown thus). These letters are invaluable directives as to how their work should be done. The New Testament does not sanction the highly organized hierarchical and monarchical system established by many, whether it be in its Roman form or in its various dissenting forms, however some may modify their practices.

Timothy was the product of a mixed marriage, his father being a Greek and his mother a Jewess. His mother and grandmother were God-fearing forebears who taught young Timothy to put his faith in God (2 Tim. 1:5). He was a convert of the apostle Paul (2 Tim. 1:2), and was chosen by Paul to be his associate in his missionary work, (Acts 16:1). This was pursuant to foregoing prophecies touching him, (1 Tim. 1: 18; 4:14), and with the approval and sympathy of the local elderhood, Timothy having been entrusted with a gift that was given to him by the laying on of hands of Paul, (2 Tim. 1:6). The laying on of Paul's hands involved the *importation* of the gift: the laying on of hands of the elderhood (presbytery) involved their *identification* with him in his future work. His gift may have been a multiple one comprising evangelist, pastor and teacher. It would seem so. He was evidently not too strong in body, hence Paul advised him to use a little wine for his stomach's sake and oft infirmities, (1 Tim. 5:23). Maybe also he was rather timid in nature, and needed to be reminded that God had not given us a spirit of cowardice, but of power, love and discipline, (2 Tim. 1:7). He was a young man, but the Greek word *motes*, used of him in 1 Timothy 4:12, is used of adults in the full vigour of life.

Titus is referred to several times in 2 Corinthians in chapters 2, 7, 8 and 12. He may be the one mentioned in Galatians 2:3. He was a Greek, and a convert of Paul, (Tit. 1:4). Paul well sums up the character and work of Titus in 2 Corinthians 8:23, "my partner and fellowhelper".

It should be observed that, while Paul exerted no dictatorial authority over his fellow workers, they did manifest a healthy submission to his authority. He "sent" them here and there, and on one occasion his communication is called a "commandment" (Act. 17:15). In Paul's missionary team there was a very happy absence of either dictatorship on the part of Paul, or independence on the part of his companions.

The Object of the First Epistle to Timothy is plainly set out in Chapter 3:15. It was to give direction as to how Timothy and people in general should behave in "the house of God, which is the church of the living God". Paul is not alluding to a building of stone, but to a congregation of persons who owned the Lordship of Jesus. Conduct in the local church, then, is the main theme of this letter. It touches purity of doctrine, the audible exercises in the gathering, restrictions imposed upon teaching, the qualifications of those who undertake the care and service of the church, widows, servants, the rich – the whole range of matters as relevant today as they were at the time when Paul wrote. These things Timothy was expected to transmit to "faithful men, who shall be able to teach others also" (2 Tim. 2:2).

The Object of the Second Epistle to Timothy is not so plainly stated, though the circumstances in which he wrote, and the proximity of the end of his earthly life are clearly in view. Paul has in mind the devolution of responsibilities to Timothy, and from him, in due time, to others also. The four chapters may be respectively labelled: Be courageous, chapter

1; Be careful, chapter 2; Be constant, chapter 3; Be considerate, chapter 4. Or we may say that here we have Paul's bequests to his son Timothy. They are: An Unfailing Saviour, chapter 1; A Sure Foundation, chapter 2; An Infallible Guide, chapter 3; A Confident Hope, chapter 4. All this we will develop, as God helps, in due course.

The Purpose of the Epistle to Titus was multiple. It was to give guidance in the ordaining of elders, the inculcation of proper behaviour on the part of various people in the church, as old and young, men and women, servants and subjects, and how to deal with heretics. The importance of such authoritative guidance for today is not only plain, but cannot be over-rated.

The Place of Writing. It is not apparent from what place the first letter to Timothy and that to Titus were written. Conjecture is of no spiritual value. It is, however, clear that the second letter to Timothy was written from the prison at Rome where Paul was on trial for his life. Paul, under the guidance of the Spirit, and with the well-being of the churches lying heavily upon his heart, felt the importance of putting into writing the things he had so often made the subject of his verbal teaching (1 Tim. 1:3). His other letters had covered much ground such as the Gospel of God, God's plans for His earthly people, order in the local church, and many other matters. It only now remained for him to give directions to these apostolic delegates, encouraging a shepherd heart and conduct in them, so that those who read these letters after their decease might have a like spirit.

We shall not, in these articles, give a verse by verse and line by line exposition of the Epistles. This has been done in various commentaries, all of which should be read discriminately, sorting out the chaff from the wheat. We shall here merely content ourselves with giving the gist of the chapters, emphasising what we deem to be points that need most to be stressed in our present time.

1 Timothy 1

The age in which we live is accurately described in verse 9: "lawless and disobedient (unsubject)" – man-ward; "ungodly and sinners" – Godward; "unholy and profane" – self-ward. Some details are given by Paul which are remarkably descriptive of our own days: children actively and physically opposing parents, murderers, fornicators, homosexuals, kidnappers, liars, perjurers, and any other thing that is contrary to the spiritual and moral teaching of the holy Gospel. God's inflexible law applies to such and its inevitable penalties will be ultimately exacted from the offenders, for the grace of God has not displaced the government of God, even in this present era, Romans 1:27.

The Gospel in a Corrupt World

This is a day calling for plain speech, not profitless discussion. As in Paul's day, so today; there are plenty who are desirous of being theological teachers, though they do not understand what they say nor the things about which they make such confident assertions. They do not understand either the statements they make, or the cases with which those statements deal. They but engender questions and leave their hearers all confused and in doubt. What they should do is to teach the true Gospel which is designed to produce love out of a pure heart (the inward spring), and of good conscience (the inward monitor), and of unfeigned faith (the inward sight). This sacred word "love" (in the Authorised Version translated "charity", which today has a different nuance) is now much abused, and used in all manner of unworthy associations. It is not uncharitable when one attempts to curb the harmful teaching of others, which teaching occupies the minds of people with things that get them nowhere, solves no problems, and leaves the mind full of doubts, instead of building up a solid structure of faith. Such are many religious leaders today, who, anxious to be recognised as such, have no real understanding of the matters with which they profess to deal, yet speak so confidently. They have a religious "jargon", but when it is measured by the standard of Scripture it is found to be wanting both in accuracy and usefulness.

It was no easy thing for Timothy to be left in Ephesus to care for the saints and to propagate the gospel, seeking at the same time to hinder its corruption by others. He might readily have been prone to despair in a city noted for its spiritual "wild beasts", 1 Corinthians 15:32, but for his encouragement Paul recounts his own conversion. Who, desirous of the salvation of sinners now-a-days, does not have a similar feeling of inadequacy in view of the wickedness and hardness of the ungodly in the midst of whom we are placed? Yet Paul was a blasphemer of God, a persecutor of Christ, and a "hectoring bully" of the saints, but he obtained mercy because he did not know the real nature of his hostile actions. The situation would have been far different had he known the real nature of his enmity. But as with his nation, so with him. "I know", says Peter, "that through ignorance ye did it, as did also your rulers", Acts 3:17, and the Lord Himself prayed "Father, forgive them; for they know not what they do", Luke 23:34, Saul's question on the Damascus road, "Who art Thou, Lord?", revealed that he did not understand that, in persecuting the Christians, he was persecuting the Lord of glory.

Paul could never forget the mercy shown to him, the chief of sinners – the "longsuffering" of God that waited and yet waited till He was apprehended on the Damascus road. The conversion of Saul of Tarsus is, next to the resurrection of Christ, the outstanding miracle of Christianity. He himself recognised that God had made him an exemplary case for the encouragement of all other sinners that afterwards should believe, and we may add for the encouragement of all who are interested in, and are prayerful about, the conversion of longstanding and bitter opponents of Christ.

Before the New Testament Scriptures were in circulation, certain phrases became current among the early Christians which are referred to as "faithful sayings"; see 1 Timothy 1:15; 3:1; 4:9; 2 Timothy 2:11; Titus 3:8. The emphatic words in 1 Timothy 1:15 are "sinners" and "chief": Paul puts them in a place of emphasis. And Paul so records it to stress the "mercy", the "grace", the "love", and the "longsuffering" of which he was the undeserving object, but which called forth such abundant thanksgiving as he utters in verse 12. He attributes the eternal glory of it to "the King eternal, incorruptible, invisible, the only God" in verse 17 R.V., which verse should not be read in isolation: its immediately preceding context lends force to it.

Such spiritual work as was entrusted to Timothy was of a militant nature. He would have many enemies to face and it was imperative that he should keep fast both faith and a good conscience. Were he to allow doubt or unbelief to creep into his mind, and were he to allow sin and inconsistency to enter into his behaviour, defeat would be sure. Others had done so with calamitous results. Hymanaeus and Alexander had thrust these things from them: personal faith and a good conscience were thrown overboard: no marvel they had made shipwreck concerning "the faith", that is, concerning that body of revealed truth presented to us for our acceptance. With apostolic authority, Paul had delivered these individuals to Satan that they might learn by discipline not to blaspheme. This authority cannot be exercised by any today, but such persons should not be allowed to remain in the church; they should be excommunicated. The phrase "deliver unto Satan" is a very solemn one. It is again found in 1 Corinthians 5:5. It denotes that, when a person is thus dealt with, he is put into a sphere where Satan has power, even over his body. It might have been experienced in the form of disease or death. Of course, if the person were a genuine believer Satan could not touch his spiritual life. In each of these passages the spiritual good and recovery of the persons are in view. Note in this connection the phrases "that the spirit may be saved in the day of the Lord Jesus", and "that they may learn not to blaspheme", 1 Corinthians 5:5; 1 Timothy 1:20.

Paul twice joins "faith" with a "good conscience", verses 5 and 19. These must not be divorced the one from the other. Orthodoxy must be accompanied by proper conduct. Belief and behaviour must agree. Belief without a good conscience tends to hypocrisy. A good conscience without faith is like a ship without a rudder, it lacks guiding control. It can degenerate into prejudice. The surrender of either one may be the cause or the effect of the abandonment of the other.

1 Timothy 2

The Gospel – its Bearing on Prayer

Prayer is the first subject-matter on which Paul gives direction. Its range must encompass all men from the highest to the lowest, for each can disturb the tranquillity of society as we well know in our present times. The word "supplications" denotes the existence of urgent need: "prayers" is a more general and wider kind of petition and communication with God. By "intercession" is contemplated the uninhibited approach of an inferior to a superior on behalf of one's self or of others: "thanksgivings", R.V., is a self-evident and appropriate attendant in such exercises. The authorities existing in Paul's day were anything but desirable or just, yet prayer on their behalf was not to be withholden for that cause. Similarly, today, whatever one may think of the existing powers that be, either in one's own land or other lands, prayer for them, as well as submission to them, is the path to be trodden by the Christian. The object is that we may lead a "quiet and peaceable life in all godliness and honesty". The word "quiet" has to do with the state arising from without, and "peaceable" has to do with the state arising from within – one's circumstances and one's condition respectively. Prayer can affect both.

Paul brings forward the attitude of God towards all men in support of this exhortation. God desires all men to be saved (this is not His irrevocable purpose but His unrestricted desire).

His desire covers all without distinction. In accordance with that desire Christ Jesus gave Himself a ransom for all, "for all" relating to its potential benefits, not to the application of those benefits. If it be said that men, high or low, do not deserve our prayers then it may effectively be said that neither do they deserve to be provided with a ransom which, if they will but avail themselves of it, will prove effective for their deliverance. But God does not act on a principle of merit in this matter.

Of "God our Saviour" certain things are said:

1. He desires all men to be saved and to come to a knowledge of the truth. This "all" is both without distinction and without exception.

2. He is the only God, unique – One God; see verse 5. This is directed against idolatry of all sorts.

3. There is only One Mediator between God and men, Himself Man, Christ Jesus. This is the answer to the long standing desire of Job for a daysman, Job 9:33; see also John 14:6 and Acts 4:12.

4. That Mediator gave Himself a ransom for all. His death was entirely voluntary, notwithstanding that it was a murder on the part of men, and a judgment on the part of God. The phrase "a ransom for all" must not be construed quantitatively but qualitatively. A true vicarious substitution, or literal mathematical equivalent, is not here contended for. The New Testament recognises no such thing as a limited atonement.

The emphasis is on the One who gave Himself as the Ransom, and seeing He is an Infinite Being, His Ransom must be of an infinite nature. Matthew 20:28 shows that the ransom was given instead of "many". The Greek preposition there is *anti*, that of the scales, as one thing is put over against another of equal weight and, therefore, the passage is strictly substitutional, and consequently limited in scope to "many". Christ's propitiation is unlimited: His substitution is limited. The notion in the word "ransom" is that of a price paid to secure the freedom of another. To whom the price was paid is not discussed in Scripture, and perhaps the nearest we can say with accuracy is that it was paid to the principle of Justice. Someone has said that "all intelligent Calvinists (that is, those who give undue weight to election) readily grant that that persuasion of theirs does not transmute an infinite into a finite expiation" (that is, that their theory does not limit the potential of the death of Christ).

5. The testimony to this is to be given in its own season; see 2 Corinthians 6:1 and 2. The season is now.

6. Paul was the divinely appointed original trustee of this message, the word "preacher" having to do with that which he heralded, an "apostle" having to do with the sphere to which he was sent, and "the Gentiles" (nations other than Israel) the audiences which he addressed. This Paul did "in faith" Godward (i.e. faithfulness), and "truth" (R.V.) manward (i.e. truthfulness).

Paul now proceeds to regulate the manner of public prayers in the "house of God", 1 Timothy 3:15, when the church is gathered together. The audible expression of such prayers is to be made by the men – i.e. men in contradistinction from women. Their character and attitude must be consistent with such a holy exercise; "without wrath" towards others, and without "doubting" or reasonings within their own minds. The phrase "in every place" seems to equate "in every church"; see 1 Corinthians 1:2.

Women and Public Prayer

The words "in like manner also", verse 9 A.V., represent but one Greek word ὡσαύτως which is a copula and may be rendered 'also'. To render it as suggesting that Paul means that the "women pray also" makes an impossible construction, with two infinitive verbs in one sentence, i.e. "to adorn themselves" (stated) and "to pray" (understood though not stated). This suggestion seems to spring from a desire to justify women speaking audibly in the church, a thing which is forbidden in 1 Corinthians 14:34. We cannot here enter into a full discussion on the scope of women's ministry, but we cannot resist observing that the notion that "silence" is not silence (because of the Revised Version translation "quietness") lacks common-sense support. If in a public library one room has "quietness" placarded on its wall and another has the word "silence", the two must be synonymous. The Oxford English Dictionary gives a meaning for "quietness" as "silent". The Greek word *hēsuchia* involves silence. It is not merely a quiet state of mind, as a consideration of the New Testament occurrences of the noun and verb would show. Of course, according to the context, "quietness" and "silence" can have different connotations, but no Scripture contradicts another, and we must always observe the rule that what is plain must govern our interpretation of the obscure. Yet we do not think that either 1 Corinthians 14:34 or 1 Timothy 2:8-14 is obscure. One, surely, needs but ask: Why did Paul specify the "men" (Greek: *andres*) in verse 8 for praying, and the women in verse 9 for adorning, if he intended that both alike might publicly pray? Paul certainly in his Greek has anacolutha (lack of grammatical sequence) and parentheses, but we need not make any for him where he has not made them himself.

Paul here is giving Timothy directions as to the conduct of

meetings in local churches, and they may be summarised as follows:

1. Men as distinct from women are to lead in prayer publicly.

2. Women should adorn themselves with good works rather than with tinsel and finery

3. Women should learn in silence and submissiveness.

4. Women are not to teach in the church neither to have authority over men, but are to keep silent for the two good reasons, (a) man's priority in creation and (b) woman's priority in sin.

5. The woman's proper sphere is the home and that of motherhood, and she may count on God's mercy in such case if she continues in faith, love and holiness.

Let us beware of two perils: one of extending 1 Corinthians 14:34 and 1 Timothy 2:12 beyond their proper limits, for plainly a woman may at times teach (see Titus 2:3-4); the other of evading a plain meaning by the introduction of untenable affirmations.

1 Timothy 3

In this chapter, Paul gives directions as to those things which qualify a man for doing the work of an overseer, and similarly for a man or woman doing the work of a servant. "Bishops, priests and deacons" are three "orders" recognised in the established church but they have no such likeness in the New Testament. The Scripture teaches that all believers are priests, that some believers are servants and a lesser number are overseers. The New Testament (A.V.) translators were not permitted to alter recognised, ecclesiastical terms, for their sponsors could see what untold damage to their established systems would be done were proper translations to be given. The word "bishop" should be replaced by the word "overseers" (which in Acts 20:28 the A.V. translators did, though the R.V. restored the word "bishops"), the word "deacons" by the word "servants", the word "baptise" by "immerse", and so on.

Overseers - their Character and Work

The phrase "office of a bishop" represents but one word, which might be rendered "overseership". It occurs again in Acts 1:20 relating to Judas. There is no word corresponding to "office" in the Greek and, as the reader can test for himself, all references to such work denote a self-sacrificing service rather than an official position. The Revised Version translators were at least fair in that they put the word "overseer" in the margin of 1 Timothy 3:1.

The word "bishop" is but a shortened and anglicised Greek word, and the word "deacons" also is an anglicised Greek word. Both are misleading as tending to suggest divine approval of a vast system of archbishops, bishops, deacons and various subsidiary officers all foreign to the early days of Christianity and of the New Testament.

It is a "good", or beautiful, work to take care of the church of God but plainly anyone who does so must be spiritually and morally qualified to do so. Although the word "bishop" is here used in the singular, it is only used in a generic sense, for in Ephesus, Philippi and elsewhere there was a multiplicity of bishops *in* one church, whereas now-a-days in certain circles there is but one bishop *over* many churches. Such is topsy-turvy Christendom. The qualifications are essential - note "must" in verse 2. They are not optional. If today we can find no-one fully so qualified, it seems that we must seek God that we may approximate nearer and nearer to the divine standard. There must be personal, domestic and social fitness.

As to the qualifications we may remark: "husband of one wife" is restrictive, not injunctive. An unmarried man or widower is not disqualified because of this. But in places where polygamy was current, a polygamous man would be disqualified from such a position but not disqualified from church fellowship. If Paul had meant that only a married man could serve as an overseer then he would have disqualified himself, for it would seem that he was a widower. (As a member of the Sanhedrin previously he would have been at that time a married man.) Besides he would have contradicted his own statement in 1 Corinthians 7:32. See also Matthew 19:12. The present writer recalls that he owes an enormous debt to two bachelor overseers in the days of his childhood and early manhood.

The reader should consult the Revised Version and other reliable translations to get some idea of the wide range of thought covered by the various words used. "Of good behaviour" is rendered elsewhere as "orderly", "dignified". "Apt to teach" does not necessarily involve the idea of public preaching; a man may be very apt to teach privately but have no gift of public speech. But clearly if one is to care for the saints he must be thoroughly acquainted with the Word of God and its meaning. He must be master in his own house, for plainly if he cannot rule his children, then he reveals incompetence "to take care" of the church of God. Luke 10:35 is to the point here. The definite article before the word "devil" both in verses 6 and 7 leads one to the conclusion that Paul is alluding to Satan, and not to "slanderers" in general as some suggest. A reference to Ezekiel 28 and also to 2 Timothy 2:26 would also seem to justify this conclusion.

Deacons and their Work

This word relates to those who perform any service specifically for the church. It is the Holy Spirit who appoints overseers but the church chooses *its* servants (see Acts 6 and compare also v. 10). Here again the reader should consult as many reliable translations as he is able and also W. E. Vine's *Expository Dictionary* to get the idea of the wide range of thought covered by the various words used. For the performance of any particular service there should be competency, and this can only be discovered by prior testing. If the prior test is satisfactory, then "let them serve" in that particular capacity. This service appears to be open both to men and women, though restricted to their appropriate spheres, verse 11. Phebe was one such, Romans 16:1. Those who serve the church well gain to themselves a good standing before the saints, and great boldness in the faith, knowing that their lives commend it, and it does not condemn them.

There seems little doubt that "overseers" and "servants" were two recognised groups of believers within the framework of the church (see Phil. 1:1), entrusted with specific work on behalf of the church, the former caring primarily for the believers' spiritual well-being, and the latter caring *also* for the material things relating to the daily affairs.

A Local Church - Described

In verse 15, the apostle describes a local church. The definite articles are omitted, for he is specifying its character, and it would seem making provision thereby for the sad times later to be when not all believers in one place could claim to be *the* house of God, *the* church of the living God, or *the* pillar and ground of the truth in that place. Originally it was so. But the division has come in, breaking up the unified witness. The omission of the definite article shows the character or nature of the company. It is God's house, for the ordering of which He has the right to specify what should and what should not be done. It is a congregation of a living God, not an assemblage of people interested in dead idols. It is pillar and ground, stay or bulwark of the truth. Just as Nelson's Column in Trafalgar Square, London, elevates the man and is firmly based at its foot, so too a local church should give prominence to the truth. Ephesus was noted for its magnifical temple to Diana and its strong pillars, but that of which Paul writes is spiritual and not material. If the Ephesians cried, "Great is Diana (Artemis) of the Ephesians", Paul could counter that with, "Great is the mystery of godliness".

If verse 16 is an extract from an ancient hymn, as is asserted by some, then here we have given in poetic form a credal statement touching the Lord Jesus. The Revised Version appears to give the correct reading. We prefer "He who", the pronoun, *referring to the Lord Jesus,* making the following phrases easier to understand.

Each phrase is antithetical to the other, being arranged in three pairs. Flesh, spirit; angels and Gentiles; world and glory. Only as to the first and the last do they appear to be chronological: His manifestation and His ascension.

The *manifestation* of the Lord Jesus in flesh implies His prior eternal being and His dual natures, i.e. His deity and humanity. The reader should refer to John 1:14; 1 Peter 1:20; 1 John 1:2; 3:5, 8 and other similar passages.

His *justification* in Spirit may relate to the anointing by the Spirit at His baptism, or if we read Spirit with a small 's', it may refer to His own inner consciousness of ever pleasing the Father. His resurrection also may be in view.

His being *seen of angels* need not be limited, for they were attendant at His birth, His temptation, His experience in the garden of Gethsemane, at His resurrection and at His ascension.

His being *preached among the nations* is recorded in the book of the Acts as the fulfilment of His command to His apostles after His resurrection, Matthew 28:19; Mark 16:15.

His being *believed on in the world* is self-evident, the existence of churches here and there demonstrating it.

His being *received up in glory,* R.V. (*not* "into glory"), is recorded by Mark and Luke, and mention is made of it by the Lord Jesus in John's Gospel.

1 Timothy 4

Features of Later Times

Paul could see the trend of things, and knew that in "later" times there would be an apostasy from the faith (the A.V. has "latter" times). In its place the vacuum would be filled by seducing spirits and demoniacal teachings. Satan would use men to achieve this end, men whose consciences were branded or seared as with a hot iron.

The Spirit of God through Paul had expressly foreshadowed this in his second letter to the Thessalonians, and history has confirmed the truth of this forecast. Celibacy and vegetarianism have been imposed upon persons without the slightest scriptural sanction. Marriage was not only instituted by God but has His specific sanction as being an honourable estate, to be preserved as such by man and woman, Hebrews 13:4. Furthermore, Paul had already written to the Roman believers to the effect that no food was unclean in itself, Romans 14:14, and here he repeats his same conviction. Also what both he and Peter recognised (see Acts 10) had already been affirmed by the Lord Jesus in Mark 7:18.

Three things should be observed, (1) Every creature of God is good. He said so in Genesis 1:25, 31, and He extended His permission to cover animal food, excepting its blood, in Genesis 9:3. (2) These are to be received with thanksgiving by those who believe God's Word touching them, and know the truth of the matter, 1 Timothy 4:3. (3) The food is sanctified by God's Word referred to above and by prayer, that is, by seeking God's blessing upon it. "Grace at meals" should be no formal matter, much less should it be abandoned. Acts 27:35 is an excellent example for us all.

Another matter discussed in this chapter is that of "bodily exercise", (Greek: *gymnasia*). Paul is careful not to write off as altogether worthless physical exercise; he recognises its temporary benefits, but owns that comparatively they are small when placed beside the benefits of "Godliness", that is, Godfearing behaviour which observes the spiritual commandments and warnings given by the apostle to Timothy. The benefits of these extend beyond this life. This explains why Paul and Timothy devoted their energies to such a physically hazardous service as disseminating the truth, risking their own personal safety, knowing that the Living God is the Preserver of all men in general, specially of those who put their trust in Him, verse 10. Whether verse 9 relates to what precedes or immediately succeeds is a moot point. Finality seems impossible.

Counsel to a Young Man, Chapter 4:11-16

Timothy was a comparatively young man – maybe about 38 years old – and it may well be that some of the elders with whom he would have to do would be his senior. The tendency would be, therefore, to despise **him** on account of his age, but nothing is so effective in gaining respect and confidence as a good example. His "speaking" should command their hearing; his "manner of life" in general should commend his teaching; his "love" to the saints should beget their confidence; his personal "faith" both in God and His Word should manifest his convictions; his "purity" of behaviour would encourage the same in those who had but recently been converted from a corrupt society.

Timothy was enjoined by Paul to give attention, or heed, to the public reading of the Scriptures, verse 13. These may include both Old and what are now known as the New Testament writings (see, e.g., Luke 4:17; Acts 13:15; 15:21; Col. 4:16; 1 Thess. 5:27). He was not to neglect the gift that had been given to him which would enable him, not merely thus publicly to read, but as a consequence and relative to what had been read, to exhort the saints and to teach them. Note the order: exhortation has to do with conduct, teaching with belief. Both should be in harmony with each other. Timothy must himself observe this order and take heed to himself as well as to his teaching, lest what he is contradicts what he says. Luke writes of "all that Jesus began both to *do* and to *teach*", Acts 1:1, and Paul himself could refer the Philippian saints to what they had "seen in him" as well as heard from him.

The "presbytery", 1 Timothy 4:14, is the recognised body of elders, first appointed by the apostles, Acts 14:23, and thereafter appointed by the Spirit who manifested in the persons concerned the requisite qualifications of which we have spoken in chapter 3. They are "overseers". Acts 15:6 gives the precedent for such elders to meet together from time to time to discuss matters which affect the wellbeing of the saints.

In Timothy's case the charismatic gift was given to him by the laying on of the hands of Paul, 2 Timothy 1:6, but it was also attended by the laying on of hands of this elderhood, 1 Timothy 4:14, which did not involve the impartation of the gift but implied identification with Timothy in his consequential work. The presumptions of so-called prelates today in this regard are to be eschewed. As a limb which is not used will atrophy, so a gift which is not exercised will lose its usefulness. Hence Timothy must not neglect his gift.

He must be "diligent in these things", verse 15 R.V., or "occupy thyself with these things", J.N.D. He must "be wholly in them", J.N.D., - give himself wholly to them, so that his progress may be plain to all.

Timothy must remember that he does not live to himself, and further that he is in a specially responsible position having been entrusted with a divine gift which is not for his benefit but for that of the church. By taking heed to himself and to the injunctions here given by Paul, he will both save himself and those that hear him from many a pitfall into which they would otherwise come, verse 16.

1 Timothy 5

The Church's Personnel – their Duties

The church is made up of young and old, male and female, and Paul now gives Timothy instruction as to how to deal with each. He is not to rebuke an elder, that is, a man of years (not necessarily an overseer) but to exhort him as a father. He is to respect his years. He should regard the younger men as his brethren and deal with them on that level. The elder women he should treat as mothers, and the younger women as sisters always recognising the necessity for avoiding any impropriety.

Paul has a good deal to say about widows, of which there were many as was the case when the Lord was here; for example, Anna, the widow of Nain, and the widow noted for her two mites, and perhaps also Mary the mother of the Lord was later a widow. Widowhood in those days was attended with many difficulties not now existent in a "welfare state" which makes certain provisions for such. All these directions, therefore, in this chapter should be read in the light of the present existing conditions.

It is to be feared that present-day conditions have engendered in the minds of many younger people an unhealthy disregard for their parents and senior relatives, assuming that the state has relieved them of their moral obligations. But the requital of parents is a principle to be observed always, for that is acceptable in the sight of God. It is the children's duty to look after their living needy forbears. But in the case of those who are "widows indeed", that is, women bereft of their husbands and devoid of family help, these are to be honoured by the church, such honour including monetary assistance. Nevertheless, the relatives should remember that if they fail to make provision for such, they are worse than the heathen who, at least, do care for the old folk. In addition, they have given a practical denial of the faith they profess.

Everything was to be done decently and in order. A list was to be kept of these widows, but only those with certain qualifications. All must be over sixty years of age; they should have been married only once. Like Phebe, they should be noted for good works; like Lois and Eunice, they should have brought up children; like Lydia, they should have entertained strangers; like Mary, they should have washed the disciples' feet; like Dorcas, they should have relieved the afflicted; and like Persis, they should have followed every good work. But none of this is to be construed so that those who have widows in their family circles may evade their responsibilities; they should relieve them and the church should not be burdened, 1 Timothy 5:16.

The enrolment seems to be for the purpose of receiving church relief, though those thus qualified would doubtless be willing to lend a helping hand in church affairs as was necessary and desirable. Like Anna, they do not have their eye on the visible and material; they continue in supplications and prayers day and night to God on whom they have set their hope, verse 5.

But in these days of the welfare state monetary help is not the only assistance needed by those who are widows indeed. The sympathetic and loving care of younger ones will intuitively discern those things which are necessary, and which they can supply, to make up for the deficiencies of the life of the widow or the lonely.

As to younger widows, seeing that there is always the likelihood of their remarriage, and/or the possibility of their earning a living for themselves, they are to be refused admission to this "roll". Time heals many wounds, and while in the initial stages of their widowhood they recognised God as their only support, yet as time wore on they would desire to remarry and have a more visible support. Were they to be put on the "roll" they would learn to be idle, and Satan finds something for idle hands to do. Some would fill their time with gossip, visiting, and becoming busybodies with all its ill-spoken accompaniments. Paul's wish for such is that they should remarry, establish families, exercise themselves in their proper sphere, the home, and thus avoid giving occasion for reproach. Paul knew cases where they had already "turned aside after Satan", verse 15. We may observe that now-a-days there are ample avenues of appropriate service for women whose domestic duties do not occupy all their time. Such things as Women's Meetings, Sunday School classes, Old Folk visitation, babysitting to enable mothers to get out to meetings, and the like, come to mind.

From verse 17 to 25 Paul has chiefly in mind elders, that is, overseers. Those that rule well are to be counted worthy of double honour, specially those that labour in word and teaching. Verse 18 clearly shows that this honour has to do with material support. In this connection, see Deuteronomy 25:4; 24:15; 1 Corinthians 9:9; Luke 10:7 (this latter citation shows that Luke's Gospel was regarded as Scripture). The ox is to be allowed his nibble when at his work; the labourer is to be rewarded for his work. In the case of churches which rightly reject a one-man ministry this principle is oftentimes overlooked. This ought not to be, for the church should reimburse those who at the cost of time, money, energy, shoe leather, and so on, give themselves to caring for the saints.

It would appear that verse 19 specially has in mind an overseer. The word "elder" here is used in that sense. Because by reason of their work they can the more readily become the target of ill-minded persons, an accusation against them is not to be accepted unless it be adequately attested, Deuteronomy 19:15. In the case of proven guilt such are to be reproved in the presence of all the church so that the other elders as well as the church at large may fear. Paul solemnly enjoins Timothy to do these things without prejudice and without partiality (treating any preferentially above others).

Then, again, as to the appointment and recognition of elders, Timothy is enjoined not to lay hands suddenly on anyone. He may find, if he does so, that he will implicate himself with their sins. Some men's sins are self-evident going before into judgment, but in the case of others they take time to reveal themselves and, therefore, Timothy might unwarily be caught. He must see to it that he does not become involved in the wrong-doing of others. At all costs he must keep himself pure. He must remember that time will tell; it will bring to light a man's sins, and it will bring to light a man's good works; he must not act precipitately.

Sound judgment is largely dependent upon a healthy body. Therefore the apostolic advice to Timothy was that he should use (note the verb) a little (note the quantity) wine for his stomach's sake and chronic weaknesses (note the object).

1 Timothy 6

The Personnel of the Church – their Perils

It will be observed that neither Paul nor the Lord Jesus made an onslaught upon the principle of slavery. What they did rather was to create an atmosphere in which such a degrading custom could not survive (see especially the letter to Philemon).

Slaves are to honour their masters with the view of safeguarding the esteem in which the name of God and Christian doctrine are held. They are not to take advantage of the fact should it be that their masters are also believers; rather they should serve them because the benefits from such service will be enjoyed by believers, saints beloved. Today the principle of master and servant, the principle of a bargain of so much service for so much pay, is apt to cause Christians to overlook the fact that God has set His children in different stations and relationships of life, but the New Testament not only recognizes their existence but states the respective duties that devolve upon the various occupants (see e.g., Eph. 6:5-9; Col. 3:22; 4:1).

Timothy must expect opponents and contradictors, but he is entrusted with the health-giving teaching that relates to the Lord Jesus Christ and which will promote practical godliness, 1 Timothy 6:3. Those who teach differently are marked by pride and controversy. Paul calls them "proud", verse 4, who are themselves sick, marg. What they promote is envy, strife, railings, evil surmisings, wranglings of men corrupted in mind and bereft of the truth. They wrongly suppose that Godliness is a way of gain, reflecting the covetousness which is in their own heart.

This leads Paul to discuss the subject of the Christian's attitude to wealth. Contentment should mark him, for he came into the world empty-handed and it is certain that he will go out in like manner. Anything amassed in the meantime will either be used for the glory of God, or for self-gratification, or left behind for the consumption of others in ways of which he may disapprove. This vexed the Preacher, Ecclesiastes 2:18. But if he is content with his divinely appointed lot, 2 Corinthians 9:8, and couples with it Godliness, he is in the veriest sense rich. Conditional guarantees of food and clothing were given by the Lord Jesus, Matthew 6:33, and having these what more could we desire? But discontent is apt to creep into every heart and a craving to become rich. Money itself is not evil, for its proper use may lead to many a God-honouring benefit, but the love of money is a root of all kinds of evil. One has but to think of Achan, Gehazi and Judas, and to consider their ends to see how true this is. Those who aspire after wealth are like the wild beast which, leaping at the bait hung over the pit, falls into it and is impaled on the spike below. Paul's words are very descriptive: "a snare" entrapping the aspirant after wealth; drowning in the attempt to clutch at the unobtainable; "seduced", 1 Timothy 6:10 marg., from the faith so that they are without an anchor in the sea of life; "pierced through" with arrows of their own making. Contrast the end of Micah's priest, Judges 18, with that of the apostle Paul. Paul coveted no man's silver or gold or apparel, his own horny hands which plied at the canvas tent bearing witness to his selfless labours for his own needs and those of his associates. Materialism is the bane of our present age. It not only affects the world but it affects the people of God. Vying with one's neighbour, "keeping up with the Joneses", indeed endeavouring to go one better than they, cause the child of God to spend unduly on himself and his family, to the loss of the furtherance of the work of the Lord. If only we could remember that we have "only one life, 'twill soon be past; only what's done for Christ will last", then we should be saved from the snare of materialism. We should learn from the example of the Lord: "Buy those things that we have need of", John 13:29, and of Paul, whose hands had ministered to his necessities and to them that were with him, Acts 20:34.

Paul addresses Timothy as "man of God", 1 Timothy 6:11; he is God's man as were the prophets of old. He must flee, and follow and fight, verses 11-12. The things under review, covetousness in all its forms, must be eschewed. He must follow after righteousness, Godliness, faith or fidelity, love,

He must fight the good fight of the faith and lay hold on the life eternal, instead of seeking to seize as much of the things of this life as he could. To that he had been called; and there were many who could witness that this was his goal in life.

Timothy is charged to keep the commandment until the appearing of our Lord Jesus Christ, verse 14. This is significant. Paul does not say until Timothy passes on by death. It is a consistent principle of his writings never personally to legislate to the saints.

Verse 15 relates to the Father, despite the fact that almost similar words are used of the Lord Jesus, Revelation 17:14.

God is unique, supreme, immortal, unapproachable, invisible, worthy of honour and power everlasting.

Paul reverts to the matter of riches and those who possess them, 1 Timothy 6:17-19. He does not condemn them but exhorts them not to be high-minded (a very easy propensity) nor to set their hope upon those riches which can so easily disappear.

Paul adds one final plea, addressing his words with, "O Timothy". He feels things deeply. He has in mind the "deposit", that body of Christian doctrine with which he himself had been entrusted, and which now he was passing on to Timothy and which he was expected to transmit to others (see 2 Tim. 1:12, 14; 2:2). Attacks will be made upon it; it must be guarded as diligently as Shammah defended the field of lentils, 2 Samuel 23:12. The oppositions of "science falsely so called" must be avoided. Some having gone in for such knowledge have missed the mark as regards the faith. Intellectualism has intruded into the assemblies of God's people. Believers tend to forget that the natural man receiveth not the things of the Spirit of God; to him they are foolishness, 1 Corinthians 2:14. Mere knowledge (otherwise termed "science") puffs up. Mere knowledge *per se* is a dangerous tiling. It has to do with things, but eternal life consists in the knowledge of "the only true God, and Jesus Christ", John 17:3. This is the "most excellent" thing, and Paul made it his aim in life, Philippians 3:8, 10. He did not lack academic learning; yea, he excelled in it, yet after his conversion he had another aim in life. No wonder his "unlearned" brother Peter wrote, "Grow in grace, and in the knowledge of our Lord and Saviour Jesus Christ", 2 Peter 3:18. "Grace be with you", R.V., terminates the letter. "You" is not the colloquial "you" of modern speech, but the plural embracing all the saints who were associated with Timothy.

2 Timothy 1

'Be Courageous'

This is the last recorded letter that came from the apostle Paul. It was written from a Roman dungeon, which was devoid of every trace of comfort. From it, Paul was to go forth to his martyrdom. Its value and pathos are, therefore, tremendous indeed.

In both his letters to Timothy he writes as an apostle of Christ Jesus, called and appointed by Him as such on the Damascus road; see Acts 26:16. He was not self-appointed. His apostleship was by the commandment and conforming to the wish of God our Saviour, and Christ Jesus our hope; cf. 1 Timothy 1:1; 2 Timothy 1:1. Both God and Christ Jesus are conjoined, in recognition of their essential equality. As the Messiah was the "hope" of the nation of Israel, so now Paul recognises Him to be the hope of mankind, and his great work was to proclaim the promise that God would give eternal life to all who believe; see e.g., Romans 6:23.

"In Christ Jesus" is a key phrase of this letter; see chapter 1:13; 2:1,10; 3:12,15. Timothy was no spurious convert. He was a "true (genuine) child in the faith", 1 Timothy 1:2 R.V., indeed a "beloved child", 2 Timothy 1:2 R.V. As always there were good and bad fish caught; wheat and tares grew together; but the genuineness of Timothy had been proven, and this endeared this "beloved child" to his spiritual father.

We have earlier suggested that this chapter might be labelled with the words "Be courageous", and well we may, for in verse 12 Paul says, "I am not ashamed"; in verse 16, referring to Onesiphorus, he says that he "was not ashamed", and in verse 8 he enjoins Timothy not to be ashamed. One can listen to such exhortations when they come from a man who manifestly is suffering because of his unabashed boldness in the gospel.

In verses 9-11 Paul sets out the work wrought by the gospel: God "saved us", which was itself consequential upon His calling us with a holy calling, having had its roots in His eternal sovereign purpose which sprang from His sovereign grace. Thus he traces things back to their ultimate source: grace issuing in a purpose, resulting in a call, and that call resulting in salvation. That purpose and grace were given to us in the eternal past, and therefore could have had nothing whatsoever to do with "our works". God acted altogether independently of any thought of merit in the objects of His purpose.

These abstract truths became manifest in the incarnation, crucifixion and resurrection of the Lord Jesus. The "appearing (or *epiphany*) of our Saviour Christ Jesus" broke in upon man's darkness and showed God now to be operative in effecting His eternal designs. Christ Jesus put death out of action, for He "death by dying slew", Hebrews 2:14, and brought life and incorruptibility to light through the gospel. He Himself was raised from the dead in the power of an endless life, not having seen any corruption when in death. He was raised with a body of glory.

Of this Paul was appointed a *"herald"* (having to do with the message), verse 11 R.V. marg., and a *"teacher"* (having to do with the persons whom he addressed). He uses the emphatic pronoun "I" in this verse, thus magnifying the grace of God that should place such an one as he had been into such an honourable position.

Because of his fulfilling his commission, he was at the time of writing this letter suffering persecution and imprisonment, and facing martyrdom. False accusations may have been lodged against him charging him with incendiarism or worse, but the real cause of his trouble was his loyalty to Christ and the gospel.

Nevertheless he was not ashamed. For he had an *unfailing Saviour* and of Him he could say, "I know whom I have believed". His past experience of the faithfulness of his Lord assured him that He would not at this time fail him, however extreme his case might be.

Not that Paul was pre-occupied with himself or his own safety. He was, it would seem, pre-occupied with "the deposit", verse 14 R.V. marg., that body of truth which he had committed to Timothy, 1 Timothy 6:20, and which he again enjoins Timothy to guard, verse 14. No servant of God is indispensable. His work will continue even if His workman is removed. He is able to guard that deposit unto "that day".

The day of the Lord Jesus was constantly before Paul as his many references to it show, a day when the Lord Jesus and His gospel would be shown to be ultimately triumphant despite all the oppositions that it might encounter.

The R.V. in its text agrees with the A.V. and reads, "that which I have committed unto Him". The marginal reading of the R.V. is, "that which He hath committed unto me" and seems to be more in line with the context. Surely we may rightly say that there was a mutual transaction on the Damascus road, when Saul of Tarsus handed himself over unreservedly to the Saviour, and when that same Saviour appointed him as the official trustee of the Gospel to the Gentiles. In neither case would that Saviour fail either him or his trust.

Onesiphorus was an outstanding example of loyalty to the apostle despite the defections of others such as Phygellus and Hermogenes who, with all that were in Asia, had turned away from Paul. Nothing is known of these two persons, or of the cause of the defection in verse 15. Maybe those involved could not find courage to stand openly with this notable prisoner at that time. But Onesiphorus, who had oftentimes refreshed him, had made it his business when in Rome to search out this prisoner. Of course he would not have asked for "the apostle Paul" but for "Prisoner Number so and so", and despite several rebuffs from the officials he did not give up his quest till he had found and contacted Paul. He was not ashamed of his chain nor to be identified with such an one. Now it would appear that he had passed away by death. Paul expresses a wish for mercy to be given to his house. And he expresses a wish that Onesiphorus will also find mercy in "that day", for any rewards for faithfulness here will but magnify the mercy that takes knowledge of such things done by those who, but for the grace of God Himself, would have acted altogether otherwise. We must not construe verse 18 as if the eternal salvation of Onesiphorus were in doubt, nor that this verse authorised prayers for the dead.

There are three couplets in this Epistle of great significance: Phygellus and Hermogenes are those who abandon the truth; Hymenaeus and Philetus, chapter 2:17, corrupt the truth; and Jannes and Jambres, chapter 3:8, resist the truth.

Timothy. Having regard to the fact that Paul was not ashamed and that Onesiphorus was not ashamed, Timothy indeed should not be ashamed. He was the subject of Paul's incessant prayers; he longed to see him, either by release and his being able to revisit Ephesus or by Timothy coming to Rome: the latter would be more likely as release seemed impossible. Paul refers to his having served God with a pure conscience from his forefathers, and he now recollects the forebears of Timothy, his grandmother Lois and his mother Eunice, both of whom were Godfearing women and had taught young Timothy accordingly. They had an unfeigned faith in God; theirs was no hypocritical belief as was that of Simon Magus. The "faith" referred to in verse 5 is evidently the Christian faith; Acts 16:1 would lead one to believe that Timothy's mother was in the Christian faith before Timothy. Paul recalled the tears of Timothy when he was forcibly separated from him and had been left alone in such a place as idolatrous and fanatical Ephesus. He urged him to rekindle the gift of God which was in him, which gift had been imparted by the laying on of Paul's hands. Paul was not the donor of the gift; it was the "gift of God", some special charisma which he must not allow to lie unused or to die within him. He may indeed feel himself to be inadequate for the task, but God had not given him a spirit of cowardice but of power, and love and discipline. Any natural timidity must be overcome by faith. He must not be ashamed either of the testimony of the Lord or of Paul *His* prisoner. Paul did not regard himself as the prisoner of Nero. Timothy must endure hardship with the gospel not in his own strength but according to the power of God. He must hold fast the pattern of sound (health-giving) words which he had heard from Paul. This he must do *in faith* (i.e., personal conviction of their truth), and *love* (bearing in mind that Christian doctrine was designed to disseminate the knowledge of God's love to man and to promote it in man). The good deposit (that is, the truth committed to Timothy which is, veritably, a beautiful [good] thing) he must guard from the enemy's onslaughts, not in his own strength, physical or mental, but by the Holy Spirit which had been given both to him and to Paul.

2 Timothy 2

'Be Careful'

This chapter we have labelled, "Be careful", for in it Paul urges Timothy to "shun", "depart", "purge", "flee" and "avoid" certain perils that beset his path. At the end of the chapter he speaks of those who have been caught alive by the devil and entrapped, and trusts that, through Timothy's efforts, they may awake to a true consciousness of their state, be released from the snare of the devil and made free to do the will of God.

For his onerous task, Timothy may find all requisite grace in Christ Jesus, grace which will impart to him strength, verse 1. He must transmit the things he has heard from Paul among many witnesses to faithful men, who will be able to teach others also. Thereby a relay service will be established, and the truth will be passed on from one to another throughout the age till the Lord come, verse 2.

Paul then uses *three illustrations* to enforce upon Timothy certain important lessons, (1) The soldier on active service does not entangle himself with the affairs of this life, since he has but one aim in view, to please the one who enlisted him. The man who has a business for which he is solely responsible cannot carry on that business and simultaneously be engaged in armed warfare. The one must be abandoned if the other is to be prosecuted. Timothy must have no divided interest; he cannot serve two masters. He must be solely occupied with the *will* of his Superior. (2) Paul then alludes to the athlete who competes in the games. He must adhere strictly to the rules, and failing to do so, he would be disqualified from receiving the prize. He must be occupied with the *word*. So, too, Timothy will find the Word of God a sufficient guide for him in the contest in which he is engaged. (3) Again, the farmer must concentrate on the work before he can expect to partake of the harvest. He may be assured of the fact that he will be the first to participate (as now-a-days, in the case of a bankruptcy, wages must be paid before dividends), but he must *work* first, then partake secondly.

Verse 8 should read as in the Revised Version, for it is not the recollection of a fact but the remembrance of a person: "Remember Jesus Christ, risen from the dead, of the seed of David". Although the Lord Jesus was of the seed of David, He did not have His rights prior to His death. They are established and assured in resurrection. He is the pre-eminent example of One who sought ever to please His Father and to do His *Will*. He was the One in whose heart was the *Word* of God, Psalm 40:8, and it was He who said, "I must *work* the works of Him that sent Me, while it is day", John 9:4.

The Lord Jesus had suffered and come through triumphantly; Paul was then suffering and he was assured of a triumphant issue. Timothy may, therefore, resolve for himself likewise. Men may bind the preachers; they cannot bind the word.

In verse 10, Paul uses words that stretch from eternity to eternity: "elect" casts the mind backwards, Ephesians 1:4, and "eternal glory" throws it forward, while in the centre is "the salvation" of which he has already spoken in chapter 1:9. He regards the "elect" as the Lord did – "the excellent, in whom is all My delight", Psalm 16:3, and this enabled him to endure for their sake.

This backward and forward look leads Paul to mention some "faithful saying" well-known to the saints of that time, verse 11. (1) Identification with Him in death assures identification with Him in life, (2) Present endurance of adversity will be followed by victoriously reigning with Him, (3) Present denial of Him will result in His future denial of us. For confession of Him is an indispensable necessity for salvation; see Romans 10:9; Hebrews 13:15; Mark 8:38. A temporary failure through lack of courage, as in the case of Peter, is not here in view, but rather a determined course which knows no repentance. (4) Faithlessness on our part will not change the Lord; He abides faithful, He cannot deny Himself. He changes not.

Timothy must charge his brethren not to engage in a battle of words; it yields no profit, but rather tends to subvert the hearers. He has been entrusted with the "word of truth", verse 15, and he must use every possible endeavour to present himself a workman approved unto God that has no need to be ashamed. He should handle the word of God alright or, as the A.V. and R.V. marg., "rightly dividing" it. His handling of Scripture should be done in spiritual intelligence, ensuring that both the motive of the interpreter and his exegesis are proper, verse 15.

Salutary Warnings

Timothy must shun profane babblings (godless chatter) for they will but lead people into more ungodliness, and instead of their word being sound teaching, it will prove to be of a cancerous nature, gradually eating away healthy tissue. Such was the case with Hymenaeus and Philetus, men who had erred concerning the truth. They affirmed that the resurrection had passed already, possibly mixing up Paul's doctrine of a future resurrection in 1 Corinthians 15 with the believer's experience of having already been raised with Christ as taught by him in Ephesians 2:6 and Colossians 3:1. This was a clear case of not handling aright God's Word. It was upsetting the faith of some, but not, thank God, of all. Nothing could subvert the firm foundation of God which had, as many constructions have today, a double inscription-seal: the one Godward, "The Lord knoweth them that are His", and the other manward, "Let everyone that nameth the name of the Lord depart from unrighteousness", R.V. This latter is the sole way by which we may judge whether a person is real or false.

Verse 20 is an illustration used by Paul to illustrate the fact in the Christian profession there are two classes, the vessels to honour and those to dishonour; that is to say, there are those utensils which find their use in the dining room, whilst others never appear there but are used in the kitchen. In the former case, the master of the house uses them; in the latter the servants in the house use them. If therefore, I am desirous of being used by the Lord Himself, I must purge myself from "these", verse 21. To what does "these" refer? It cannot mean that I must purge myself from the other vessels; that would never make one useful. It seems that Paul has in mind purging one's self from the babblings of verse 16 and the babblers of verse 17. Verse 21 denotes those from whom we are to disassociate ourselves, and verse 22 indicates those with whom we are to associate ourselves.

As to the word "purge", verse 21, which Paul uses here, it only occurs elsewhere in 1 Corinthians 5:7. There the "wicked man" has to be purged out of the company: here the man has to "purge himself" out from the other things and persons.

The verb is here strengthened by the addition of the Greek preposition *apo* (from).

It is well-known that verse 26 is difficult to render into English, but the writer regards its sense as follows. The verse relates to those who "oppose themselves" to the truth; Paul trusts that God will use the endeavours of Timothy to bring these opponents to repentance, and the acknowledgement of the truth that they have before opposed. They have allowed themselves to come into a state of stupor, and are unaware that the devil has caught them alive in his snare. The Revised Version margin seems to the writer to give the proper sense, namely "and that they may return to soberness out of the snare of the devil, having been taken alive (and captivated) by the devil, unto the will of God".

It is nature to those who seek to defend the truth so to act that they lack the gentleness and meekness that marked the Lord, thereby making strife, even in the cause of truth. Such things ought not to be, verse 24. Ponder carefully verses 22 to 26. Opponents are much more likely to be won if these exhortations are heeded, than if we resist them ungraciously by mere argument.

The word Paul uses for "patient" (R.V. and A.V. marg. "forbearing"), verse 24, occurs nowhere else in the New Testament. It means suffering evil patiently – a thing hard for unaided human nature. It is a medical term for suffering an illness bravely.

2 Timothy 3

'Be Constant'

We have labelled this chapter, "Be Constant", because of the exhortation in verse 14. The taunt of many that we have submitted ourselves to the teaching of our mothers and our grandmothers is apt to injure our personal pride and our desire to be regarded as independent thinkers. We are prone, therefore, to cast overboard our early training. But Paul exhorts Timothy to continue in the things which he had learned and been assured of. He had not only been taught them but, by personal examination, had assured himself of their veracity. Why then abandon them? Lois, Eunice and Paul had been his early tutors. From his childhood he had been acquainted with the "sacred writings" (J.N.D.: "sacred letters") and he is enjoined now to continue.

The Holy Scriptures are the infallible guide which is bequeathed by Paul to Timothy and to us all. They are sacred in nature. As to their *capacity,* they are able to make one wise to salvation (salvation in the most comprehensive sense, both present and future). They are *Christocentric* and designed to inculcate faith in the Lord Jesus. In *origin*, they are God-breathed; men from God spake as they were borne along by the Holy Spirit. In *utility*, they are profitable for teaching, rebuke, correction and training in righteousness. Their *purpose* is that the man of God may be perfect, complete, up-to-date, fitted out for every good work.

"All scripture is given by inspiration of God", that is, is warm with His very breath; hence Scripture has today as much power as when it was first uttered. The translation of this verse has been the subject of much discussion and we shall not reconsider the subject here. Our preference is for the A.V., though one would never dare to say that the R.V., "Every scripture inspired of God is also profitable ..." is wrong. It all depends how one interprets the word "scripture", whether exclusively of the Holy Bible or whether more extensively of "writing" in general. In Scripture itself the word "scripture" is only used for the sacred writings, but Paul's statement here is so worded that it embraces what we now call the New Testament, as well as the Old, and certainly, however we translate it, excludes all uninspired writings (uninspired by God, that is).

The Last Days

This chapter commences with a reference to the "last days". Though this term may apply particularly to the last phase of the present period just prior to the return of the Lord Jesus, 1 John 2:18 shows clearly that it may be interpreted to embrace our own present era. It is clear from verse 5 that Timothy was living in them. Their features show that the decalogue would be spurned. Men infringed the first item by loving themselves rather than God. They infringed the third by being blasphemers; the fifth by being disobedient to parents; the seventh by being unholy; the ninth by slander; the tenth by being covetous. If Romans 1 describes heathendom, this describes spurious Christianity which retains a religious form but in practice denies its power. Like Jannes and Jambres, such people resist the truth, their minds are corrupted, and as regards the faith they are altogether spurious (counterfeit). They are false religionists who prey upon the guilty consciences of silly women, creeping into their houses knowing that they will listen to anybody, though they never arrive at a knowledge of the truth. Paul is assured that, like as these ancient magicians were halted and their folly exposed, so it will be with these deceiving teachers (see Exodus 7:8-12; 9:11). The action of Elymas the sorcerer should be compared with all this, Acts 13:8.

Paul reminds Timothy of what his own behaviour had been, which was in strong contrast to this. His had been a life of persecution, suffering, endurance and deliverance. He could promise nothing better either for Timothy or for any who would wish to live Godly in Christ Jesus. In fact things will gradually get worse and worse, and evil men will increasingly deceive others while they themselves are also being deceived. The Godly would more and more find a strong tide of opposition to them. Notwithstanding, Timothy should continue and not allow himself to be deflected.

Paul not infrequently called attention to himself, aware that his conduct had pleased the Lord and had set a worthy example for others to imitate, verse 10. Paul had proved the truth of Psalm 34:19. Read also Matthew 16:24 and Acts 14:22.

2 Timothy 4

'Be Considerate'

We have labelled this chapter, "Be Considerate", because it contains the touching last requests of the veteran apostle to his junior aide in circumstances that imply that he is at the end of life's journey.

He urges Timothy to do his utmost to come to him shortly, verse 9, as he longed to see him, chapter 1:4. He wants him to do this "before winter", chapter 4:21, when travelling would be, at least, very difficult and hazardous. In the mercy of God he has Luke, the medical man, with him but all others have left him. Demas had allowed the world to get a grip on his heart and he had gone to Thessalonica, Crescens to Galatia and Titus to Dalmatia.

He wishes him to collect on the way Mark, who had defected on Paul's first missionary journey, but who had later proved himself to be a very useful servant. The R.V. better renders the phrase as "useful to me for ministering" rather than as in the A.V. "for the ministry", verse 11. This latter has now acquired a restricted and religious meaning which it did not originally possess. Tychicus in self-sacrificing devotion had Paul sent to Ephesus, presumably with this letter; hence of his travelling companions the only one left was Luke. It is apparent from verse 21 that there were other believers near at hand, so that verse 11 must be interpreted in relation to his erstwhile fellow-workers.

The love of Demas for this present age, verse 10, is manifestly set in contrast with those "that have loved His appearing", verse 8 R.V. The pull of the unseen had given way, as far as he was concerned, to the pull of the seen.

In view of the approaching winter, Paul wants a cloak which he had left at Troas with Carpus (long standing doubts as to the meaning of the word translated "cloak" have not yet been finally resolved; see Vine's *Expository Dictionary*). Paul not only wants something for his body but also something for his soul and his spirit; hence he desires Timothy to bring the books specially the parchments, verse 13. Maybe the latter were writing material. Did Paul wish to write further letters?

In our present day, when the younger sometimes have little regard for the older, such requests might appear so trivial that they would be apt to be ignored, but Timothy must be considerate of his spiritual leader, and in view of his very trying circumstances and gruesome prospect he must not regard matters such as cloak, books, parchments, and haste as things which can be forgotten. Besides, could Timothy so treat his loved chief?

The Last Words of Paul.

Timothy has been left in Ephesus. In view of the fact that the Lord Jesus is about to judge the "quick" (i.e., living; see Matt. 25:31) when He returns to earth, and the "dead" at the great white throne, Revelation 20:11ff; in view of the fact that He is not always to be absent but will in due time appear; and in view of the fact that His rights on earth will then be acknowledged and that He will have His kingdom, Timothy must now "preach the word", verse 2. He had been assured of its true nature and capacity at the end of chapter 3; this word he must now preach, or "herald". Both Paul and Timothy are accountable to the Lord; hence Paul gives his solemn charge in the sight of God and of Christ Jesus, and Timothy must heed and comply with it accordingly. If he has not opportunity he must make opportunity – in season or out of season; he must reprove (margin, bring to the proof), rebuke, exhort; it will take patience and diligent teaching. This is all the more imperative because the time will come (and by our day has come) when people will not endure sound teaching (healthy doctrine). Note how Paul describes the message entrusted to Timothy: "sacred writings", chapter 3:15 R.V.; "all scripture", chapter 3:16; "the word", chapter 4:2; "sound doctrine", chapter 4:3; "the truth", chapter 4:4. To unregenerate men the "truth" is unpalatable, and consequently they turn away from it, and governed by their own likings they heap to themselves teachers who will speak things which are palatable to them but in reality are merely myths (fables).

Timothy must be sober in all things. He must allow nothing to control him excessively. He must suffer hardship, verse 5 R.V.; chapter 2:3, and he must do the work of an evangelist and fulfil the specific service that had been entrusted to him. This is all the more urgent because Paul affirms that his work is finished.

I am, he says, already being poured out as a drink offering, verse 6 R.V. marg. He foresaw this as a possibility when writing to the Philippians, 2:17, but now it was being realised. The time for him to strike tent and to "go home" (cf. 2 Cor. 5:8) had come; the time for him to loose his moorings and to set sail for the eternal harbour had arrived. Paul has no fears; rather a joyful prospect lies ahead of him.

He reviews his life. "I have fought *the* good fight", verse 7 R.V.; not, "I have fought well", but the cause in which I have been fighting has been a splendid one (Greek: *kalos*). Possibly the thought is not so much of a fight as a games-contest, (see Heb. 12:1-2), and this may agree with the second item mentioned, "I have finished my course", a thing that he earnestly desired when speaking to the Ephesian elders, Acts 20:24. He had kept the faith (that good deposit to which he referred in 1:12).

Thus Paul imitated his Lord whose great contest and ultimate victory is mentioned in Hebrews 12:2. The Lord Jesus said, "It is finished"; Paul the apostle said, "I have finished". He had enjoined Archippus to "fulfil" the service entrusted to him, Colossians 4:17; Timothy must do likewise.

Paul had been the subject of much adverse criticism, as his letters to the Corinthians in particular show, but there is a "righteous judge" or the Lord Himself from whose hand Paul was sure he would receive a victor's crown because He would righteously assess both his motives and his work at that day. However, he has no exclusive monopoly in this as it is open for all to gain, providing that they have loved His appearing. The perfect tense which Paul uses frequently here is important, for it denotes a thing done, the effects of which abide.

At the end of the journey of the life of king Saul, he had to bemoan, "I have sinned: ... I have played the fool, and have erred", 1 Samuel 26:21. At the end of the earthly life of our blessed Lord Jesus, He could say, "I have glorified Thee on the

2 Timothy 4

earth: I have finished the work ... I have manifested Thy name", John 17:4, 6. And now Paul has his three triumphant notes.

Alexander, whose identity cannot definitely be fixed, is said to have done many evil things to Paul – when and where is not stated. The latter part of verse 14 is rendered in the A.V. as the expression of a desire, but in the R.V. as the assurance of a future penalty. Certainly the latter conforms more with the Christian spirit, while the former agrees with the Old Testament imprecations. In view, however, of the fact that this Alexander had greatly withstood Paul, Timothy should be specially wary of him.

Paul then alludes to his first hearing before Nero. Unhappily no one was prepared to accept his brief, and argue his case on his behalf. He had to be not only prisoner in the dock, but counsel for the defence. Yet, though apparently standing alone, he was not really alone, for the Lord stood with him, and at that time he was delivered from the lion's (Nero's) mouth. The case was apparently deferred.

Read in the light of chapter 1:15, it would seem that none had the courage in those hard days to stand by Paul and espouse his cause. But, as always, he found the Lord standing by him, faithful as ever. He had been with him in the difficult days when he first visited Corinth, Acts 18:10, and again when he was in peril in the midst of the Euroclydon storm, Acts 27:23, and again in Jerusalem, Acts 23:11. It was so with the three men in the fiery furnace, Daniel 3:25, and with Daniel, Daniel 6:22. We may count on His like presence, Hebrews 13:5. But how mysterious, in view of all this, was the cry of the Holy Sufferer!, Psalm 22:1.

Paul has no hard thought against his fellow believers who

deserted him in this hour of legal trial. It seems from the language of verse 17 that Paul took advantage of his dual position, prisoner in the dock and counsel for the defence, to proclaim the gospel to a crowded court before the ruler of the Roman world and all who were there assembled. It was a unique and splendid opportunity. Who can tell what were its eternal issues?

Yet Paul knew that martyrdom was not far off and that it would prove a deliverance from every evil work, however extreme. It would but be the means of his entrance into the heavenly kingdom. He employs the title "the Lord" in verse 18 as referring, of course, to the Lord Jesus – not to Nero who claimed the title for himself. But Paul recognised the Lord of all lords whose purposes could not be frustrated, and whose eternal glory would be assured by whatever happened to him.

Paul salutes Prisca and Aquila (Prisca, a shortened form of the name in affectionate regard, as we often do now-a-days) and the house of Onesiphorus, who had presumably passed on by death.

Trophimus Paul had left at Miletus sick. Had he possessed the gift of healing to be used indiscriminately upon any and all, this could only be regarded as callous in the extreme; but, of course, such a gift was entrusted to no one for such haphazard use.

In the last verse, we see what a loss modern translations incur for us when they jettison "thee", "thou", and similar second person singular pronouns. As in the A.V. Paul expresses in verse 22 two wishes, one for Timothy, and one for all saints. For Timothy: "The Lord be with *thy* spirit". For all saints: "Grace be *with you*" (plural).

Titus 1

God is Faithful

It would appear that this letter was written to Titus after Paul had made a recent visit to Crete (possibly with Titus), and had left him there in order that he might set in order certain things, verse 5. This is the only place where Paul describes himself as a *bondslave* of God, verse 1. Though he was born free, yet he gladly accepts this bondservice. He equates it with "an apostle of Jesus Christ", thereby implying the equality of Christ with God. This apostleship stood "according to", "with regard to", "in order to bring about" the faith of God's elect, called in verse 4 a "common faith". Perhaps "faith" in verse 1 is subjective, referring to the fact that God's elect believe, while "faith" in verse 4 may be objective, referring to that common body of truth which both Christian Jew and Christian Gentile acknowledge.

As Paul frequently does, he spans the whole range of what we call "time". He casts his mind back to eternity in the past and reflects on the promise which God, who never lies, made, and then he throws his mind into the eternal future and speaks of "eternal life" as being the subject of that promise; he calls it a "hope". This has been manifested in its own seasons in the preaching with which Paul had been specially entrusted (he uses the emphatic pronoun "I", v. 3 R.V.) according to the commandment of God our Saviour. (For the phrase "our Saviour" used of God and of the Lord Jesus see 1:3; 2:10; 3:4; 1:4; 2:13; 3:6.) The one preposition "from" governing both "God the Father" and "Christ our Saviour", verse 4, declares them to be equal with each other.

We may state the matter thus:

In the past: God is eternally incapable of falsehood: He made a promise before time began; in sovereignty He elected those who were the objects of His purpose.

As to the future: He gives the hope of eternal life.

In the present: God made manifest His promise in the word of the gospel, through the preaching of His authorised bondservant, who had been commissioned and sent by Jesus Christ, so that these "elect" might be discovered, might believe, might acknowledge the truth, and adjust their lives according to godliness. One of such was Titus, a genuine child who, though a Gentile, was embraced within the compass of the message, for it was "common" to Jew and Gentile; see Acts 11:8-18.

Paul is thus seen here as a bondservant, an apostle, a trustee, and a father. He felt on leaving Crete (whensoever he visited that island is not clear) that there was much needing to be put in order, and he therefore wrote to Titus enjoining him in this regard and giving him guidance in the matter. We must not read verse 5 as if Paul authorised "elders" to have authority in sundry churches in one particular "city" or "town". In those early days, all the believers in one town would comprise the church in that town. It is, unhappily, not the case now-a-days, seeing that church testimony has been so sadly fragmented. But, as we have seen earlier in considering Paul's letters to

Timothy, he envisaged a multiplicity of elders in one church. He sets out the requisite qualifications for overseers.

The family of an overseer should be such that the children in it are reliable, dependable, honest, (cf. the same word translated "faithful word" in verse 9). The word does not appear to mean that they *must* be believers of the gospel, though it is to be hoped they would become such. But having regard to the acknowledged anomaly that in Old Testament times some good men had bad sons, and some bad men had good sons, and bearing in mind Isaiah 1:2 and the parable of the Prodigal Son, it seems that the sense of verse 6 here is that the overseer's children must be faithful. Biblical "faithfulness" is the fruit of being just. Hence many take the meaning to be that the elder should have children who are believers. It is plain from verses 5 and 7 that "elders" and "overseers" are identical. (See our remarks on 1 Tim. 3 as to the word "bishop".)

An overseer is God's steward, and as such he is to take care of the church of God. Paul was God's steward of His mysteries, 1 Corinthians 4:1, and all believers are "stewards of the manifold grace of God", 1 Peter 4:10. In all such cases it is required that a steward be found faithful. Negative and positive characteristics are enumerated as qualifying for overseership. He must firmly hold the faithful word as he has been taught for the dual purpose, firstly, that he may be able to exhort in the healthful teaching, and, secondly, be able to convict the gainsayers. Any discrepancy between conduct and teaching will inevitably weaken the healthy influence of any who are placed as overseers in the church.

We have already learned that the love of money is a root of all kinds of evil. Therefore the overseer is reminded that he must be free of greed, because it is that very thing that results in the evils mentioned in verses 9, 10 and 11, where we read of profitless talking, deceptive teachings, activities which subvert whole houses, and right at the bottom of it all is a greed of "filthy lucre". The Jews, not content to dog the steps of Paul and to hinder his work, did not in his absence give up their nefarious activities. Acquainted as they were with a monotheistic religion, they could easily prey upon the early Christians who, of course, also believed in only one God. But their activities were characteristic of the race of the Cretans, one of whose prophets had described them as persistent liars, dangerous wild beasts, lazy gluttons (the quotation is from Epimenides - see also another quotation from the same context found in Acts 17:28a). Paul affirms this description to be true - he may well have had personal experience of it. Judaism and Christianity cannot mix, and these false teachers must not only have their mouths stopped, but they must also be sharply rebuked for their own benefit, so that they may be sound in the faith.

Reading between the lines, one can detect the kind of teachings which he has in mind: Jewish myths, commandments of men who turn away from the truth and add to the sacred Old Testament Scriptures such things as put men in needless bondage. They were teaching the gnostic errors alluded to in Colossians 2:22. They failed to understand that it is not what enters a man that defiles him, but what comes out from him. To these who are unbelieving and defiled nothing is pure; their mind and their conscience are defiled. There is a disconformity between their profession and their conduct, verse 16, and it is no wonder that Paul uses such strong words as these in this verse.

Titus 2

Christian Behaviour and its Effects

The key to this chapter is the English word 'that' (Greek: *hind*) found in verses 4, 5, 8,10,12,14.

Titus is to teach the aged men that they are to be sober (R.V., temperate), grave (or serious), sober minded (sensible), healthy in their personal *faith,* and in their *love* to others, and in their *patient endurance* of testing circumstances. He is to teach the aged women that their behaviour should be reverent, their tongue and their cravings should be controlled; they would thereby be able to teach good things, and to train the younger women to love their husbands, to love their children, to be workers at home, to be subject to their husbands, *in order that the word of God be not blasphemed*. In our present day these exhortations are urgently needed, for modern looseness has brought the Word of God into discredit. "If that's what your Bible teaches you, I don't think much of your Bible" is the retort of the ungodly when they witness disordered domestic life on the part of professing Christians. The Bible gets the blame.

We cannot here expand at undue length the scope and nature of women's ministry. We have already made comments on 1 Timothy 2 (which see). Also, in commenting on 1 Timothy 5, we referred to Phoebe, Lois, Eunice, Lydia, Mary, Dorcas and Persis. A study of these cases will show that the sphere of their work was in the home. It is significant that no woman is ever recorded as a preacher in the New Testament, nor did God use any woman to write any part of the Holy Scriptures. The present day clamour for the equality of the sexes overlooks the governmental arrangements of God. The head of the woman is the man, but this does not imply inequality, else what shall we say about the phrase "the head of Christ is God"? He was equal with God, but voluntarily accepted the subordinate place. The climate of the world is so apt to affect the climate of the churches, and outside clamours are apt to intrude inside. Let us beware.

The importance of sober-mindedness is manifested in that Paul reverts to it constantly (see 1 Tim. 2:9, 15; 3:2; 2 Tim. 1:7; Titus 2:2, 4, 5, 6, 12). We cannot do better than quote Trench on this word: "It is that habitual inner self-government, with its constant rein on all the passions and desires, which would hinder the temptation to these from arising, or at all events from arising in such strength as would overbear the checks and barriers which *aidos* (shamefastness) opposed to it" (Trench, *New Testament Synonyms*, Sec. xx end).

The younger men next come under review: Titus is to exhort them to be soberminded concerning all things - or maybe concerning all things should be attached to verse 7, "showing thyself an ensample of good works; in thy doctrine showing uncorruptness (a word that is the counterpart of "virgin"), gravity (self-respect, dignity), sound (or healthy) speech, that cannot be condemned; *that he that is of the contrary part may be ashamed,* having no evil thing to say of us (the apostle and Titus)", R.V.

Bond slaves are next dealt with. They must be subject to their masters (despots), in everything well-pleasing, not answering back, not pilfering, but showing utter fidelity so *that they may adorn the teaching of our Saviour God in all things,* verse 10 R.V. Instead, therefore, of giving men occasion to blaspheme it, they rather make it attractive to them, for their actions will speak much louder than any words that they may utter.

In verses 11 to 13 Paul speaks of two appearings: the appearing of the grace of God which brought salvation within the scope of all men, and the appearing of the glory of the great God and our Saviour, Jesus Christ, at His second advent. First "grace", then "glory", in accordance with Psalm 84:11, "The Lord will give grace and glory".

This "salvation" is not merely a deliverance from a future penalty but from the danger of the present life. God's grace not only shows us unmerited favour but it teaches us by discipline how to live. It was given *in order that having once and for all repudiated ungodliness* and worldly lusts (or passions, not necessarily gross, but all such desires as are essentially earthbound), we shall live soberly (selfward), righteously (relative to others) and godly (Godward) in this present age.

This salvation further gives the believer a hope. Like Simeon, Anna, and Joseph of Arimathea, Luke 2:25, 38; 23:51, he is "looking for ... the glorious appearing of the great God and our Saviour Jesus Christ". This phrase does not speak of two persons being governed by one definite article; it refers to our Lord Jesus Christ under the comprehensive phrase. Similarly there are not, it would appear, two items of the "hope", but we feel the phrase should read, "the blessed hope, even the appearing of the glory". The word "and" (Greek: *kai*) is better rendered "even" here, as the phrase "the appearing of the glory" more fully explains the earlier phrase "the blessed hope", and as with the other phrase the two words "hope" and "appearing" are governed by only one article.

Of the Lord Jesus it is said that He gave Himself for us, *in order that He might redeem us from all lawlessness,* and purify unto Himself a people for His own special possession zealous of good works.

The death of the Lord Jesus was voluntary; He "gave Himself". It was vicarious; "for us". It was purposive, in order to redeem us from all lawlessness negatively, and positively that He might cleanse or purify to Himself a peculiar people (who are) zealous of good works. The reader should consult Ephesians 5:25-27 and Hebrews 10:10-14 in connection with the sanctification of the believer.

All the foregoing directions Titus is to speak, not dictatorially but hortatively, and where necessary he is to reprove since he has apostolic authority so to do, should any challenge him. He must see that he gives no occasion for anyone to despise him.

Titus 3

The Christian and the State

The believer has been redeemed from all lawlessness, and he should be zealous of good works. He must, therefore, be subject both to the law of God and the law of man, however irksome he might find the Roman yoke. In our present times of labour unrest and strikes, these exhortations are specially relevant. Paul reminded the Romans of their duty in this regard, Romans 13, and Peter likewise reminded the believers to whom he wrote, 1 Peter 2:13-17. There should be subjection, obedience, a readiness to participate in what is essentially good (beneficial to men), to speak evil of none. Believers should not be quarrelsome but yielding and meek towards all men. In verses 3-7 Paul joins himself with these Cretan believers, and speaks of *(a)* their former state, *(b)* the discovery that they made, (c) the relief which it brought to them, and *(a)* the hope which they now possessed.

(a) *Their Former State.* This is stated in verse 3. Paul uses an emphatic "we", a pronoun which included himself and Titus, the Jew and the Gentile, the old and the young. Godward they were disobedient; selfward they were deceived, and enslaved; and manward they were malicious and envious, hateful and hating one another.

(b) The Discovery. This was the appearance of the kindness

and the love of God to man, verse 4; it had been mentioned in chapter 2:11. Contrary to the thoughts of the heathen, God's attitude to man is one of benignity and philanthropy (see Acts 27:3; 28:2). He is "God our Saviour".

(c) *The Relief Brought.* "According to His mercy He saved us." Negatively it was not according to our works done in righteousness, for as Paul had insisted everywhere and in all his writings, by the deeds of the law no flesh shall be justified before God. But positively it was "according to His mercy" of which Paul had spoken in 1 Timothy 1:16.

All three Persons of the Holy Trinity were engaged in this wonderful operation. It was God's love to man, for God is our Saviour. But He worked "through Jesus Christ our Saviour", verse 6, bringing about our regeneration by the Holy Spirit.

The phrase "washing of regeneration" implies the removal of the former state and the commencement of a new one. Similarly the "renewing of the Holy Spirit" is another way of saying, "Old things are passed away; behold, all things are become new", 2 Corinthians 5:17. The ideas in this verse are similar to that in John 3:5, and that passage appears to revert to Ezekiel 36:25-27 with which Nicodemus was expected to be well acquainted. Paul does not appear to be referring here to baptism when he speaks of the "washing of regeneration" (laver, R.V. marg,). The Holy Spirit was poured out, Acts 2:33; Romans 5:5, on the day of Pentecost by the Lord Jesus, Titus 3:6.

(d) *The Hope Received.* This is stated in verse 7. Our present state is that we are justified by His grace, a doctrine fully dealt with by Paul in his letters to the Romans and the Galatians. Our future prospect is that we are "heirs according to the hope of eternal life". Many Scriptures assure the believer that he is the present possessor of eternal life, but it is not yet manifest what we shall be. He hopes for its full manifestation in glory of which he is an heir.

Verse 8 appears to have in mind the contents of what has just preceded. Good works are to be maintained. This phrase "good works" is most comprehensive and embraces every aspect of life. The phrase, "they which have believed in God" (some omit the word "in"), alludes to their present attitude, not merely to a past event. They did believe and they continue so to do; God is the object of their faith.

If Titus teaches what Paul here enjoins, he will speak what is profitable, but he must avoid the various things named in verse 9, to which he has before alluded when writing to Timothy, 1 Timothy 1:4; 6:4, and which are unprofitable and pointless. Should anyone persist in a self-chosen idea or course he is to be admonished, and should he refuse the first admonition a second is to be administered. After that he is to be avoided, given the cold shoulder. This may not involve excommunication, though it may go on to that. The offender is "perverted" (a medical term for dislocated), verse 11 R.V. The word "heretic" refers to one who has chosen an idea or course which is not commonly acceptable to the company. It had not then acquired its modern meaning.

Nothing is known of Artemas, verse 12. There are several references to Tychicus, Acts 20:4; Ephesians 6:21; Colossians 4:7; 2 Timothy 4:12. Nothing certain is known of Zenas. Whether or not he was a Roman lawyer is not known. Much is known of Apollos as The Acts and the Corinthian letters reveal. "Set forward on their journey", verse 13 R.V., is a word of frequent use in The Acts and Epistles, denoting that the persons journeying are furnished with all things requisite. In this other believers besides Titus may share; the whole weight should not fall on his shoulders. Paul's example, Acts 20:35, may be compared with this verse. Cases of urgent need will not be hard to find, whether they are among the Lord's servants or His people. This "practical Christianity" is a pleasing fruit (see 2 Pet. 1:8; Phil. 1:11; 4:17; Col. 1:10).

All who were with Paul at that time saluted Titus. Who and where they were is not clear. Paul had a specially warm place for the saints in Crete who were affectionate towards him; he could wish that all were. But to these he sends a special greeting. Whether "faith" in verse 15 is subjective or objective is not certain; the A.V. favours the latter; the R.V. the former. Even so, Paul finishes his letter with the comprehensive words, "Grace be with you all". He will be no partisan, nor will he acknowledge any sectarianism (with which the word translated "heretic" has to do). His heart goes out towards them all.

Him That Endured

A Short Commentary on the Epistle to the Hebrews

Foreword

It is a privilege as well as a pleasure to be allowed to write a foreword to a book by Mr. E. W. Rogers, to whose ministry, both written and oral, one has been indebted for so many years. Those years have not diminished the author's gift for clear and succinct exposition, and for that careful comparison of Scripture with Scripture which is essential if the message of the Word is to be truly understood. In the ten chapters of this book, Mr. Rogers deals with the great themes of the Epistle to the Hebrews, and gives us guidance especially on those portions which have provided difficulties for some, in particular the warning passages of Chapters 5, 6, and 10. Most of all, however, he brings out the master theme of the Epistle, the Supreme Excellence of the Person of Jesus Christ our Lord, Son of God and Son of Man, Apostle and High Priest, Sacrifice and Servant, and exalted King: the One Who in His own Person and Work both surpasses and supersedes all that had gone before Him.

Wisely, as I think, Mr. Rogers deals only briefly with the unsolved and probably unsolvable question of human authorship, and on this and other debatable points he gives weighty and cogent reasons for his conclusions.

This book should prove a valuable guide to those who come to the serious study of the Epistle for the first time, and may well provide new insights for those who already know it well.

A. E. DALE

Introduction

Apostasy – the repudiation of one's faith – is an ever-present peril to the people of God, and the New Testament in many places warns us against it. 'Will ye also go away?' (John 6:67), asked the Lord, as He noticed many leaving Him because of His teaching. 'To whom shall we go?' replied Peter, 'Thou hast the words of eternal life'. Apostasy reveals the true state of the heart and makes manifest the unreality of the profession. As dogs return to their vomit, and sows to their wallowing in the mire (2 Peter 2:22), so do mere professors return to their former things, or even go to something worse. Those who, out of a pure heart, follow the Good Shepherd are genuine sheep, and should they, at times, wander they ultimately return to the Shepherd and Bishop of their souls (1 Peter 2:25).

The profession of one's faith must be tested to prove its genuineness. Faith is a precious thing, more precious indeed than perishable gold (1 Peter 1:7), and if gold is tried by the fire, who shall wonder that faith likewise is put into the fiery crucible to purge away the dross and leave the pure residue that is sterling in quality? Where there is genuineness there will be continuance, but not otherwise. Hence, both Paul (Col. 1:23) and the writer to the Hebrews use the word 'if' (Heb. 3:6, 14) when addressing those who regarded themselves as, and posed as, true believers. They say, 'We shall know whether you are true or false by whether you continue, or otherwise'. God's purpose is to 'present you holy and unblameable and unreproveable in His sight *if* you continue in the faith' (Col. 1:22-23). He cannot do otherwise.

The Epistle to the Hebrews warns against apostasy and gives means whereby professors may test themselves. Rightly understood, it affords the utmost encouragement to the people of God. Only when the eye of faith is diverted from Christ and becomes wholly occupied with self is it likely to create misunderstandings, and is assumed to support doctrines which are not in agreement with the general tenor of the rest of the New Testament.

This letter recognises the parallel truths of divine sovereignty and human responsibility. The will of God and the work of Christ relate to the former: the 'if' sections and hortatory parts have to do with the latter. Each must be given full weight and not be modified so as to accommodate the one to the other. Resting fully on the work of Christ, we may regard our eternal destiny as absolutely secure. But recognising the subjective duties of our faith, we should give heed to all that is here written touching continuance, holding fast, unbelief, and disobedience, lest it should prove that we have never had the root of the matter in us.

As, when the gospel is preached, the preacher should recognise that everything depends in one way on the work of God's Spirit, and in another way on his preaching and the response of his hearers, so in this other matter. In one way our eternal security depends solely on the effectiveness of the work of Christ, yet in another it depends likewise on our genuineness and continuance. We must prove 'ourselves' to see whether we are in the faith (2 Cor. 13: 5).

In no other letter is Christ more exalted than here: the sufficiency of His sacrificial death to make the sinner meet for the Holy Presence of God is crystal clear. Every encouragement is given to faith, but the sternest warnings are given as to the results of apostasy.

The following pages have been written with the desire to help in the understanding of this rich portion of Scripture. Difficult parts have not been avoided, though readers may not at first agree with the explanations given. Reasons for conclusions reached have been set out, and readers should 'prove all things; hold fast that which is good, and abstain from every appearance of evil' (1 Thess. 5:21-22). Yet let them not reach a hasty decision to reject what to them may be new. 'Consider what I say; and the Lord give thee understanding in all things' (2 Tim. 2:7).

My sincere thanks are due to Mr. David Ellis, B.D. and Dr James Naismith, M.D., who have very kindly gone through the manuscript carefully and made useful suggestions which have been adopted.

May God, in His rich mercy, be pleased to own this small endeavour to His glory.

E. W. ROGERS
Oxford,
England

Chapter 1

Authorship

The authorship of the Epistle to the Hebrews has received, perhaps, more consideration than that of most of the other books and epistles of the New Testament. Though some of these books contain no name of the original writer, no letter has given rise to more guesses and speculations than has that to the Hebrews. Many and diverse conclusions have been reached, though plainly only one of them can be right. Therefore, the present writer does not intend to offer any suggestion whatsoever; he does not know who wrote it; certainty is not attainable by any. An ancient writer has said: 'Who wrote it, God only knows.'

It is hardly necessary to remark that the heading of the Epistle, as shown in most A.V. Bibles, is not part of the original writing, and in this case assumes what cannot be proved, that Paul wrote it.

It seems as if God intended to allow this letter to remain anonymous because He wished to emphasise throughout that He is speaking. 'God Who *spake* ... hath at the end of these days *spoken*' (Heb. 1:1-2). 'See that ye refuse not Him that *speaketh*' (12:25). 'Today, if ye will hear *His voice*' (3:7). 'The *word* of God is living and active' (4:12 R.V.).

There is another reason for anonymity. The Lord Jesus is spoken of as 'the Apostle' as well as 'High Priest' (3:1), and it would, plainly, be inappropriate to introduce the name of another and lesser Apostle.

Furthermore, the quotations from the Old Testament in this Epistle, which, for the most part, are taken from the LXX,[1] are given without indicating the human author or the place in the canon where it is to be found. Now the writer was, surely, not ignorant of these things. He displays too much acquaintance with the Old Testament in general to suppose that he did not know the places from which he was quoting and who wrote them. The fact seems to be that the Spirit of God caused him to omit mentioning them, for the same reason, namely, to re-emphasise that, both in the Old Testament and 'in these last days', it is God speaking to man.

Some have assumed that 2 Peter 3:15 gives ground for supposing that Peter, who certainly wrote to the Hebrews, was affirming that Paul was the author of this letter to the Hebrews. But the words, 'as our beloved brother Paul also, according to the wisdom given unto him, hath written unto you', do not necessarily relate to this epistle. It is a mistake to suppose that all Paul's letters have been preserved for us. Stronger ground than that which this passage affords is required before we can attribute the Hebrews epistle to Paul.

Others suggest that the seed was sown when Stephen said

---

[1] The LXX (Septuagint) is the translation into Greek of Old Testament Hebrew Scriptures made two or three centuries before the birth of the Lord Jesus. In many places it paraphrases rather than translates, and by no means all the citations of the Old Testament in the New are taken from it. It is called the LXX because it is believed that a body of seventy men were engaged in its translation.

he saw Jesus 'at the right hand of God' (Acts 7:56), because our epistle frequently mentions this fact. But that is no proof of Paul's authorship. Other writers in the New Testament have mentioned this, and with no stronger plea the epistle might be attributed to any one of them.

Style, moreover, proves nothing. It is quite conceivable that two servants of God, writing in regard to Christian matters, be they personal, doctrinal or hortatory, should each adopt a similar style, seeing that both are writing on similar subjects.

If Paul were the author, it may pertinently be asked, why should he conceal his name and write anonymously? This was not his habit. In fact, he tells us that he signed all his letters. 'The salutation of Paul with mine own hand, which is the token in every epistle: so I write' (2 Thess. 3:17). More than that, it is not supposed that he would believe his letter should gain more acceptance with his national brethren if he omitted his name than if he inserted it. It is utterly unlike Paul to hide behind anonymity.

But suppose we knew who actually did write it: should we be much better off? We have the letter itself, which everywhere bears the hallmarks as having come from God. There can be no doubt of its divine inspiration and the justice of giving it a place in the canon of the New Testament. It covers a territory of truth which is dealt with by no other New Testament writer. We should suffer an irreparable and immeasurable loss were we deprived of it simply because we cannot trace it to one particular person.

Therefore, we leave the question of its authorship as it has wisely been left by others: we do not know who wrote it.

Chapter 2

The Aim of the Epistle

Though not specifically stated, it is everywhere apparent in the letter that those addressed are Jews who had accepted the Lord Jesus as their long-promised Messiah, although the nation had judged Him to be worthy of death. This resulted in persecution, confiscation of property, imprisonment, and what came little short of bloodshed (12:4; 10:32-34).

The attitude that they had adopted towards Jesus was one which virtually condemned their nation for rejecting Him and putting Him to death. They were on the side of Jesus, whom they owned as Lord: the nation was against Him.

This resulted in their being ostracised from their fellow nationals and their exposure to severe sufferings. In these circumstances, the temptation to recant and go back on their decision, and to return to their fold, is understandable. They might have argued that they did not suffer under Judaism, which was given by God through Moses, and attested by miracles. Why then should it be that they suffered under Christianity, which it was alleged was also given by God through Jesus, and likewise attested by miracles? Since both systems were apparently of divine origin, given through human agency, might they not revert to the former and so avoid suffering through adhering to the latter? Who, after all, could say which was the better of the two systems?

Hebrews Chapter 2, The Aim of the Epistle

The liability to apostatise was very real, and it was to prevent this that the letter was written. The genuineness of their faith would be proved by their continuance. The writer assumes their profession to be real. Nevertheless, it must be tested, and in this letter he gives means whereby they may know if they have the root of the matter in them.

The ritualistic system of Jerusalem, in vogue when the letter was written, does not form its background. The writer rather takes the Old Testament sacrificial and Aaronic priestly ordinances for that purpose, and, in particular, the ritual of the Day of Atonement. The ritual was, of course, substantially the same in each case, but the writer consistently refers to the Tabernacle and not to the Temple (9:11,21). The Tabernacle in the wilderness, and not the Temple in the land, is used by him to throw into relief the superior blessings of Christianity over against Judaism. He is writing to a pilgrim people, and what could be more suitable than to take the Tabernacle in the wilderness as his object lesson? They are Hebrews – passers over – going through the wilderness of this world to their heavenly country. They are strangers here. They, therefore, must guard against the twin evils of 'disobedience' ($ἀπείθεια$) and 'unbelief' ($ἀπιστία$).

And so, by comparing and contrasting the Levitical system with the new order of Christianity, he shows the superiority of the latter to the former. He constantly employs such words as 'better' (7:22; 8:6), 'substance' (10:34), 'eternal' (9:12,14), 'more excellent' (8:6), and 'greater' (9:11).

Replying to the taunt of their adversaries that they had nothing visible or tangible - that they had no priest, temple, sacrifice, or altar - the writer repeatedly uses the words 'we have' (8:1; 4:15), showing that, though in one way these taunts were correct, yet the believers were not without the spiritual counterparts of these visible things, which, after all, are vastly superior.

He urges them to recognise that all they had was held by faith, and that faith has to do with eternal and invisible realities. The visible was soon to pass away by judgment, as was bitterly experienced when Titus ransacked the city of Jerusalem and destroyed its Temple. What they had, however, could not be lost.

This letter differs from others in the New Testament, as might be expected. For example, Romans is occupied with showing the reader how guilty criminals may be pardoned; Hebrews shows how those pardoned criminals have constant right of access to the throne of God. Romans tells how the guilty may get out of the criminal court; Hebrews shows how they may even have entrance into the Holiest of all. Romans has to do with the unsaved; Hebrews with those who are already saved. Romans is occupied with the sinner; Hebrews with the people of God. Romans tells how redemption may be obtained, but Hebrews assumes that the people are already redeemed. Romans begins from Exodus 12; Hebrews from Exodus 24. Not often do we hear of pardoned criminals being welcomed into the royal palace, but it is so here.

Other contrasts may be drawn. For example, the letter to the Ephesians envisages the believer as being already seated with Christ in the heavenlies, but Hebrews regards him as still travelling through a wilderness.

The mistake of the Galatians was that they were seeking to alloy the gospel – mixing up together law and grace, works and faith, the flesh and the Spirit. That was not the case with the Hebrews. The mistake they were apt to make was to abandon grace, faith, and the Spirit's work altogether, and to revert to law, works and carnal ordinances. Their danger was apostasy, not corruption.

But would they really give up the substance, the blessings of the gospel, the realities behind all their Levitical types and shadows, in order to secure a little worldly comfort? Whoever heard of anyone giving up the substance of anything in order to have merely its shadow? Yet that is precisely what they were liable to do!

The General Argument

The supremacy of the Lord Jesus, the Son, over angels is first considered in Chapter 1. This was important, for the Jews held angels in high repute: they figured largely in their ancient national history. For example, the law was given by the administration of angels, but the Son of God is infinitely their superior.

Chapter 2 continues in a like strain, only here the emphasis is on the Manhood of Christ, whereas in Chapter 1 it is on His deity. The 'habitable world to come' has not been subjected to angels, but to 'Man'. This is not a little startling, since man was originally made a little lower than angels. Moreover, man does not seem to be master of creation now, whatever may have been the position of the first man. The whole question is discussed in Chapter 2.

Here, then, is One who is both God and Man. In this He stands altogether unique, 'Jesus, the Son of God'. It follows then that none of the heroes of Hebrew history, however illustrious, could be compared with Him. He is without a peer, He stands alone, for He embodies in Himself two whole and perfect natures, full deity and full and real humanity. Many of these heroes are brought forward in this letter with a view to showing the excellency of Christ over each one of them. Could these Hebrews, then, even entertain the idea of abandoning such an One as Christ in favour of adherence to a system that had to do with these much lesser lights?

Chapters 3 and 4 draw lessons from the failures of Israel in the wilderness. They fell and did not attain to the 'rest' which was before them. These Hebrews must guard against the same peril.

At Hebrews 4:15, the writer resumes what he had incidentally mentioned in Hebrews 2:17 – the High Priesthood of Christ. He discusses it at length until the end of Chapter 8. From Hebrews 9:1 to 10:18, he is concerned with the one great final sacrifice, showing that in Christ the Old Testament sacrificial system had its complete fulfilment, with far better benefits. The rest of the epistle is largely hortatory, with some warnings. Chapter 13 is not, as some have supposed, unrelated to the main argument: it is not by a different hand. Indeed, it rather sums up the argument in the words, 'Let us, therefore, go forth to Him outside the camp, bearing His reproach'. The Hebrews were in danger of returning to the camp of Judaism, by which they hoped to escape the reproach attaching to Christianity, not recognising that the former was effete.

The practical bearing of this letter for us Gentiles, and for our present times, is important. If the earthly organised and ritualistic religion of Judaism, which was in the first instance ordained by God, and was the only such thing ever owned by Him, is now superseded, what shall we say of the camp of Christless Christendom? It is but an amalgamation of effete Judaism with corrupt paganism: that which once was divinely sanctioned, with that which at no time had any such sanction. 'Let us, therefore, go forth to Him outside the camp' (Heb. 13:13).

Chapter 3

God Speaks in His Son - Hebrews 1-2:4

Chapter 1 should really end at the fourth verse of chapter 2.

We quote with comments these four verses: 'Wherefore we ought to give the more earnest heed to the things that were heard, lest haply we drift away from them. For if the word spoken through angels proved steadfast (that is, the law of Moses ordained through angels - Gal. 3:19) and every transgression (sin of commission) and disobedience (sin of omission) received a just recompense of reward (and the man who gathered sticks on the Sabbath day was stoned - Num. 15:32-36), how shall we escape (the penalty of a broken law) if we neglect (disregard, make light of) so great a salvation (from that penalty), which having at the first been spoken through the Lord (as recorded in the four Gospels) was confirmed unto us by them that heard (that is, by the Apostles), God also bearing witness with them both by signs and wonders (such as the healing of the lame man at the entrance of the temple - Acts 3:2ff), and by manifold powers, and by gifts of the Holy Ghost according to His own will?' These signs, wonders and miracles, having now served their confirmatory and validating purpose, are no longer to be expected (Mark 16:20; Heb. 2:4). Christianity has received adequate divine authentication once and for all. There would be no point in continuing these miracles.

Hebrews Chapter 3, God Speaks in His Son

It will be seen that there are three levers which the writer employs on the fulcrum of his argument. In view of (*a*) the dignity of the speaker, (*b*) the finality of the message, and (*c*) the nature of the offer, they are duty bound to give more attention than they ordinarily gave to the things heard, lest they should drift away from them. 'Drifting away' would be 'apostasy'; 'neglecting so great salvation' is ceasing to be interested in it, while, at the same time, professing a nominal adherence to it. They must beware against drifting under the influence of adverse tides, lest the place of safety be hopelessly lost. If they 'hold fast to the end', well and good, but if they neglect it and drift back to a legal system, there can be no escape from the righteous penalty due to infringement of the Mosaic law. Let us consider Chapter 1 and see how the matter is argued.

Old Testament prophets were but channels: they were neither authors nor commentators. They were reporters, transmitting a message from a higher authority. 'Thus saith the Lord' (e.g. Jer. 13:1), 'the word of the Lord came unto me' (Jer. 2:1), was often on their lips. Sometimes, too, God spoke by dreams (Gen. 37), visions (Isa. 1:1), wall-writing (Daniel 5), or in other ways. At times He came in an appearance - a theophany - (Gen. 18), but at no time was His revelation complete. It was 'by divers portions' - here a little and there a little; line upon line, precept upon precept (Isa. 28:10). There was always something more to be added until the times of Malachi, when the canonical prophetic word ceased.

But now, 'at the end of these days', or, as expressed in another epistle, 'when the fulness of the time had come' (Gal. 4:4), God has spoken all His mind, not piecemeal nor in a variety of ways, but 'in' One who is 'Son'. Note the aorist – $\dot{\epsilon}\lambda\dot{\alpha}\lambda\eta\sigma\epsilon\nu$ – He spoke, a completed action. He has no more to say; His word is final. The word 'Son' here is *anarthrous* (used without the article), as also elsewhere in the letter (Heb. 5:8), and therefore it is best to regard it as a proper noun and we should spell it with an initial capital S. The force is, 'such an One as Son', and not a mere prophet. The title has a unique significance in which none others can have part, even though the word 'son' is sometimes used of them (Gal. 3:26; 4:6-7).

In His case, 'Son' connotes equality with the Father, as John 5:18ff clearly shows, where this equality is both affirmed and proven by the Lord. We must not import into the word 'Son' those ideas which relate to human generation, juniority, dependence. In His case, it denotes co-existence. He is co-eternal and co-equal with the Father. This is, indeed, implied in what follows: He ever is (ὤν) the effulgence of God's glory, just as the sunbeam and the sun are inseparable. He ever is (ὤν) the impress of His substance (R.V.), just as the wax impression corresponds exactly and always to the seal which made it. In all respects there is equality, and that eternally.

'In Son' means Son-wise; not only what was spoken by the Son, but that He Himself is God's full and final message to man. His being, nature, work, position, and all else that relates to Him, is God's message to man. It was perilous to have ignored God's word through His prophets; how much more when it is spoken in the Highest of all. To refuse to listen to the Queen's envoy would be serious, but to refuse to listen to the Queen herself would be far worse and more dangerous. So, to refuse to listen to God in His Son is to incur an inescapable judgment.

We have said that God has no more to say. This does not mean that there were no more inspired writings to be given after the Lord Jesus had returned to heaven, but all New

Testament writings (every one of which was written after His ascension) are written communications pertaining to the wonderful glories to be found in the Son. This, indeed, is the force of 'In Son', for in these writings not only are we reminded of the sayings of Jesus in the days of His flesh, and not only does the Spirit take of His present 'things' (John 16:14) and show them to us, but He also shows us 'things to come' (John 16:13), pertaining to His future manifested glories.

But there is more. The writer calls attention to the greatness of His Person, and that in relation to the universe. Scientists are constantly exploring the universe, but its infinity defies them, as it ever will. The heavens above cannot be measured, nor can the depths of the earth beneath be searched by man (Jer. 31:37). Man asks if matter is eternal, or how did it all come to be in the first instance? How is it being kept in such amazing order, coordinated with such exact precision, functioning harmoniously despite the multiplicity of its several parts? To whom does it belong? To man, or to whom? What is His name? Can He be found by searching?

Our writer replies, 'By whom also He made the worlds'. The word he uses is $αἰῶνας$, which is sometimes translated 'ages': it has to do with the time-state in this matter world. The N.E.B. translates it, 'all orders of existence'. It denotes the universe. Elsewhere we read, 'All things were made by Him' (John 1:3); and again, 'By Him were all things created, that are in heaven and that are in earth, visible and invisible' (Col. 1:16). He was the great Originator in Creation. Not only so, He 'upholds all things by the word – $ῥῆμα$ - of His power' or, as elsewhere we read, 'By Him all things consist' - $συνέστηκεν$, hold together (Col. 1:17). 'He spake and it was done' (Psa. 33:9); He now speaks, and by His word the whole universe ($τά\ πάντα$)

works harmoniously. Seasons follow each other in proper sequence: day follows night; tides ebb and flow; the earth and other bodies revolve on their axes and go round in their orbits without mishap or collision. Creation in all the infinity of its marvellous detail, with its apparently contradictory laws, such as the centripetal and centrifugal forces, works together as a united whole. God has appointed His Son, moreover, to be 'heir of' it all. It all belongs to Him: 'All things were created by Him and for Him' (Col. 1:16). 'For Thy pleasure they are, and were, created' (Rev. 4:11). Men and nations seek to acquire as much of earth's territory as they can. Wars of aggression for territorial aggrandisement have stained human history; man forgets that the Lord Jesus is the rightful and eternal Owner of it all, and that the day will come when He will enforce His rights.

Did these Hebrews apprehend His dignity? His humble birth, poverty, and death as a felon were known to them. They knew, too, of His vindication in resurrection. But did they realise, in fact, Who He was? Did they know He was before and above all the limitless universe? Sun, moon, stars, and all else are His. The recent amazing discoveries of the immensity of the universe only add glory to Him Who planned and brought the whole into existence.

Yet note another thing. The perfection of His work is stated thus: 'When He had made purification[1] of sins, He sat down on the right hand of the Majesty on High'. There was no seat provided in the Tabernacle of old, for, as the letter plainly shows, the High Priest's work on earth was never done. He was 'standing daily', but the Lord Jesus, having 'finished the work' that God had given Him to do (John 17:4), said, 'It is

---

[1] 'Made' has a peculiar reflexive force here – 'having done it for Himself' (JND). See his full note at this verse in the New Testament.

finished' (John 19:30), and then He took His own seat in heaven at the place of honour beside the Majesty on High.

The background of this, as we have already remarked, is the Day of Atonement, when the priest went outside the camp and burned to ashes the sin offering, and then into the holiest of all with its blood (Lev. 16). But he never sat down. Yet the Lord Jesus, having once and for all made purification of sins 'outside the gate', has now taken His seat in heaven. That part of His work is done.

The R.V. omits 'by Himself' and not without authority, yet some would insert it. Even though the words lack adequate support to justify inclusion, yet the fact is that He alone could do this work. *'There was none other good enough to pay the price of sin; He only could unlock the gate of heaven and let us in.'* As on the Day of Atonement no one but the High Priest was allowed to enter the most holy place, so none but Christ could make purgation of sins. He said to Peter, 'Whither I go, thou canst not follow Me now' (John 13:36). In that work He was in His loneliness as a sparrow on a housetop, as a pelican in the wilderness (Ps. 102:6-7).

But there is more in the verb even than this. It is what grammarians call reflexive, and means that the work was done in His own interests in order to satisfy His own rightful claims and gracious desires. He did it 'by or for Himself'; not that He had any need of cleansing, but to carry into effect those delights of grace which had been eternally purposed. He removed sin by the sacrifice of Himself.

Thus we are presented at the outset of the letter with the glories of Christ, His unique relationship, His essential greatness, and the perfection of His work. The writer further adds that in His Post-incarnate and risen state He is 'become so much better than angels', which was in keeping with what He had eternally been, the possessor of a 'more excellent name than they'.

This introduces the contrasts which are made between Christ and the angels, with the aid of seven Old Testament Scriptures (Ps. 2:7; 2 Sam. 7:14; Deut. 32:43; Ps. 45:6-7; 104:4; 102:25-27; 110:1). 'He maketh His angels spirits, and His ministers a flame of fire', for angels are what they are *made*, but the Son eternally *is*. 'Thou art My Son': He was not made. So far above angels is He that 'all the angels of God worship Him'. He is infinitely superior to them all. He is God, Lord, The Same.

'Thou art My Son, this day have I begotten Thee' is cited three times in the New Testament (Acts 13:33; Heb. 1:5; 5:5). In each case His incarnation is in view. Paul at Antioch cites it, not, be it noted, of His resurrection, but in support of the bringing into the race of Israel a Saviour for them. God had from time to time raised up deliverers for them when they were in trouble, and this is their great Final Deliverer. In Hebrews 5:5, the passage is again cited, in relation to His High Priesthood in heaven; and the third citation is the one before us, which stands closely linked with His future advent, a second time to this world. The 'begetting' refers, it would seem, to His incarnation, of which Gabriel spoke to Mary (Luke 1:26; see also Matt. 1:20) in words which command nothing but our wonder and worship. It would seem to be altogether inappropriate to relate them to what has been called an 'eternal begetting' (whatever that may mean), or to His resurrection, which is never so spoken of, that is, His 'being made alive' after His death.

The word, 'I will be to Him a Father, and He shall be to Me a Son', was spoken, in the first instance, to David regarding his son Solomon (2 Sam. 7:14). It is brought in here to emphasise the fact that the Lord Jesus is Son, and ever will be. He was when He first came; He is now, now that He is in heaven; and when He comes forth as the true Solomon to establish His earthly Kingdom, He will even then be Son. Of course, being a relationship of life and nature, it could not be otherwise.

But this is not His only name. He is addressed as God, and as Lord - titles which show beyond a shadow of doubt that deity was His eternally. These names could never be applied to angels, nor to men.

Over and above all this, He is King and His throne is 'for ever and ever'. The Hebrews knew that the mighty empires of the Hittites, Egyptians, Babylonians, Medo-Persians, and Greeks had all passed away. The then existing Roman Empire was destined also to vanish, as indeed has since come to pass; but, 'Thy throne, O God, is for ever and ever'. Creation itself, the heavens and the earth originally founded and made by His hands, will perish and, when they have served their purpose, will be rolled up as a worn-out garment and exchanged. But the Son is constant. His years fail not. These believing Hebrews belonged to a 'kingdom that cannot be moved' (Heb. 12:28). Would they, then, now withdraw, even though their faith brought them suffering?

One thing more. Changes will pass over creation, 'But Thou art the same, and Thy years shall not fail.' He is 'Jesus Christ, the same yesterday, and today, and for ever' (Heb. 13:8). This surely was a comfort to these believers who were suffering so much for their faith. They had lost many an erstwhile friend, who in fact had so changed as to become their enemy, but in Christ they had an unchangeable Friend.

In view of all this - the perfection of His work, the endless duration of His throne, and the unchangeableness of His character - how could they secede from Him? How could they revert to that which was so incomplete and transient? How could they abandon the eternal for the temporary, the complete for the partial, the perfect for the imperfect? His cause is sure to triumph: 'Sit on My right hand until I make Thine enemies the footstool of Thy feet'. This was never at any time said to angels. They stand and wait His bidding; they are ministering spirits sent forth by Him on behalf of those who are about to inherit salvation in all its blessed fulness. This is not an allusion to death, but to the sure end of the wilderness journey for God's redeemed people. In view of this, it may be asked, How could they contemplate throwing their lot in again with His enemies? Had not Israel been guilty of His death?

He unites in Himself offices which, in Israel's past days, were found in separate persons. He is at one and the same time Prophet, Priest, and King. As Prophet, He came out from God and spoke to men. As Priest, He enters into the presence of God and acts for men. As King, He will yet reign and enforce His rights in the earth. For all these offices He is morally fitted. He loved righteousness and hated lawlessness. His path of obedience brought Him more sorrow than any other ever had known, but God has anointed Him with the oil of gladness above His fellows. He has more joy than any of them. The Psalmist (45:6-7), whose words are here quoted, was thinking of the royal honours which He will have and which will exceed those of any other of earth's monarchs. But this epistle goes further and shows these 'fellows' to be those who, by faith, have cast their lot in with Him in the time of His rejection. Whatever sorrow they had, He knew deeper. Whatever joy they have, or will yet have, He has greater.

To sum up: In this first chapter the writer passes in review the glories of the Son of God, His unique relationship, the greatness of His person, the perfection of His work, the duration of His throne, the immutability of His character, the sure triumph of His cause. They ought certainly to give Him heed, for none could be greater.

Chapter 4

What is Man? - Hebrews 2:5-18

In His eternal deity, the superiority of the Lord Jesus to angels has been clearly demonstrated in Chapter 1. They all worship the Son; they are servants of the saints; their work was altogether different from that of the Son. He procured salvation; they are servants of those who will inherit it. In all respects, He is greater.

Even in manhood He is superior to them. This is the subject of Chapter 2. The habitable world to come is not to be subjected to angels, but to Him. Reference has already been made to this habitable world (οἰκουμένη)[1] and now it is taken up again. The administration of this 'world to come' is not entrusted to angels, but to Man in the Person of the Son – to Jesus. Daniel 10 teaches us that angels have much to do with earth's affairs at present, but the millennial age will not be administered by them, but by a Man who is also God's Son. God will then bring again[2] His first begotten into the habitable world and entrust

---

[1] Οἰκουμένη: 'habitable world', an almost technical prophetic word of the world in the age to come. Some take this to refer to the present order of Christianity, but this does not seem tenable in Heb. 2:5, whichever way we read Heb. 1:6.

[2] 'When He bringeth again.' It is only fair to say that translators are not agreed as to where, in English, to place the word 'again', whether it relates to a further citation, or whether it relates to a 'second' bringing into the world of the Lord Jesus. The present writer favours the R.V. text: the matter is of very little consequence: it does not affect the general argument.

all into His hands. This title 'First begotten' denotes priority and superiority. He then will be seen to be 'the First' of all, as well as infinitely greater than all.

Psalm 8 is cited. As we have earlier remarked, it is quoted anonymously, for the reason that God is the speaker throughout, whoever the human author was. It is not the mere expression of David's ideas, though they are his words. In one sense they express what David felt and thought, but the record of them is God's voice to man. It goes beyond David's experience. It is possible that this Psalm had in mind David's resounding victory over Goliath. He was then as but a 'babe and suckling' in his own eyes, and Goliath was 'the enemy and the avenger'. But David's words to him are never-to-be-forgotten. Through him, God had made His name excellent in all the earth. David then ponders. Many a night, when keeping the sheep, he looked at the moon and stars of heaven and wondered why God should have put them there. They certainly did help him to see at night when the wild beasts emerged from their dens and sought their prey. Plainly, they were there as a help to man, and specially to such as he, a shepherd. How else could he have spotted the wild beasts in the darkness of night and saved the flock from their ravages? But that raises the question: What is man that God should think of him, and, as one interested in his well-being, thus visit him? In kindness to man He has put night lights in the heaven. What then *is* man? The answer is a matter of fact: man is the highest order of God's creation, the chief part of the dust of the earth. Adam stood as God's vicegerent and everything in the air, on land, and in the waters was put under him. The crown of authority was once on his head. All had been brought to him to name. He then ruled under God as supreme.

God excepted nothing from his domain. 'All things' were put in subjection to man, yet we do not *now* see all things so. Something calamitous has happened. The flying eagle, the wild beast of the earth, and the sea monsters all seem to be in rebellion against their erstwhile head. These were not originally excepted from man's domain. Due to sin, the crown of authority has fallen from the head of the first man, and creation itself has been made subject to vanity; not willingly, but by reason of Him who subjected the same (Rom. 8:20).

Yet there is hope, for the 'second man' has come, the 'last Adam', the Lord from heaven. 'Jesus' - the name of His manhood[3]; the name which, wherever it stands alone as frequently it does in this epistle, is designed to emphasise His humanity - has restored all that the first man lost. He 'was made a little lower than the angels', that is, both temporarily and positionally: for a little while and to a little extent. He was not lower essentially or morally, for angels worshipped Him at His birth and ministered unto Him when on earth (Matt. 4:11; Luke 2:13). But by coming into Manhood He experienced what no angel could ever experience. He hungered, thirsted, slept, was weary, suffered pain, wept, and indeed died. These things no angel could ever know, but He shared them in common with man. He did not share man's sin, but being real man He shared the concomitants of manhood. When He became man He did not cease to be God, but conjoined with His deity another full and perfect nature, that of humanity; real in every way, for He had human spirit, soul, and body (Luke 22:43).

---

[3] It is to be deplored that the name of 'Jesus' alone is used by modern writers without adding the title 'Lord'. The apostle Paul was consistent: 'As the Lord Jesus said, It is more blessed to give...'. And, 'The Lord Jesus, the night in which He was betrayed...'. It is strange that modern writers are careful to give the prefix 'St.' to Paul and others, to which they are not specially entitled, and yet do not give the title 'Lord' to Jesus, to Whom it is due.

'Since then the children (that is, the children of Abraham, believers) are sharers (in common with each other) in blood and flesh (possibly put in this order because the Fall is not here in view: flesh had not primacy before sin entered), He also in like manner (or closely corresponding to) partook (a voluntary action) of the same.' All others were passive in the matter of their birth: they had no choice of race, or place, or date. But He was active throughout, and His entrance into humanity was His own act. He came into the world to save sinners (1 Tim. 1:15). 'The Son of Man came, not to be ministered unto, but to ... give His life a ransom for many' (Matt. 20:28). He elected to change both His position and His condition, to leave heaven and to come to earth, to manifest His deity in humanity. He elected the time of His birth, His race, nation, tribe, family, place of birth, and all else. None other ever did this.

'Partakers' and 'took part of' (Heb. 2:14 A.V.) are apt to mislead. They do not sufficiently clearly throw into relief the passive state of the human race at birth, and the voluntary entrance into that race of the Son of God.

The 'likeness' was real in all respects, though there was a vital difference between Him and all others of the human race. The word translated 'likewise' indicates this: it is a cognate word being elsewhere translated 'nigh unto' (Phil. 2:27). Jesus was God manifest in flesh: His human nature was free from all taint of sin. In this respect He was different from all. Indeed, the very beginning of His humanity was different from that of all others; yet it was real, for He 'was made in all things like unto His brethren' (Heb. 2:17). Plainly this excludes sin, for sinnership is not part of human nature; it is something which invaded it from without after it came into being. Yet this likeness includes all those experiences of life on earth which are common to man. It was essential that He should become man, for only by coming into such a state could He become a merciful and faithful High Priest in things pertaining to God on behalf of His brethren.

The writer enumerates various reasons for all this in Chapter 2, and we may set them out as follows:

Reason 1. *'Because of the suffering of death.'* Not merely death, but all that was involved in it, mental and physical: death in the fullest sense of the word. Some read, 'Because of the suffering of death, crowned ...', whilst others read, 'made a little lower than angels because of the suffering of death'. Both are grammatically tenable, as well as true. He was born with the intention that He should die. It was the main object of His coming, for, as has been well said, Bethlehem without Calvary would be a mockery. In this He was unique. He came to give His life a ransom for many. Not that He would 'kill Himself' (John 8:22), but His death was a commandment that He had received from His Father (John 10:18). It was the main, though not the final, goal of His earthly life, for 'on account of the suffering of death' He is now 'crowned as a victor with glory and honour', being in heaven clothed with garments of 'glory and beauty'.

It is just possible that 'crowned with glory and honour' relates to Him in the days of His flesh, for even then He stood as God's vicegerent in His creation, wearing the crown of authority which Adam, by sin, had forfeited. He then displayed His authority over the wild beasts of the field (Mark 1:13) and the fish of the sea (Matt. 17:27) as well as the tempestuous waters and the winds of heaven (Matt. 14:24ff). All creation was at His feet and subserved His will.

Verse 9, then, would seem to admit of two possible meanings in the writer's mind. Some think the word 'behold' (R.V.) should determine the question, for they consider it has to do with the present glory of Christ in heaven, which by faith the Hebrews could then see, and we now, though neither they nor we may have known Christ in the days of His flesh. But the context appears to require the reference to be related to the days of His flesh.

Reason 2. *'That by the grace of God He should taste death for every man.'* The word 'man' is wanting in the original, and some supply 'thing' instead. The latter, of course, includes the former. Through the death of Christ, God has ensured the recovery of fallen creation as well as making it possible for the sinner. When the 'sons of God' are manifested then the creation itself will be delivered from the bondage of corruption and be brought into the liberty of the glory of the children of God (Rom. 8:21). The lion will eat straw like the ox, and the wolf and the lamb will lie down together (Isa. 11:6ff; Isa. 35); war will be no more (Micah 4:3) – all this will flow from the fact that 'He tasted death for everything'. The death of Christ is as a stone thrown into the pond of creation, affecting every part of it from centre to circumference. In this God has acted in sovereign grace, for, manifestly, if sinful man had received the just recompense of his deeds and no grace had been shown to him, recovery would be out of the question. And how can creation be restored unless its rightful head is first restored?

Reason 3. *'That through death He might put out of action him that hath the power of death, that is, the devil.'* Just as David first stunned Goliath and then beheaded him with his own sword, so the Lord Jesus silenced the devil when he tempted Him, and later by His own death ensured the ultimate doom of the devil. Death is the wages of sin, and therefore the Lord Jesus, being sinless, was under no necessity to die. But He did so willingly and in accordance with the command that He had received from His Father. The empty grave demonstrates the conquest of the devil by his own weapon, for he it was who was responsible for bringing death into our world. Whatever he is allowed to do in this present age (for note the tense – 'him that hath the power of death') his incarceration in the abyss and final consignment to the lake of fire are assured by the victory of Calvary.

Reason 4. *'And deliver them who through fear of death were all their lifetime subject to bondage.'* The background seems still to be that of Israel trembling before their foes, and the triumphant victory of the historic David. That victory relieved all Israel from fear of bondage to the Philistines. So, too, the death of Christ delivers from the fear of death. In consequence of this, we read such things as Stephen saying, 'Lord Jesus, receive my spirit' (Acts 7:59). Paul spoke of his death as, 'departing to be with Christ; which is very far better' (Phil. 1:23); as being 'absent from the body, and at home with the Lord' (2 Cor. 5:8). Peter calls his death an 'exodus' (2 Pet. 1:15 Gk); an emancipation, much as Israel left the brick kilns of Egypt for a land flowing with milk and honey (Exo. 3:8). The Lord Jesus has now 'the keys of Hades and of death' (Rev. 1:18), and in His own due time both will have to yield to Him all they retain.

Before the cross it was far otherwise, and one has only to read the moanings of men like Job (Job 14) or Hezekiah (Isa. 38) to realise what death meant for them. Both regarded death as being the end of all joy; they did not possess the glorious light of the gospel on such a sad subject. It is all so different now that the Saviour's tomb is empty.

Reason 5. *'That He might be a merciful and faithful High Priest in things pertaining to God.'* In order that many sons might be brought to glory it was requisite that the Captain ($ἀρχηγός$) of their salvation should be fully qualified[4] to act on their behalf whilst they are on the journey thither. He must, therefore, have trodden the same path and have gone through the whole range of human experience, feeling in Himself the consequences of human sin, though never being tainted with it. He and they are 'all of one' group ($ἐξ\ ἑνός$). He is the sanctifier and they are the sanctified. They belong to the human race and He entered it also. Consequently, He is not ashamed to call them brethren.

Three Old Testament quotations are cited in support of this. As dependent Man He says, 'I will put My trust in Him' (cf Isa. 8:17). He declares God's name to His brethren: in the midst of the congregation He leads the praises (Ps. 22:22); He regards His brethren as 'children that God has given to Him' (Isa. 8:18). The Lord Jesus often made allusion to these in that way, as is clearly seen in John 17:2, 6, 9, 11, 24.

Whatever were the thoughts of the Hebrews touching angels, it was apparent that the Lord Jesus does not undertake their cause, but He has espoused the cause of the 'seed of Abraham'. This seed is the faithful: those who, like the Hebrews, have put their trust in Him. He did not become an angel in order to help angels, but He became man in order to restore men.

Moreover, it was His humanity which made it possible for

---

[4]$τελειόω$ (to make perfect) does not imply moral perfection of the Lord Jesus: there was no need for that in His case. But the word has to do with qualifying a person to enable him to fill a particular office. As a medical student must pass through all the stages of training requisite to enable him to practise as a doctor, so the Lord Jesus had to pass through all the requisite experiences of humanity to enable Him to function as a High Priest on behalf of men.

Him to 'become a merciful and faithful High Priest', dispensing mercy to us and being faithful not only to God who had appointed Him to the office, but also to us whom He represents before Him.

Verse 16 should read as shown in the R.V. It is the present tense and denotes what the Lord is now doing. He is championing the cause of the seed of Abraham before God. The ground of it is, of course, His completed work at the cross, which enables Him to be a priest 'seated on the right hand of the Majesty on high'. The A.V. is astray here. It is not His taking human nature that is in view, but His dealing with the case of those in need.

Reason 6. *'To make propitiation for the sins of the people.'* The sense really is, 'with a view to making, etc.' (εἰς τὸ). While His work on earth was done - as He said, 'It is finished' when He bowed His head and gave up the ghost - His work in heaven is continuing. Propitiation, or atonement (the corresponding Hebrew word is *kaphar*, frequently used in the Old Testament in this sense)[5] is a work now being done by the Lord in heaven. It is priestly work. It is consequent upon the killing of the sin offering outside the camp. The offerer under the Levitical economy could not offer the blood because he was a sinner; the priest must do that. But the Lord Jesus, being 'holy, harmless and undefiled', was not only both 'offerer' and 'offering', but He now has gone inside the veil as High Priest also, in virtue

---

[5]It is a mistake to say that 'Atonement' is not a New Testament doctrine. Sins, as well as their penalty, in the Old Testament times were not merely covered, they were actually removed, cancelled, lifted off. The equivalent of the Hebrew word *kaphar* in the LXX is ἱλάσκομαι. Vine's *Dictionary of New Testament Words* says: 'The corresponding New Testament words are ἱλασμός propitiation, 1 John 2:2; 4:10; and ἱλαστήριον mercy seat, Romans 3:25 and Heb. 9:5.'

of His own blood (not 'with it' - an altogether too materialistic notion). The whole period from the time He entered heaven until He later comes out is the 'Day of Atonement'. He there 'makes propitiation'; that is to say, His very presence there is the ground on which God can, in grace, deal righteously with His people, and yet show mercy in respect of their sins.

Sir Robert Anderson has rightly said, 'In Scripture, making atonement is priestly work, following and based upon a sacrificial death'. The words of the Lord Jesus uttered on the cross, 'It is finished', should not be construed to mean more than that the basic work for atonement was then finished. To say 'atonement' was completed then would assume atonement without death; for He said, 'It is finished' *before* He died. Those words indicate, as one hymn-writer has put it, that 'His work *on earth* is done', and He, therefore, could bow or recline His head (John 19:30 κλίνας). But atonement could not have been completed apart from the resurrection and ascension of Christ. It is inconceivable that there could have been atonement otherwise. He Himself is the 'atonement offering' for our sins. John does not say He *was*, but He *is* (1 John 2:2), which is in full accord with what we have in this epistle, in which He is seen as at present seated in heaven, acting as a High Priest, His earthly work admitting of no repetition. But that work was an initial and essential part of a whole; it was not the end.

The three stages must never be separated: the work outside the camp on the Day of Atonement; the work inside the veil whither the High Priest went with the blood; and His coming out with blessing for the waiting people. In fact, the incarnation, sinless life, sacrificial death, triumphant resurrection and ascension in glory, and His present priestly work, are all of one piece; not one thing can be separated from another without doing damage to the whole.

From verse 17 we learn that His High Priestly work is not restricted to the weaknesses of His people, as has been supposed by some. Chapter 4:15 shows clearly that it has to do with them; but it has also to do with sins. It is the 'sins of the people' that are in view here: sins committed in the wilderness after 'redemption' from Egypt has been experienced. Thus this aspect of His priesthood is almost identical with His advocacy of which John writes. Both are concerned with sins: the one of the people, and the other of the children of God. Of course, 'the people' and 'the children' are the same persons.

But not only so. This Great High Priest, in addition to making atonement, also helps those that are tempted, for He has suffered, being at one time in like testings. There is a difference between 'taking hold' and 'succouring': the former seems to be more general, the latter more specific. 'Taking hold' (v. 16) is almost equivalent to undertaking a cause in order to help the helpless; but 'succouring' (v. 18) is the active response to a cry for help, as $βοηθῆσαι$ implies.

These then are the objects achieved by the incarnation and death of the Son of God. It all stands in sharp contrast with that to which the Hebrews had been accustomed before they accepted the Lord Jesus as their Saviour. Could they, then, entertain the thought of abandoning all this and revert to a system which was so imperfect and incomplete? The inspired writer presents all this in such a way as to meet the peculiar difficulties with which they were beset. It is so different from the ideas which they had had hitherto, and so much better.

Chapter 5

Rest - Hebrews 3-4:13

Sin is destructive of rest. Man's history generally, and that of the Jewish people in particular, demonstrate this. Captivity, servitude and oppression followed their many sins. Nor was it only their outward circumstances which were all awry, but they found no rest of conscience, whose accusing voice was insistent. It is so everywhere and with everyone, unless the conscience has become seared. As soon as sin entered, the original tranquillity which man enjoyed was lost. Sin has disturbed the ordered creation of God, and sinful man is restless.

The chapters before us now are devoted to this subject. The Greek word for 'rest' used by our writer (κατάπαυσις) differs from that used by the Lord Jesus (ἀνάπαυσις) (Matt. 11:29). In the latter case, the thought is of *lifting up* burdens from the weary shoulders of others who were 'labouring' under the rigours of the Mosaic law, and 'laden' not only with that yoke but with all its unsanctioned and humanly imposed accretions. In Hebrews, however, the writer is concerned with the *laying down* of the legal works of Judaism, and adopting the principle of faith in its stead. In Matthew, it is what Christ does; in Hebrews, it is what they should do. Here rest is cessation from works.

The Hebrews were engaged in a great struggle: they were liable to revert to the law and to apostatise from Christ. They were, in fact, in danger of not entering into the rest which had been made possible for them. Who would have the mastery, Christ or Moses? Christ is superior to all – angels, Moses, Aaron, Joshua, Melchizedek, and all. There should be no doubt, then, as to Who was entitled to the mastery, but there were two other principles at work which made the issue uncertain. These are named in our chapters: one is unbelief (ἀπιστία), and the other is disobedience (ἀπείθεια). The meaning of the latter is literally a refusal to be persuaded as to the truth of a thing, with the result that, whatever that thing requires is not conceded; hence it results in disobedience. Unbelief, on the other hand, has to do with distrust of a person. They are as cause and effect: unbelief is the cause, disobedience is the effect.

Israel was promised the land of Canaan: that was the gospel that was preached to them (Heb. 4:2). Notwithstanding the evidence of the grapes of Eshcol, however, they remained unconvinced. They could not trust God to redeem His promise and give them the land. His promises were not believed; His ability was not trusted. No wonder they fell in the wilderness and did not enter the land. They asked, 'Can God furnish a table in the wilderness?' (Ps. 78:19). They 'limited the Holy One' (Ps. 78:41); and, though He had brought them out of Egypt, they doubted if He could bring them into Canaan.

The Holy Spirit speaks in no uncertain tone. It is He, and not men, who called upon these Hebrews. 'Today' they must listen to His voice and exhort each other before it is too late. It will be observed that Psalm 95:7-11 is quoted as the voice of the Holy Spirit.

Their true safeguard lies in constant occupation with Christ. Study His words in Chapter 3:1-2. Verse 1 is really a brief summary of what has gone before. In the words 'holy brethren', the writer takes up the two threads woven into the fabric of Chapter 2. There he had spoken of the 'Sanctifier' and them that are sanctified; here it is summed up in the one word, 'holy'. There he had said, 'He is not ashamed to call them brethren'; here that word 'brethren' is repeated. In Chapter 1 he had already spoken of 'Thy fellows'; here he repeats the same word, although it is translated differently by the word 'partakers'. He has spoken of their 'calling'; here it is a 'heavenly calling'. In Chapter 1 the Lord Jesus is seen as the great Apostle who has come out from God to men, as Moses of old; in Chapter 2:17 He is viewed as the High Priest who has gone in from men to God, as Aaron of old did. Here the two titles are combined – the Apostle and High Priest. In Chapter 2 we have a 'faithful High Priest'. Here in Chapter 3:1 the word 'faithful' recurs, but is used in comparing Him not with Aaron, but with Moses. Thus all the various strands are gathered together in one cord: they should 'consider Jesus'.

The Jews held Moses in high esteem, but the glories of Christ are infinitely greater. He was the builder of the house, Moses was but part of it, for the house here is not a stone building but one made up of living persons. In fact, He is God. In that house Moses officiated as a servant, but Christ is Son. That house, we say, is of living persons – the Hebrews to whom the letter is sent; but only 'if we hold fast our boldness and the glorying of our hope firm unto the end' (3:6). Abandonment would be apostasy, and they would then be like their forefathers, who fell in the wilderness because they did not hold fast the hope that was set before them. As we have seen, they did not trust God, who had brought them out of Egypt, to bring them into the land. They were not persuaded that the land was what they had been given to understand. They accepted the report of the ten spies, and that of the two had no effect. 'Let us return into Egypt' was their cry: the very thing these Hebrews were spiritually liable to do. Only 'if they continued' would it become evident that they were genuine; and only so would they enter into rest.

It is very easy to harden one's heart. The lesson of Meribah and Massah (Ex. 17:7) - names which are reminiscent of the sins of provocation and temptation - could too readily be forgotten, and the twin evils be all too easily repeated by these Hebrews. They must 'take heed'. 'Take heed,' says the writer, 'lest there be in any of you an evil heart of unbelief' (v. 12). It was said of Israel, 'They do always err in their heart'. If the heart is not right, it is unlikely we shall understand God's ways. Note the emphasis laid upon the heart in this section. 'Keep thine heart with all diligence,' said the wise man (Prov. 4:23). The propensity to wander is persistent: Israel always erred in heart. Backsliding begins there; it exists before it is seen by others. How grievous, as with that people, when they become perpetually erring!

Israel saw God's works but did not discern His ways (Ps. 103:7): they did not discern the principles which underlay His acts. They were only interested in the actual, not in the spiritual. Can we marvel, then, that God said, 'They shall not enter into My rest'? What is God's rest? Is it something present or future? There can be little doubt that it would appear to be both present and future - available in time, and to be enjoyed throughout eternity. It is not first entered into either at death or when the Lord comes (whichever is earlier); it is available to be enjoyed in the present life. We must not press the type of Israel in the wilderness too far. In their case, certainly the 'rest' lay at the end of the journey; but in our case it is not so. We do not have to wait for it until life's journey is ended - 'We which have believed do enter into rest' (4:3; see also v. 10). Note the present tense; we enter it now. Faith and rest are two things which God has joined together; they must not be put asunder. It is those who believe, and only those, who enter this rest.

In the Old Testament history Israel entered Canaan, and that was their land of promise - their rest (Deut. 12:9), though they failed to obtain it. But Canaan is not a picture of heaven; if for no other reason than that there was sin and fighting there and no such things are in heaven. Therefore, the type must not be pressed too far.

The 'rest' spoken of here is cessation from works. God inaugurated it on the seventh day when He rested from all His works. It is to keep this lesson constantly before His people that He enjoined them to 'remember the Sabbath day to keep it holy', and to do no work then. But what works are before the writer's mind? It would not seem to be the labours of God's servants, touching whom it is written, 'They rest from their labours'. The background of the letter must not be forgotten. It is written to Hebrews who were prone to revert to ritualistic and legalistic works, dead works. Now were they to do that, they could not possibly enjoy rest. How could they, since they would have returned again to a system which was marked throughout by imperfection and by non-completion, as the daily routine showed?

'So great salvation' (2:3) is of faith, and 'not of works'; and, as we have remarked earlier, faith and rest go inseparably together. 'Let us therefore labour to enter into that rest' (4:11).

The thought is complementary to Matthew 11:28. There it is release from the burdens of Judaistic ritualism; here it is the enjoyment of all that has been procured by the Lord Jesus, who, through death and resurrection, abrogated the Levitical ceremonial system, having fulfilled its typical significance.

The 'rest' here, then, is cessation from the ceremonial works of Judaism.

When he warns against possible lapsing, the writer is not inconsistent with the clear and indubitable fact of the believer's eternal security. His use of the conjunctions 'if' and 'lest' is not contrary to it. We must distinguish between things that differ. Relationship, the result of imparted life, is not here in view, but rather the pilgrim character of the Christian. The stress here is on human responsibility and not on divine sovereignty; on our continuance and not on our election. Everything here seems to depend on us, and not on God. We have voluntarily made a 'confession' of faith in the Lord Jesus and thus have started a pilgrimage to 'better things'. 'Let us therefore fear, lest, [under the pressure of persecution] we should seem to have come short of God's intended rest.' Note the tense: 'to have come short' implies the possibility of here and now failing to enjoy the rest which might have been ours.

The writer takes the Hebrews on the ground of their confession, and assumes it is necessarily a genuine confession. He would fain hope so, but they must examine themselves and 'take heed'. If they continue, their genuineness will be apparent. If they apostatise, it will show the contrary.

The argument of the writer seems to be this. God's rest existed from the foundation of the world, that is, when He completed His work of reconstruction. He rested on the seventh day. Creation's rest, however, was broken by sin. In due course there followed the offer of Canaan's rest, but whatever Joshua achieved, Israel did not attain to it. They fell in the wilderness and those who did enter Canaan had no settled peace: enemies still remained there. Later on, David spoke of that 'rest' as still remaining available for the people of God. Whether these Hebrews entered into it would depend on their condition of heart and their response to God's voice. 'The word of God is living and active'; that is, the particular word cited from Psalm 95, though what is true of that Psalm is true of all Scripture. Its sharp edge would be felt by hearts that had not been hardened. It pierces and reveals what men really are; it lays one bare and naked before the eyes of God. What failure and weakness it reveals! How sorely the High Priest is needed, and how gracious of God to bring Him in just at this point of the writer's argument!

Leviticus 23, which sets out the Feasts of the Lord, shows that 'rest' is the ultimate goal of God for His people. The numeral seven speaks of it: the seventh day, the seventh week, the seventh month, the seventh year, and the end of the forty and ninth year, are all there. On the seventh day God rested. There is, therefore, a *sabbatismos,* a sabbath keeping, for the people of God. God's goal for His people is that they should enjoy rest, enjoy it here and now - a foretaste on earth of what will be known in perfection in heaven.

It follows from all this that, if Judaistic works are now unacceptable to God, any other kind of work must be equally so. The works imposed by Rome, its penances and monetary payments, and all else, imposed by no matter whom, is as unacceptable as the offering of Cain. Paul is very clear on the matter: 'By the works of the law no flesh shall be justified' (Rom. 3:20). He hammers it out when writing to the Galatians. To the Ephesians he says that it is 'not of works' (Eph. 2:9). All the New Testament writers are unanimous as to this.

The 'good works which God hath afore prepared that we should walk in them' (Eph. 2:10), are not a means to salvation, but a result issuing from it. They are done, not in order to get, but because we have already received. They are not performed as meritorious acts but as worshipful ones.

Chapter 6

Our Great High Priest - Hebrews 4:14 - 5:10; 7 and 8

It is born in man that he must have dealings with an Unseen God. Hence all the world over he is found worshipping a Being higher than himself as he imagines, even though the true God be unknown. Fallen as he is, he has an awareness that he needs an intermediary to secure a favourable standing, his relations with the true God, or the god of his own mind, not being what they should. Conscience tells him this, even though he is not able to give any proper explanation of why things are so with him.

In early Old Testament times, the head of a family acted as priest, e.g. Noah, Abram and Job. Later, Israel as a nation was chosen to be a kingdom of priests, but, at their request, they renounced the position (Ex. 20:19). They fell into idolatry, worshipping the golden calf, and later into even worse whoredoms. God, therefore, chose the tribe of Levi to be His priests (Num. 25:13). They stood for the true God at the time of national apostasy, though even they also failed, as the history of Eli shows (1 Sam. 2:12). God has His resources however, and He promised to raise up a faithful priest who would do according to that which was in His heart and mind.

Israel was next given a king, but monarchy as well as priesthood was a failure, as all else that is put into the hands of man is bound to be. The kingdom was divided: ten tribes going into captivity first and later the remaining two tribes also. A remnant of the latter returned, and in their days Zechariah, by the Spirit, said that God intended to raise up a priest who should sit on His throne (Zech. 6:13). One who would unite in Himself both offices of priest and king. In this He would be unique, for such a union was forbidden under the law. Royalty belonged to Judah, priesthood to Levi. When any attempted to function in both offices, the judgment of God followed; as in the cases of the kings Saul (1 Sam. 15) and Uzziah (2 Chron. 26:16; Isa. 6:1). It is evident that our Lord sprang out of Judah, and, therefore, when on earth He could not be a priest. The union of both offices could, therefore, only be effected in resurrection, as we shall see in due course.

Melchizedek foreshadowed the Lord Jesus in this respect. It is true that David wore an ephod and offered sacrifices (2 Sam. 6:14), but the circumstances were special and prophetic. The royal priesthood of the Lord Jesus is one of the main themes of our letter. But before this could be established it was necessary that there should be a change of the law: the Mosaic law must be abrogated. There was no doubt that He sprang from the tribe of Judah according to the flesh and was, therefore, entitled to the throne. But it was not so as to the priesthood, and before He could fill that office a fundamental change of law must come into force.

We have already seen that one of the purposes of His incarnation was that 'He might become a merciful and faithful high priest in things pertaining to God to make propitiation for the sins of the people'. This has now been achieved. Therefore, it is written, 'Having then a great High Priest who has passed through the heavens, Jesus the Son of God, let us hold fast our confession.' The taunt of the Jews that, because these Hebrew believers had nothing visible, they therefore had nothing at all, was groundless. They had in Jesus, the Son of God, far more than Israel ever had at any other time. He had gone through no mere earthly curtains to God, but through the heavens themselves. For them, faith turned what otherwise could not be seen into a substantial reality.

Christendom seeks to interpose between man and God those who set themselves up as priests and intermediaries. But there is, 'One Mediator between God and men, Himself man, Christ Jesus' (1 Tim. 2:5). There is now, in God's sight, only one High Priest. He alone should come between the soul and God. He is the only Mediator for the sinner, and the only High Priest for the believer.

The inspired history of Melchizedek, given briefly in Genesis 14, is deeply instructive. It omits much which might have been of interest, but the silences of Scripture have been likened to pauses in music: they add to its harmony. To speak when God is silent spoils all. The writer of our letter considers (*a*) what the Old Testament record says; (*b*) what it does not say; and (*c*) what it implies. No mention is made of the birth of Melchizedek nor of his death, nor of his lineage or parentage, which things were of indispensable importance in the Levitical priesthood. His history was thus accommodated to make it illustrative of what is actually true of the Lord Jesus. Melchizedek was but a man, yet his historical record is so written that he becomes like the Son of God who abides a priest continually. His very name is significant: it means 'king of righteousness'. Moreover, the place of his rule is suggestive, for Salem means peace. And observe the order: righteousness comes first, peace afterwards, for only on such a principle can peace be permanent.

The high priests of Israel could only bear gently with the ignorant and erring, for that they themselves also were compassed with infirmity. But there is no such restriction to the sympathy of Jesus, the Son of God. The two words used are in contrast with each other: δύναμαι and μετριοπαθεῖν, the former being most aptly translated as 'touched with the feeling of': it is a fellow-feeling. Many a surgeon 'feels for' his patient, but should he himself have to be subjected to surgical treatment, he can thereafter 'feel with' them, having experienced the same, for experience is essential to sympathy.

Our great High Priest has none of the limitations of Israel's priests. His earthly experiences give Him competency to be a 'merciful and faithful High Priest'. He has been 'in all points tempted like as we are, sin apart'. In every class of temptation, He was tested. Sin could not appeal to Him, for there was nothing in Him to respond to it. But in every other way He was tested. All goods of merchandise are classified under a certain number of classes. So, too, all life's experiences may be classified. Although not in precise details, yet, in all essential principles of each class, Jesus when on earth was tested. He, therefore, is able to sympathise with those who in any one of these classes is tempted.

He is a 'merciful' High Priest, seated on the right hand of the majesty on high. 'Let us, therefore, draw near with boldness to the throne of grace, that we may obtain mercy in respect of the past and find grace for the present to help in time of need.' He is always available to give such timely aid. The word 'succour' is an old English word meaning 'help', and has the thought of an action in response to a cry. We cry; He helps.

Of course, He cannot, nor does He, sympathise with sin, for

He had no experience of that. He is an advocate with the Father in respect of the sins of God's children. But He is a High Priest acting in sympathy in regard to their weaknesses. His memory of His sojourn here is ever green: He was hungry, thirsty, poor, bereaved, tired, and so on.

As two harps answer the one to the other when one is plucked, so He feels all that touches us. Therefore, He said, 'Saul, why persecutest thou *Me*?' - although Saul was actually persecuting the saints.

He has 'passed through the heavens', as the High Priest on the Day of Atonement 'passed through the veil', into the holiest of all. He is now 'within the veil', in the 'true tabernacle which the Lord pitched and not man', 'in the presence of God', 'in heaven itself'. All this is real to faith; it is not demonstrable to sight. Under the old economy, none but the High Priest might 'draw near' to the throne of God in the sanctuary. But now all are invited to 'draw near with boldness'. It is an ever-present privilege at all times.

The High Priesthood of Jesus began when He had been made perfect, that is to say, when He had completed all the experiences essential to qualify Him to hold the office. Aaron was not appointed high priest until Moses, the mediator of the covenant, had made purification of sins (Exo. 29). So, too, it was not until the work of redemption had been finished and Christ had ascended to the right hand of the Majesty on high, that He was publicly addressed by God as High Priest after the order of Melchizedek. He did not take upon Himself this office, independent of God, any more than Aaron took the honour to himself.

The Melchizedek priesthood of Christ is in sharp contrast with the Aaronic priesthood. The one was a royal priesthood, but the other had nothing to do with royalty. The one belonged to the tribe of Judah, the other to the tribe of Levi. The Aaronic priesthood was temporary: its priests were mortal, and the office was, therefore, transmissible to successors. In the nature of things, this made the well-being of the people precarious, for who could tell whether the successors would be like the sons of Eli, or worse (1 Sam. 3:13)? But the Melchizedek priesthood is held by One who lives by the power of an endless life. It will be transmitted to none other.

In every way it is superior to the Aaronic system. Levi, when yet in the loins of Abraham, paid tithes to Melchizedek, showing the recipient of the tithes to be superior to the one who rendered them. Again Melchizedek blessed Abram and in so doing virtually blessed Levi, and the one who blesses is far greater than the one blessed. Moreover, the priesthood of Christ was established by divine oath. This was not so with Aaron, which had to do with a carnal commandment, and related to the flesh. The Melchizedek priesthood has to do with the spirit. All this was most encouraging to the believing Jews. It gave them an effective answer to those who taunted them, both on the ground of their having no visible priesthood, and the loss of all the privileges that they supposed accompanied it.

What are the functions of our Great High Priest? It is necessary that this High Priest should have somewhat also to offer. Of course, He does not repeat the sacrifice which was made outside the camp, but He offers His very presence in heaven as One who on earth had once for all put away sin by the sacrifice of Himself. In that way He makes propitiation for the sins of the people. He has entered heaven in virtue of His own blood. He is a priest 'for ever'. His priesthood will never terminate, not even when He returns to earth and establishes His millennial kingdom. Indeed, the history of Genesis 14 is prophetic throughout, of which we cannot here speak particularly. But when Israel are hard pressed by their enemies, their true Melchizedek will come out bringing to them the 'bread of sustenance' and the 'wine of joy'.

There can be no doubt who has the better part. These Hebrews have a High Priest, who is able to save to the uttermost[1] all who keep coming to God through Him, and who ever liveth. What more could be desired? The Aaronic priesthood had deplorably failed and, at the time this epistle was written, it was but a hypocritical system in the hands of wicked men. But their Great High Priest is 'holy, harmless, undefiled'. Though at one time He 'was numbered with the transgressors', both at His baptism and at His crucifixion, yet He 'was separated from sinners' in His burial, and ever afterwards. He has been made 'higher than the heavens'.

The Aaronic priesthood only served 'a copy and shadow of the heavenly things', but Jesus has brought in a 'better hope', and He is the mediator of a better covenant which hath been enacted upon better promises. A perusal of the terms of the New Covenant will show this. In contrast to 'Thou shalt' of the old, here there is 'I will'. Infringements under the old covenant have righteously been dealt with, making it possible 'for their sins and iniquities to be remembered no more'. As 'surety', the Lord Jesus guarantees the terms of the New Covenant: as 'mediator', He administers those terms. Although in the first instance the 'new covenant' was made with both the house of Israel and the house of Judah, and it will have its final and

---

[1] $εἰς\ τὸ\ παντελές$. The only other occurrence of this phrase is in Luke 13:11.

complete fulfilment to them later on (Jer. 31:31), the believer today comes into its benefits now.

The very word 'new'[2] implies that the former has been made 'old' and is soon to vanish. Could these Hebrew believers, then, contemplate reverting to it? Do they prefer the old, the inferior, the temporary, the ineffective, the mortal? Could they, in view of all this, really give up their 'confession'?

---

[2] Καινή, new in kind, not νέος, new in date, though the New Covenant could not become operative until the sacrifice upon which it was based had been made.

Chapter 7

The Perfect Sacrifice - Hebrews 9 and 10:1-18

Before the martyr John Brown of Ashford, Kent, England died, he was required to retract what was called his blasphemy. 'Christ was once offered,' said Brown, 'to bear the sins of many; and it is by this sacrifice we are saved, not by its repetition by the priests.' After his feet had been placed on a pan of burning coals, and he had been very tightly bound to the stocks so that he could barely move his head, he was burnt alive. How much we owe to such men who stood unflinchingly for the 'perfect sacrifice'.

The atmosphere of Chapter 9 is the Day of Atonement, when the High Priest entered into the most holy place. We say this because the golden censer is spoken of as being in that place. On other days it was in the holy place beside the altar of incense. All the various items of the furniture of both the holy place and the most holy place are deeply instructive, and the phrase 'of which we cannot now speak particularly' virtually gives the believer freedom to interpret these according to the tenor of Scriptural doctrine.

We will not go into these details now, save for mentioning one thing. The pot of manna here alluded to was not in the ark of Solomon's temple, nor indeed the rod of Aaron which budded; nothing was there save the two tables of stone. This is suggestive, for by the time when that which is signified by

Solomon's temple has come - that is, when Christ will have set up His kingdom on earth as the true King of peace - wilderness conditions will have ceased, and the provision therefore, such as the manna, will no longer be required. The inclusion here of the manna and the budded rod shows that the writer has wilderness conditions in mind.

The tabernacle in the wilderness and its ordinances declared that the way into the holiest of all was not yet made manifest. They were but a parable for the time then being, 'standing' as owned of God, although they could not perfect the conscience. They only related to carnal ordinances which had to do with the flesh and its defilement; the conscience remained untouched. God, indeed, did not intend that system of things to be permanent. It was imposed only until the time came when there would be a true reformation, or setting right of things. The cross has now done what that could not do. Christ was ever before the mind of God in all His ancient dealings with Israel.

Whether the tenses of Chapter 9 verses 9-10 are rendered in the past as in the A.V., or in the present as in the R.V., seems to make little difference. The one takes the mind back to the Old Testament, whereas the other envisages the situation as it then existed by the religious practices of the Jews in the land. In any event, what God had legislated is now 'done away' in Christ. Judaism has been superseded and can be safely abandoned.

'Good things to come' signify all the blessings of Christianity that have been brought in consequent upon the death and resurrection of Christ – they are 'the heavenly things' (v. 23). His High Priesthood has to do with a greater and more perfect tabernacle; His sacrifice is Himself; and in virtue of 'His own blood' He has entered into the presence of God. He needs not to repeat that entry annually: it is 'once and for all time' because He has obtained 'eternal redemption'; His blood cleanses the conscience from dead works and gives right of approach to God in true service and worship.

'The offering up of the body of Jesus Christ' was not a thing which He was compelled to do contrary to His own will, but He readily consented to do it in order that God's claims might be met and the desires of His heart righteously satisfied. The notion of the offering to God of a human body was obnoxious not only to the Jews, but to God Himself. It was a thing that never came into His mind nor entered His heart. His judgment followed wherever it was in practice. Yet, in the case of the Lord Jesus, God specially prepared Him a body for this very purpose. The compulsory substitution of an innocent for a guilty person or persons is against all morality, but the willing substitution of a person in the stead of the guilty is the display of the greatest possible love. Great stress is here laid on this. He made purgation of sins 'by Himself'; 'He tasted death'; 'He offered Himself'; and 'through the eternal spirit He offered Himself without spot to God'. He was manifested 'to put away sin by the sacrifice of Himself'. The initiative was always in His hands, whether during His earthly course, in the garden of Gethsemane, in Pilate's hall, or on the Cross. His death was a determinate act on His own part, and not the outcome of physical exhaustion or irresistible forces.

'The eternal Spirit' is the Spirit of God; the word 'eternal'[1]

---

[1] 'Eternal Spirit.' The humanity of our Lord Jesus had a beginning and, therefore, His human spirit, and soul and body had that beginning. The Holy Spirit who is one Person in the Godhead, however, had no beginning, for all divine attributes are His as much as they are those of the other two Persons. Some take 'Eternal Spirit' as denoting His eternal divine nature, 'His own pre-existent divine personality'. But this does not seem to be tenable. Had it been in the accusative and not the genitive there might have been something to say for it.

does not appear to be appropriate to His own human spirit. Characteristically the Lord Jesus always acted 'by the Spirit'; even at His conception it was 'by the Holy Spirit'. Irrational animals were bound by cords to the altar, but He laid down His own life. It was love to His Father and to us that 'bound Him to the tree'.

The death of Christ makes it possible for Him to be the mediator of the New Covenant, for by it redemption is obtained from the penalty which transgressions under the Old incurred. The benefits of a will are only dispensed after the death of the one who made it, so our spiritual benefits do not depend on a conditional covenant in which there are two covenanting parties, but on a 'will' made in sovereign grace. It becomes operative because the testator has died.

If the importance of 'blood' in the Old Testament ritual cannot be over-rated, what shall we say then of the 'blood of Christ'? 'Without the shedding of blood there could at no time be remission of sins.' The word 'almost', which indicates there were some exceptions in connection with 'the pattern of things in the heavens' (Heb. 8:5), could never be used in respect of 'heavenly things'.

From verse 24 to 28 the writer refers to the Day of Atonement, and calls attention to its three phases: (*a*) 'outside the camp', where the sin offering was made; (*b*) inside the veil, where the priest is functioning; and (*c*) his coming out thereafter.

He first speaks of Christ's presence before God 'inside the veil'. This is the chief point and is, therefore, put first, for he wishes to impress on his readers that it is of first importance. Faith should lay hold upon it, that 'Christ *now* appears in the presence of God for us'. But that presumes that He has already made the offering for sin outside the camp, and the fact is that He has done that 'once and for all time' without need of any repetition. 'At the consummation of the ages' of man's earlier history - when it had been proved beyond dispute that, apart from Christ, man was utterly without hope - He appeared for the specific purpose of putting away sin by the sacrifice of Himself. This was a never-to-be-repeated offering, for had it been necessary to repeat it, it would not have suffered merely to have gone back to the days of Israel's wilderness pilgrimage. One must go back right to the foundation of the world, for sin did not originate with Israel but with Adam.

The writer is not particularly concerned with the efficacy of the death of Christ to meet the needs of 'all', but shows its particular value to those who exercise faith. He is content to say, 'He was once offered to bear the sins of many', though we know in fact, 'He gave Himself a ransom for all' (1 Tim 2:6), and 'He is the propitiatory offering not for our sins only, but for the whole world' (1 John 2:2). The intrinsic worth of His offering is not in view here, however, but its imparted benefits to the 'many', 'the called', 'the sanctified'.

The offering then has been made: the priest has gone inside the veil and is now there. But soon He will come out, not again to deal with the question of sin ($\chi\omega\rho\grave{\iota}\varsigma\ \dot{\alpha}\mu\alpha\rho\tau\acute{\iota}\alpha\varsigma$) – as the High Priest of old did year by year – but to complete altogether the 'salvation' which 'the people' already enjoyed in part. 'Them that look for Him', is not an oblique exhortation to be watchful, but a characteristic of 'all the people'. In the wilderness days, only Israel was interested in the ceremony of the day of Atonement; it did not concern others. So it is believers now who await Christ: the world does not await Him.

We cannot stress too strongly the importance of keeping in mind the background of the letter, and the Day of Atonement and its ritual with which the work of Christ is contrasted. Unless we do this we shall fail to see how this letter agrees with other epistles. The writer is not here concerned with details of the Lord's second advent. He rather regards the work of Christ as all of one piece, yet in three separate stages; each inseparable from the other, but integral parts of a whole. The reader is reminded of what we have said touching *Reason No. 6* on page 354.

Chapter 10:1-18 is a development of the whole theme. The three Persons of the Godhead, in their respective activities, are each seen to have cooperated for the eternal good of the believing sinner, providing benefits infinitely exceeding the temporal benefits accruing from the now effete Levitical ritual. First, he speaks of the will of God; secondly, he presents the work of Christ which had in view the doing of that will; and thirdly, he cites the witness of the Holy Spirit that God's will has been achieved through Christ's work.

The will of God may be stated thus. He desired that man should be 'perfected', that is, made fully acceptable to all that is appropriate to God's justice and holiness. It is not here a matter of perfecting character, but rather of their state, that they may be able to appear before God. In order that this may be done, however, they must be 'purged' from their sins. In fact, God desired that man should have 'no more conscience of sins'. He wished man to be without an awareness of personal guilt, not because ostrich-like he blinded himself to it, nor because of self-righteousness he denied the fact, but because it has been removed in a righteously satisfactory way. In a word, God desired that sin, as a root principle, be irrecoverably put away.

That He was desirous and ready to forgive was evidenced by the Levitical sacrifices. The Day of Atonement declared it most eloquently, but God knew that these sacrifices could never take away sins. He merely gave them as object lessons to teach His people their need of such a provision and of His readiness to clear them from their guilt. These sacrifices were but the shadow and not the substance. They were ineffective and could give no lasting blessing. Their constant repetition was proof of this: that they offered 'oftentimes the same sacrifices'. Year by year the blood was taken into the holiest; year by year the scapegoat was sent into the wilderness after the people's sins had been confessed over its head. In them there was a remembrance made of sins every year, but there was no final removal of sin.

The wish of God, therefore, remained unsatisfied. Because of this, the Lord Jesus declared His willingness to 'come to do His will'; it was so written of Him in the volume of the book. His willingness thus to come can be traced throughout the whole of sacred Scripture. Certain words should be noted.

'Wherefore', that is, because of the inherent inability demonstrated throughout the age of 'the blood of bulls and goats to take away sin', the Lord Jesus undertook to come and do what was outstanding.

'Then' indicates the point of time as being 'when He came into the world'.

'Above' or 'higher up' referring, as it appears to the writer, to heaven from whence He came. It was there that the undertaking was given. (In like manner, the earth is referred to as 'the lower parts', Eph. 4:9.)

Because the whole system of sacrifice and offering, whole

burnt offerings and offerings for sins, did not satisfy God - 'Thou hast not desired', and because they gave Him no delight - 'Thou hast had no pleasure therein', the Lord Jesus undertook to come personally, and Himself do what they had failed to accomplish.

The difference in the citation from the text of Psalm 40 should be noted. There it reads, 'Mine ears hast Thou digged' (margin); here, 'a body hast Thou prepared Me'. The reference in the Psalm is not to the law concerning the boring of the ear, for the details are different (Ps. 40:6). There it is 'boring'; in the Psalm it is 'digging'. There it is 'an ear'; in the Psalm it is 'ears'. Evidently the LXX translators considered that the Hebrew was a pictorial allusion to the formation of a body, the sculptor having reached the ears. Hence they gave the sense, 'A body hast Thou prepared Me'; and the Holy Spirit has set His *imprimatur* on this, citing it in His own later letter to the Hebrews. An author has the right to alter when citing his own former work. This the Spirit of God does here. Had the authorship in each case been different, no such right would have existed. Strict adherence to the letter would have been morally required when quoting. But neither David, the penman of the Psalm, nor the writer to the Hebrews were strictly the authors. They were but instruments, taken up in their respective personalities, to convey the mind of God in their own times.

The Lord Jesus, then, in willing submission to His Father, to whom His ear was opened morning by morning, undertook to travel the course that inevitably led to the accomplishment of His will. The agony of the garden and the well-known words, 'Not My will but Thine be done', reveal the victory that had already been won in submissive resolve before the actual conflict of Calvary.

The result of this was that the Levitical order, 'the first', was taken away, and it became obsolete. God tore the veil from top to bottom. He had finished with that system. 'The second', that is, the will of God and all that pertained to it, was established and it superseded the first. Therefore, any continuance nowadays of the old economy - in however Christianised or, more accurately, paganised a form - is but an anachronism and the prolongation of something long since effete.

God's will has now been done by the 'offering of the body of Jesus Christ'. These words are most striking. They denote, as we have earlier remarked, the wholehearted willingness of the Lord Jesus to become the sacrificial victim. He was under no duress in the matter.

Several things are stated of His offering. It was *unique*, 'one offering'; there was none other like it. It was *final*, the offering has been made 'once for all time'. It was *vicarious*, the offering was 'on behalf of sins'. It was *permanent*, it was offered in perpetuity, so that its repetition was unnecessary. It was *finished*, the offerer 'sat down in perpetuity', a thing impossible in Levitical times. It was *preliminary*, for He is now expecting the subjugation of all His enemies under His feet, He having initially dealt with the intrusion of sin into God's creation. It was *effective*, for by it 'He has perfected for ever them that are sanctified'.

All this is in sharp contrast with the Jewish ritualistic system. How, then, could anyone contemplate reverting to it after having known these things? There many priests functioned; here there is one. There they stood daily: here He sits. There they offered oftentimes: here but once. There the same sacrifices were repeated; here only one was offered.

The words of Jeremiah are cited; acknowledged to be the words of the Holy Spirit. They relate to the New Covenant which has now become operative (see pp. 370-372). Although the words 'covenant' and 'testament' represent the same Greek word (διαθήκη), the word 'covenant' appears to be better suited to the Mosaic law, and 'testament' to that which has been brought in consequent upon the death of Christ.[2] A testament is made by one party and is, normally, without conditions. It expresses the wish of the testator as to the disposition of his estate and comes into force after his death. Likewise, new testament blessings flow from the death of Christ. This testament is that God would write His laws 'upon their hearts', so that they might love them. He further would write them upon 'their minds', so that they might do them. He adds, 'Their sins and iniquities will I remember no more'. His own wish has thus been achieved. This is exactly what He desired to be done. The work of Christ has given righteous ground for God to promise this. Sin was 'brought to mind' once and for all when Christ died to put it away. Now God promises He will not remember it any more. That is doubtless why in Chapter 11, where so many Old Testament worthies are named, none of their failings is mentioned. Only their faith is cited.

This renders unnecessary any further offering concerning sins. God has been satisfied by the work of His Son, and He is able now righteously to confer on His creatures, who believe,

---

[2] Διαθήκη. Despite all that has been said to the contrary, it seems that Chapter 9:16-17 admits only of the translation of 'testament'. Old Testament covenants were ratified, it is true, by sacrifices (see Gen. 15:9ff), but in this passage in Hebrews there is both the death of the testator and the fact that the testament is of no force while the testator is alive. In the Old Testament manner of ratification of a covenant, there is not the death of the testator, though there is the death of the sacrifices. Before discarding 'testament' in favour of 'covenant', a satisfactory explanation must be given of these two verses.

that which He has always longed to bestow. Of course, He forgave in Old Testament times, but then it was a 'passing over of sins that are passed' (Rom. 3:25), in view of the fact that Christ would later die. They were 'forgiven on credit'. The forgiveness then given was as real and lasting as that now given, only then it was in anticipation of the death of Christ and now it is because He has died.

The constant repetition of the word 'once' ($ἅπαξ$) should not escape attention; not 'once upon a time', but 'once for all'. He offered His body: 'Once in the consummation of the ages He appeared to put away sin'; 'He was once offered to bear the sins of many'. The offering up of a sacrifice for the sins of the people He did once, when He offered up Himself. By His own blood He entered in once into the holiest: 'There remaineth no more a sacrifice for sins'; 'There is no more offering for sin.' The writer is clear beyond the slightest shadow of a doubt touching this. For the godly Jew this meant a cessation of all his laborious daily and periodic sacrifices; to the God-fearing Gentile it means the solution of all his spiritual problems.

The death of Christ is described as 'better sacrifices': a plural of excellence, for it wrapt within its folds all the actual truths signified by the various offerings under the antiquated Levitical system. The death of Christ stands out in all its solitary grandeur and excellence as that to which all God's previous dealings with man pointed, and from which all His subsequent actions towards man flowed.

His death was penal: it was 'for sins'. This is time and again emphasised. He makes propitiation for the sins of the people; He was offered to bear the sins of many. Since He was personally sinless, His death must consequently have been for the sins of others - it must have been a *vicarious* death.

Indeed, it has a far wider range. Not merely were sins dealt with, but sin itself was put away, for He then finally and for ever dealt with the root principle of the evil that has blighted God's creation and man's life.

The infringers of a law have no right nor power to prescribe a penalty, much less the means to satisfy it when God's law is at issue. But God, who imposed the penalty, has provided the escape from it through the death of Christ. By it alone can the sinner be 'sanctified' and rendered fit for God's holy presence. By it alone can he be 'perfected', and be regarded as having no guilt.

The resurrection and ascension of the Lord Jesus prove that His sacrifice was efficacious: 'He sat down for ever.' It matters little with which verb we associate the words 'for ever'; grammatically either, 'He offered ... for ever', or, 'for ever sat down', is tenable, but the context appears to favour the latter. Old Testament priests were given no seat, their work was never regarded as finished. Eli was seriously at fault when he sat down at a time when his priestly work was so much needed (1 Sam. 4:18). But no less than four times in this letter is the fact mentioned that our Great High Priest has sat down (Heb. 1:3; 8:1; 10:12; 12:2). His work on earth was done; He has taken His place of honour 'at the right hand of God'. Joseph recognised that the place of honour was the right hand (Gen. 48:13-14). The Holy sufferer of Psalm 109 is given the place of honour in Psalm 110. The Lord Himself drew consolation from the fact that this lay ahead of Him when He was risen from the dead (Ps. 110:1; Matt. 26:64). Both Mark and Peter tell us it is now a realised fact (Mark 16:19; Acts 5:31 R.V.). Paul from his prison cell looks up by faith and lays hold on the truth also (Eph. 1:20). What greater evidence could there be that the sacrifice of Christ is the 'perfect satisfaction' given to God, admitting of no repetition, than this: the Sacrificial Victim is now the enthroned High Priest?

He sits there expecting the day when every foe will be put beneath His feet, and the universe cleared of all trace of sin or rebellion. This looks beyond the millennium and goes on to the eternal state when God shall be 'all in all'.

Chapter 8

Earnest Warnings - Hebrews 5:11 - 6:20; 10:19-39

In addition to those sections that we have already considered, in which the writer of the letter warns the Hebrews against apostasy (e.g., Chapter 2:1-4 and 3:7 - 4:1), there are other passages which we should consider.

Melchizedek having been mentioned in Chapter 5:6ff, the writer finds himself somewhat embarrassed in proceeding with his exposition because of the state of the believers to whom he writes. He, therefore, breaks off into a parenthesis which occupies the remainder of Chapter 5 and most of Chapter 6. As it seems to the present writer, this section is not so much a warning against apostasy as it is a warning against immaturity.

It appears to the writer that the application of this section, especially Chapter 6:4-6, to mere professors, who lack reality, fails altogether to do justice to what is actually written. It would seem the whole section affords the strongest proof of the eternal security of the believer and the impossibility of repeating the initial work of God's grace in the soul. The passage assumes this eternal security: it is not written to affirm or to prove it.

On the supposition that those contemplated in verses 4-6 have never really been saved, and do not really belong to the people of God, but are spurious, the following points should be considered. They must not be avoided, but should be fairly construed, if we are to be satisfied that our interpretation of the section is sound. It is all too easy to blindly follow what others have said; we must satisfy ourselves.

1. They have been once for all enlightened. Note the word 'once' (ἅπαξ): it is not once upon a time, or at some time or other, but once for all. We have earlier discussed this word in relation to the work of Christ: it speaks of finality and unrepeatability. Moreover, the word 'enlightened' is used elsewhere of true believers who have received 'inward light' (Eph. 1:18; Heb. 10:32). How can this be true of a mere professor?

2. How can the words, 'made partakers of the Holy Ghost', be true of any but genuine believers? The phrase cannot, it is submitted, be fairly construed to mean that those referred to have only come under the influence of the Holy Spirit and His works. In this epistle, the word 'partakers' is used in other connections, but only in the sense of a real and not a nominal partaking or sharing. There is an actual partaking of 'blood and flesh' (Heb. 2:14); an actual partaking of milk (Heb. 5:13 Gk.); and so it is in every other use of the word in this epistle, there is an actual participation in the thing concerned. Why, then, should it be necessary to modify the sense in this passage, and regard it not to mean an actual partaking of the Holy Spirit but merely a coming under His influence? Besides, the words 'were made' (γενηθέντας) imply a change which was experienced – a becoming something which they were not before.

3. 'The powers of the world to come' are spoken of separately, which seems to disprove the interpretation given by some

that this is the same as partaking of the Holy Spirit. This undoubtedly refers to the miracles that characterised early Christianity.

4. It seems too much to say that 'fall away' (παραπεσόντας) is equivalent to apostasy. The word occurs nowhere else in the New Testament, and so we have no guide save the context and the etymology of the word, though this latter is insufficient to determine the significance of its use. It means to 'fall alongside', as one might fall out of the ranks of a regiment of soldiers, not by way of desertion but because of inability to maintain the pace. This seems to accord with the sense here, where there has been decline and a need of milk has recurred: strength has waned, and strong meat can no longer be digested.

5. Nor must the force of 'taste' be reduced to merely that of sipping. The word is used of the Lord, Who 'tasted' death for everything: He actually experienced it.

6. The constant repetition of the word 'again' is a key to the true meaning (as the present writer supposes) of the section. They need to be 'taught again'; they need milk 'again'; but no one lays the foundation 'again'. It is impossible to 'renew again', for that would entail 'crucifying again'. The force of all this is that the work in the soul, once done, cannot be done again.

If the section is made to apply to false professors, then the interpretation creates a class for whom there is no hope of repentance whatsoever. It may be answered that this is so, only 'while they are crucifying afresh the Son of God, etc.', but the writer of the epistle did not use the word 'while' - unless it be claimed that in English it is required to give the sense, and cannot be properly translated without it. Grammarians may affirm or deny this. We must be careful not to make our grammatical rules according to our theological views.

What then does the section mean? We suggest as follows:

The writer of the letter says that he has many things to say touching Melchizedek, which are difficult to express, not because of the complexity of the subject, but because of the low spiritual condition of the Hebrews. They ought by that time to have been able to teach others, but they had gone back and had become themselves in need of teaching of the first oracles of God, or 'the beginning of the oracles of God'. They needed to start all afresh, right from the very beginning. They had reverted to babyhood and needed milk, not strong meat. They were without spiritual teeth.

We should carefully note the twice repeated, "Ye have become': 'Ye have become dull of hearing'; 'Ye have become such as have need of milk'. Their spiritual health was bad. They were going back to the beginning of things such as those set out in Chapter 6:1-2. These were common both to Judaism and Christianity, elementary but basic. The things peculiar to Christianity these Hebrews, or some of them, were not at that time able to digest.

But the writer is desirous of 'going on': 'Let us go on unto full growth.' It is pointless to remain on the foundation without advancing further. No builder ever does that; he proceeds with the edifice. The foundation cannot be laid again: once laid, the building should proceed. How, then, is it they need to be taught again? How is it they need milk again? 'It is impossible to renew to repentance again': the initial work cannot be repeated.

'Repentance' headed the list of six items of basic things, and it would seem that this is selected as representative of the other five. 'It is impossible to renew again to repentance.' Therefore, seeing this is so, we will go on - 'This will we do, if God permit'.

It is as though he would say: 'Consider, brethren, what is involved. If the work has to be repeated, then you cannot stop at the initial work of repentance; you must go back to the furthest possible point. It will entail crucifying again the Son of God (v. 6), and that would put Him to an open shame, in that manifestly His first death was insufficient. But this could not be, as he proceeds to show incontrovertibly in the later part of his epistle.

No one can do without the foundation, any more than a Christian can dispense with the six cardinal items of verses 1-2. But he should not remain there. To linger is pointless, the foundation is firm: 'Let us go on ...'

The experiences of verse 4, for the purposes of the argument, are supposed to be real. The persons were, in fact, once for all enlightened; they had actually tasted of the heavenly gift; they had actually partaken of the Holy Spirit; they had tasted the good word of God and the powers of the world to come. They are, the writer of this commentary supposes, genuine believers, but weak ones at that. Their hands hang down; their knees are feeble; they have fallen out of the ranks due to weakness, but they have not deserted.

The illustration which follows depicts two classes, each of whom has been privileged, but with different results. When the rain falls on the earth, good fruit results in some places, thorns and thistles in others. Verse 8 is similar to 1 Corinthians 3:15, the product is burned up. Where there are worthless results of all the labour expended upon these Christians, such 'results' will be consumed. Yet the writer is persuaded better things of these to whom he writes, for he cannot but recall their work and labour of love which they have shown towards the name of Christ, in that they have ministered to the saints and were, in fact, then doing so. But he earnestly desired that this should continue and they should not be sluggish (the same word as is translated 'dull' in Chapter 5:11).

If the results in the one case would be burned, in the other they would be rewarded. God would not be forgetful. He wanted them to continue as they had begun. They had shown love to His name, and he desired them to show the same diligence right on until the end, and not to become slothful or sluggish. Consider Abraham: with others, he was marked by faith and patience and they inherit the promises. They should imitate him. He patiently endured and he obtained the promise: Isaac was born. God promised to Abraham, and He ratified it by an oath. The immutability of God's counsel was demonstrated in that He not only made a verbal promise, but did so by a sworn oath: the promise and the oath made the blessing sure.

We are the children of Abraham because of our faith. Therefore the promise and the oath give us 'strong encouragement' who have fled from the abrogated and judged system of Judaism to lay hold of the hope set before us.

The figure in verse 19 is taken, we are told, from the practice that prevailed in olden times in the harbours of the Mediterranean Sea. There may be seen in every harbour to this very day a great stone, immovably embedded in the ground near to the water. That rock was called the Anchoria, and sometimes the ship could not make its way to the secure mooring of the harbour by means of its sails. In such a case, the forerunner would go ashore in a little boat with a line which he would make fast to the Anchoria. This was sure and steadfast, and therefore those on the ship had but to work on the line, hand over hand, and by this means draw into the shore.

In our passage the 'anchor' is out of sight, but it is our 'hope'. Our forerunner is Christ and He has gone within the veil. Therefore, though the sea of life may be very stormy because of persecution, there is no need to abandon ourselves to it or revert to our former way of life. 'Let us go on.'

Such seems to be the gist of Chapter 6. But one or two remarks may be made on its details.

The third person used in verse 6 and the second person used in verse 9 would seem to be in keeping with the view set forth here, though it has been urged in support of the view that verse 6 envisages empty professors. But surely the third person is essential for the general argument working out the logical issue of a certain course, and the second person is essential when the writer expresses his hope of the state of the Hebrews. It is true that a 'mixed multitude' came out of Egypt, but it must not be forgotten that all save two fell in the wilderness.

As we have said, the principles referred to in verses 1 and 2 are common to both Judaism and Christianity. Repentance was found in David and faith in Abraham, to say nothing of others. The 'doctrine of washings' is that which is taught by the ceremonial washings of Old Testament times, such as the washing of regeneration. The teaching of 'laying on of hands' is that of identification and substitution, such as is seen when the hands were laid on the Scapegoat. The 'resurrection of the dead' and 'eternal judgment' are things found in the Old Testament, although in a dim light.

The Day of Atonement is still before the mind of the writer. The High Priest has gone inside the veil and is there as our Forerunner. The people are waiting outside, expecting Him to appear. Much stood to the credit of these Hebrews, and God would not forget how they had occupied the waiting time. Their work and labour of love would not go unrewarded, but they must not lose heart; they must show the same diligence to the full assurance of hope unto the end, and not give up before.

Now let us consider Hebrews 10:19-39.

From verse 19 the writer of this letter exhorts the saints to use their privileges and to appropriate in a practical manner the truths he has set out. Verses 19-25 are exhortatory, verses 26-31 are cautionary, and verses 32-39 are consolatory.

Not only has the High Priest gone into the holiest, but the believer may also do so with boldness. He may freely open his mouth in praise or petition; he need not stand there speechless. Such is the force of παρρησία. He has right to be there due to the constant efficacy of the 'blood of Jesus'. It is a 'new' way which has not hitherto been available, having but recently been opened by the death of Christ. It is a 'living way' in that it has to do with a Risen Christ: it was opened by His death and is kept open by His life. The rending of the temple's material veil denoted the death of Christ, because of which we may draw nigh to God. Moreover, we are priests, having had our hearts 'sprinkled' and our bodies 'washed' - the two requisites at the consecration of the Levitical priests. Their bodies had both to be sprinkled and washed.

'Let us draw near'; 'let us hold fast'; 'let us consider one another', 'not forsaking the assembling of ourselves together', for that would be the beginning of apostasy. By obeying these injunctions, we shall keep faith, hope, and love alive. We should each encourage the other, for by so doing we shall be mutual helpers of one another's faith. And this is all the more urgent as we see the day approaching when the Priest will come out.

The word 'For' of verse 26 is important. It shows that what follows flows out of what has gone before. Forsaking, abandoning the assembling of ourselves together is, as we have said, the first step to apostasy, and 'if we sin wilfully after we have received the knowledge of the truth', and abandon not only our gatherings together but also our position altogether, nothing whatever can help us. It has been shown that the Levitical sacrifices are useless and cannot take away sins; the death of Christ alone can do that. If, then, Christ is abandoned there remains no other sacrifice that can prove effective. What then? Assuredly there can be no alternative, but a certain fearful looking for of judgment and fiery indignation from the Lord who will devour the adversaries. To the penalty of a broken law, which is inescapable, there is added the guilt of 'sinning wilfully', that is, abandoning Christ, which is apostasy. This is far more serious.

Under the Mosaic law, where there were two or three witnesses, judgment was without mercy. Here there are three indictments which call for far severer judgment. (*a*) They would have 'trodden underfoot the Son of God'; (*b*) They would have regarded the 'blood of the covenant wherewith they were sanctified a common thing'; and (c) They would 'have done despite to the Spirit of grace'. By professing faith in Christ they had taken a place separate from the nation and were positionally 'sanctified' or 'set apart', but, should they apostatise, it would reveal there had been no reality. Their profession was but nominal.

There was the likelihood that these Hebrews were a 'mixed multitude': some true, some spurious. Some were like Ruth, who would go on, and some were like Orpah and would draw back. The apostates must beware, for they become 'adversaries' (not, be it noted, an enemy, *echthros*, but *hypenantios*, one who has taken an opposing stand), and they must remember that the Lord has said, 'Vengeance is Mine, I will repay'. On the other hand, His own people can take courage in that 'the Lord shall judge His people', and vindicate them before their adversaries. It is, indeed, a terrible thing to fall into the hands of the living God.

The 'sinning wilfully' (v. 26) is not deliberate sin of any kind, but the specific sin of apostasy: abandoning one's professed faith in Jesus. It is the sin of unbelief, of 'shrinking back', and God has no pleasure in such as do these things.

These believers were in an infinitely better position than the Jews who still adhered to Judaism. Why, then, give it up? They had a very praiseworthy record so far. After their illumination and early confession of faith in the Lord Jesus, they had given proof of reality by their endurance of a great conflict of sufferings, partly in personal injuries and partly in sympathy with fellow-saints. They had shown sympathy (*sunepathēsate*) with those in prison, and the confiscation of their property had been accepted with joy. They knew that in heaven they had a better and an abiding substance. Their confidence would be handsomely rewarded: why then cast it away?

Faith and patience are indispensable requisites. Both will be rewarded; the one by receiving the promises, and the other by seeing Him Who is now unseen, inside the veil. 'Yet a little while' and He will come out (v. 37). The words are emphatic: 'A little while' (lit. how little, how soon) and 'the Coming One will come, and will not tarry'. Our hope is real; our faith is well-founded. The writer could say, 'We - we ourselves - are not of them that draw back unto perdition; but of them that believe to the saving of the soul' (v. 39).

Chapter 9

Faith - Hebrews 11; 12:1-4

The emphasis in this epistle on the importance of faith and the perils of unbelief has already been noted. The writer stresses this because of the special circumstances of the Hebrews, and to give them an answer to the taunts of their fellow nationals. All their spiritual blessings were held by faith. They could not be seen, but were none the less real. 'The just shall live by faith' - the pilgrimage journey commenced on this principle, and it must never be abandoned until faith gives place to sight.

Chapter 11 is devoted entirely to this subject.

Faith is basic. It bridges the two eternities, for we can know nothing of the past or of the future save by believing what God has revealed in His Word. We believe that the visible things were made by the spoken word of God out of things which are not seen. Creation can be accounted for in no other way, for scientific research cannot discover the origin of things. Science has only to do with the things which exist; it halts when it is a question of discovering how they came to be.

Further, faith turns into substance things hoped for, so that they become as real to the soul as if they were factual and visible. Faith gives inward conviction of the reality of unseen things. What is visible is temporal, transient, and has the stamp of death upon it; 'the things that are not seen are eternal'. Faith does not busy itself with explanations, it accepts unquestionably what God has said. The dictionary defines it as 'spiritual apprehension of divine truth apart from proof'.

The eleventh chapter of our epistle is not merely a record of the faith displayed by certain Old Testament worthies chosen at random. It is a carefully selected list, appropriate to the main theme of the writer, which is calculated to show the excellence of Christ over all others, and to encourage the Hebrews to go on and not to take the retrograde step of reverting to Judaism and abandoning Christ.

Abel is mentioned first. He approached God with his offering and was accepted. This is exactly what the Hebrews have been urged to do: to draw near to God in virtue of the Offering of Christ, which alone could prove acceptable to Him. To revert to 'dead works' would be but to repeat the error of Cain, and to stain one's hands with blood far more precious than that of Abel.

No man hath seen God at any time. He dwells 'in light unapproachable; Whom no man hath seen, nor can see' (1 Tim. 6:16). If, therefore, anyone comes to God ($\pi\varrho o \sigma \varepsilon \varrho \chi \acute{o} \mu \varepsilon v o v$), as Abel did, he must first believe that He is and that He is the rewarder of them that seek Him out. This is an initial prerequisite.

'Enoch was translated by faith that he should not see death ... for before his translation he had this testimony, that he pleased God.' In that way the LXX renders the Hebrew, which is 'Enoch walked with God' (Gen. 5:22). 'Two cannot walk together unless they be agreed' (see Amos 3:3), and seeing that Enoch and God walked together it follows that he must have been well-pleasing to Him. But the God with whom Enoch walked was invisible: he walked 'by faith', a faith which gave to him the reality of the Person and Presence of God. Like Enoch, these Hebrews had not even the Shekinah glory of Jehovah between the cherubim. It had long since been withdrawn, but the absence of that visible token of His presence made room for the fuller exercise of faith.

Noah is cited next. He certainly did not 'neglect so great a salvation', of which God had told him. By faith he prepared the ark by which he and his house were delivered from the flood. The relevancy of this to the Hebrews is plain, for they were liable to neglect their great salvation.

Abram is next mentioned. He went out in obedience to the call of God, and he left all. That is what these Hebrews should do: they should 'go forth to Him without the camp', and, as Abram left his city, so should they leave theirs and all that pertained to it.

Not only he, but his sons Isaac and Jacob could, if they had been so minded, have returned to Ur of the Chaldees. They were not without the opportunity to do so, but they desired a better country than that to which they had come: they desired a heavenly country. And were not these Hebrews called 'with a heavenly calling', so why should they ever entertain the idea of returning to the Judaistic fold?

In keeping with the faith in which they lived, so they died. Even death did not quench it. 'They all died in faith, not having received the promises, but having seen them and greeted them from afar, and having confessed that they were strangers and pilgrims on the earth.' Surely these Hebrews could not wish to come behind the 'father of the faithful' in this respect!

But there was more. Abraham offered up to God Isaac his son, in whom were centred all the promises of God, reckoning - though he had no precedent - that God was able to raise even the dead. Why then should death be a deterrent to these Hebrews?

They had made their 'confession' with their mouth; like Isaac of old, who by faith blessed both Jacob and Esau; like Jacob, who blessed the two sons of Joseph, and like Joseph, who, when his end was near, made mention of the exodus of Israel from Egypt and gave commandment as to the transportation of his bones. Faith is strengthened when there accompanies it such a confession of the lips. Paul said so (Rom. 10:9), and the writer of this letter urges the saints to 'confess His name' (13:15).

Moses next comes on the stage (11:23). His case is much to the point, for he renounced earthly and providential advantages, throwing his lot in with the people of God, choosing rather to suffer affliction with them than to enjoy the pleasures of sin for a season. How pertinent this is to the case of the Hebrews! Had they not chosen to throw in their lot with the true 'people of God'? Were they not suffering for the 'reproach of Christ'? Well, then, let them consider Moses: he did not flinch nor did he return to the palace and his forfeited comforts. He positively refused to be called the son of Pharaoh's daughter, choosing rather to be ill-treated with God's people than to enjoy sin's pleasures, which are but for a season. He knew which were 'greater riches'. He forsook, and he endured: the one the Hebrews had done when they left Judaism, the other is what they are exhorted to do, to 'endure to the end'.

Faith gives courage. The parents of Moses 'were not afraid of the king's commandment' nor did Moses fear 'the wrath of the king'. So why should these Hebrews fear their adversaries? The writer has in mind Exodus 3 to 12, not Chapter 2.

By faith Moses kept the Passover and the sprinkling of the blood. Israel's very safety from divine judgment and from Egyptian cruelty depended upon it. They could not, dare not, dispense with it. Then why were these Hebrews even contemplating giving up, and 'sinning wilfully' by apostatising from their only hope?

The writer says nothing as to the faith in the wilderness. That was a scene of failure.

Faith is the highway to victory over the enemy, as the inhabitants of Jericho fell before the oncoming armies of Israel. Moreover, had not Rahab thrown in her lot with God's people and been saved as a result?

Let them look at the long list of the heroes of faith, time failing to name all who could be mentioned. Some triumphed, some suffered; each by faith. These Hebrews had not yet suffered such things as the fiery furnace or the lion's den. They had not suffered 'unto blood', as their Lord Himself had. No one can read Hebrews 11 without being profoundly moved. Its pathos grows as the chapter draws to its close. As we walk up and down and look at the monument erected to one after another, each and all of whom laid hold on the unseen, we are challenged and, if there be in our hearts any unbelief or tendency to 'shrink back', they stand as witnesses against us.

Without exception, they all had testimony borne to them through their faith, yet they received not the promises. That awaited the development of God's ways with others - with us. He having foreseen some better thing concerning us (v. 40). That 'better thing' was the better hope, the better testament, the better covenant, the better promises, the better sacrifice, the better possession (Heb. 10:34), and the better resurrection (11:35). Until these were brought in, it was impossible for these Old Testament worthies to be 'made perfect'. Sacrifices which are offered according to the law cannot, as touching the conscience, make the worshipper perfect (see 9:9); those who draw nigh under such a system can never be made perfect (see 7:19). But, as we have previously seen, 'by one offering Christ hath perfected for ever them that are sanctified' (10:14). And that sacrifice has both a retrospective and a prospective effect. It benefits those who lived in the times of the Old covenant who were marked by faith, as well as those who live on earth after that Offering was made. The death of Christ has made perfection available for them all, so that those who are dead are now spoken of as 'the spirits of just men made perfect' (12:23).

Notwithstanding all that is said of those named in Chapter 11, not one of them is faultless, though their faults are not named. This is in accordance with the promise, 'Their sins and their iniquities will I remember no more' (8:12). Nevertheless, there is One who is perfect, who had trodden the path of faith on earth. That One is Christ, who is both the Author and Perfecter of faith (see 12:2). The pronoun 'our' is better omitted. He is the One who had trodden the whole course from beginning to end. He began His earthly life in faith ('Thou didst make Me hope when I was upon My mother's breasts', Ps. 22:9); and He finished His life in faith. When He was about to enter into that realm in which He had never hitherto been, He said, 'Father, into Thy hands I commend My spirit' (Luke 23:46). Moreover, there was no lapse in His faith during the whole of His earthly course from the manger to the

Hebrews Chapter 9, Faith

cross. This could be said of none other. It could not be pleaded that His circumstances were easier than those mentioned in Hebrews 11: He 'patiently endured' a felon's gibbet, 'despising the shame' attached to it. He won His way through by faith, and 'is set down at the right hand of the throne of God' (12:2).

As we have remarked, the lapses of others are not mentioned, though they existed. Abraham, for example, went down to Egypt and denied his wife Sarah, and brought back with Hagar no end of trouble; Moses spake unadvisedly with his lips. And so we could go on as to others, but it is not proper to do so, seeing the Spirit is silent as to all this. In the case of the Lord Jesus no failures existed: He stands supreme at the head of the line ($\dot{\alpha}\rho\chi\eta\gamma\acute{o}\varsigma$), altogether blameless.

Yet these others constitute 'a cloud of witnesses'[1] to the great principle of implicit confidence in God and His word, and the record of their lives is with the view that we should 'run with patience the race that is set before us' (12:1). They beckon us on, and we should lay aside every encumbrance, just as the athlete not only keeps his weight down but strips himself of all unnecessary things calculated to hinder his progress: his aim is to succeed in the contest.

One thing in particular beset these Hebrews; it was 'the sin that doth closely cling to us', or, 'that is admired of many'. This was the sin of unbelief. It was that to which they were most likely to fall, and had they done so their fellow-nationals would have admired them for their courage to return to the fold. They must guard against the praise of men.

---

[1] 'Cloud of witnesses.' This does not mean that departed saints are observers of what transpires on earth. Scripture does not support such an idea. They are witnesses to a life of faith which they themselves had lived when on earth.

The witnesses with which they were surrounded did not go back nor give in, though they were sorely tried and hard-pressed. They dare not ignore their testimony and they should imitate their faith.

Yet there was One supreme above them all. Turning their eye off (ἀφορῶντες) from these, they should 'look unto Jesus', God's perfect Son, who perfectly trod earth's pathway of faith right on through death to the goal of heavenly glory.

The force of ἀντί in verse 2 is not 'instead of' but 'in consideration of', 'in view of', 'in order to obtain'. To translate it by the words 'instead of' is not tenable, nor indeed does it accord with facts. The grammatical construction is the same in verse 16 regarding Esau, who, in order to secure one mess of pottage, sold his birthright. So the Lord Jesus endured the cross in order that might obtain the joy set before Him. 'The joy that was set before Him' was not cancelled and substituted by the cross, but the cross was the way by which the joy was reached – the inevitable way. What was the joy? Surely nothing less than all the blessed issues that flow from His death, both for the glory of God, and the blessing of mankind and creation itself, which was in view at the beginning of the letter (2:9).

The Hebrews were being persecuted by their adversaries, but would they forfeit all that lay ahead of them in order to secure mere temporal ease? They must beware against self-indulgence in every shape and form: even that which is not sin but may be a hindrance – 'every weight'. They must guard against unbelief and apostasy; their eye must be fixed on the Perfect Man of Faith. They should consider Him, never forgetting that patiently He 'endured the cross', and 'endured such contradiction of sinners against Himself' (vv. 2-3)

They knew something of suffering, but not to the extent that He knew it. They had not resisted unto blood as He had. They should strive against sin in all its aspects: sin on the part of their adversaries, and sin as besetting them through unbelief. They must maintain their stand and not yield to their foes, nor to their self-interest. The fight must go on.

Chapter 10

Will Ye Also Go Away? - Hebrews 12:5 - 13:1-25

There was another aspect of their sufferings which the Hebrews were apt to forget. Their sufferings were part of the Father's disciplinary dealings with His children, and proof not only of His love for them but of their relationship to Him. Chastening is the hallmark of sonship. It is found in every well-conducted family, though, when applied to God's children, its aims are far greater than those of any earthly parent. God has in view 'our profit, that we may be partakers of His holiness' and that there may be 'the peaceable fruit of righteousness' (12:10-11). Those that are without such chastening are not true sons.

Thus, what men inflict on God's people is used of Him for their good, and the persecution of these early believers became His method of developing their Christian character. They should not despise it, or treat it as a little thing; nor should they faint under it, for it is common to 'every son whom He receiveth' - He is not partial (vv. 5-6). If we respect our earthly parents who trained us in childhood, how much more should we be subject to the Father of our spirits, and not rebel against or chafe under it!

These believers are viewed as a band of pilgrims on the march through an enemy's country. Their hands should not hang down limply, nor should their knees be feeble. They should tread an even path, not merely for their own sake but for the sake of those that are lame. Peace and holiness should mark them.

Care must be exercised, 'lest any fall back from the grace of God; lest there be any root of bitterness troubling others as well as themselves' (see v. 15). They must not forget that they do not live to themselves. An uneven path can drive the lame out of it; a bitter root among the pilgrims can be a source of trouble, and many of them become defiled. To fall back from the grace of God is to abandon the sovereignty of divine grace and to revert to Judaistic principles. It might seem to be a sensible course, calculated to ease their circumstances, but they must consider not themselves but their fellow-pilgrims and the effect that their vacillation may have on others.

Esau is introduced as a warning to them. He was utterly profane and cared only for temporary and immediate self-gratification, cost him what it might. For a morsel of meat he sold his birthright, and later he lost the blessing, only to discover that he could not get his father to change his mind despite his urgent and tearful entreaties (Gen. 27:38). He was no true child of God: he had no room either for the true God or, for that matter, for any other so-called god (see Obadiah). These Hebrews were liable to be enmeshed in a similar snare, and, in the interests of present ease, to forfeit all that grace might have given, or that which belonged by right to sonship.

The undoubted superiority of Christianity over Judaism is the theme of verses 17-24. Mount Zion is far better than Mount Sinai: the former speaks of grace, the latter of judgment. The terrible scenes that accompanied the giving of the law spoke of the severity of God, when judgment had to be executed without mercy. Who would prefer that to His sovereign grace? The heavenly Jerusalem is far to be preferred to the earthly: the latter was destined to destruction, as came to pass, but the former cannot be shaken. 'The church of the firstborn ones enrolled in heaven' is a far greater conception than 'the church in the wilderness'. In the new order they were linked with 'the spirits of just men', now perfected by the accomplished sacrifice of Christ, and so brought into an association far more precious than mere association with its fellow nationals on earth. The new covenant, with its unconditional promises, is much to be preferred to the old covenant, with its stern obligations and penalties. The *blood of sprinkling* - 'precious blood' as Peter calls it - tells of better things than Abel, who though dead still speaks. Abel's offering spoke of one yet to be; Christ's offering tells of a finished work. Abel's blood called for judgment, but Christ's calls for mercy.

The writer seems to have reached a crescendo of contrasts. These believers professed to have left the ground of law and to have taken their stand on that of grace; to have left Moses for Christ, the old for the new. But they must not allow their present troubles to lead them into graver sins than those which marked their forefathers. Should anyone have refused to listen to Moses, he would have found that there was no way of escape from punishment. But Moses spoke on earth, not from heaven. It follows, then, that there cannot possibly be any escape whatever, should we refuse to listen to Him who speaks from heaven. The writer comes back to his earlier remarks: 'Therefore we should give the more earnest heed ... for how shall we escape, if we neglect ...?' (see 2:1-3).

The giving of the Mosaic law was attended with an earthquake, for all that has to do with earth must inevitably be shaken. God has forecast the shaking again, not of earth only but of heaven also (12:26). These believers need not fear, however, because they have an unshakeable kingdom. They, therefore, should hold fast to grace and not revert to law; were they to do that, they would discover that, even in Christian days, 'our God is a consuming fire'.

It is said, 'A fellow feeling makes us wondrous kind.'[1] And so it should. When our brethren suffer for their faith it affords a peculiarly opportune occasion to show brotherly love. When they are ousted from their homes we can, and should, show them hospitality, and in that way manifest real sympathy (13:1-3).

Suffering is a purifying fire, but God allows His people to have times of ease as well. The enemy, however, is all too cunning, and he would use such times to lead the saints into moral corruption and the ways of the world. They must not forget, therefore, the fundamental laws of human society which God has established. Marriage must be held in honour and there must be no illicit conduct. If earthly governments do not punish the sins of fornication and adultery, God will do so. There should also be a healthy spirit of contentment with God's dealings with them. To be discontented is to doubt both His wisdom and love. They can safely rely on the never-failing presence and help of God, and need not fear anything their enemies might contrive to do.

They should remember their 'guides' and how they finished their course, bearing in mind that they encountered precisely the same difficulties and had the same temptations. In their days, opposition was no less fierce and the desire for earthly comfort no less attractive; yet they held fast to their course and kept their faith in God. They should imitate the faith of these

---

[1]Alexander Pope, 1688-1744.

guides, for the object of their faith remains unchanged though they have passed on: 'Jesus Christ is the same yesterday, and today, and for ever' (v. 8). He is unaltered and unalterable.

Furthermore, the Jewish system had its altar[2] and ritual, but, as we have seen, the fulfilment of the typical significance of all this has now been accomplished by the death of Christ. He suffered without the gate, just as the sin offering was burned outside the camp. They should 'go forth therefore unto Him outside the camp [of established Judaism] bearing His reproach' (v. 13). The 'tent of meeting' was now outside the camp of the apostate nation. They should, therefore, leave 'the camp' and go forth' unto Him (see Ex. 33:7). Admittedly, there is a stigma attaching to association with the Lord Jesus, but what of that? Moses, who estimated 'the reproach of Christ greater riches than the pleasures of Egypt', took the same line. They can afford to abandon Jerusalem for it was, in any case, soon to be destroyed. Here they have no continuing city, and believers characteristically seek one to come: 'the city which hath foundations, whose builder and maker is God' (11:10). In this they are in the company of Abraham, whose quest was the same.

Offerings? High Priest? They have both. 'By Him therefore let us offer the sacrifice of praise to God continually [not at stated times], that is, the fruit of our lips giving thanks to His

---

[2] Heb. 13:10. There appears to be no room for doubt that 'we have an altar' refers to the Jewish sacrificial system: the 'we' means 'we Jews'. The whole argument in verses 10 and 11 shows that the writer is referring to the earthly sacrificial law and altar. Nowhere does there appear to be any justification for the Christian claiming to have an altar. Certainly the Cross is not it; nor is there need of one in heaven now, since the sacrifice of Christ is once and for ever accomplished. The word 'for' in verse 11 seems to be decisive as to this. Verse 11 explains verse 10: 'We have' of verse 10 may be read impersonally as 'There is'.

name. But to do good and to communicate forget not ...' (vv. 15-16). There must be both word and action, not the one without the other, for confession without action is hypocrisy, and action without confession speaks very little. God is well-pleased with such sacrifices. In animal sacrifices He has no pleasure, but His heart is pleased when He hears the lip of praise, confessing His name, and when His eye sees the kindly deed, sharing with others what in His providence He has given.

They should obey their guides, submitting to their rule. These guides watch for their souls in that watchfulness that often keeps them awake at night ($ἀγρυπνοῦσιν$), conscious of the many wild beasts that would prey upon the flock: a flock for which they will have to give an account to God. Where there is obedience and submission, the watching can be done with joy. But where it is otherwise it causes grief to the guides and loss to the sheep.[3]

Nothing can be plainer than that the spiritual wellbeing of these Hebrews lay heavily on the heart of the writer of the letter. He solicits their prayers, being assured of a good conscience before God as to the manner of his living. He desires to be among them in order to help them further, for he is deeply aware of the immensity of the subject and of the brevity of its treatment in his epistle. He hopes to bring Timothy also: a specially suitable person, having regard to the fact that his mother was a Jewess, though his father was a Greek. In the mouth of two witnesses, and witnesses such as these, every word would be established.

What more apt prayer could be offered than that which closes the epistle. 'Now the God of peace, that brought again from the

---

[3] Heb. 13:17 'that they may do this with joy and not with grief'. 'This' refers to watching, not the giving account.

dead our Lord Jesus, that great shepherd of the sheep, through the blood of the everlasting covenant, make you perfect in every good work to do His will, working in you that which is wellpleasing in His sight, through Jesus Christ; to whom be glory for ever and ever. Amen.'

The writer, as we have said, was aware of the immensity of his theme, and the brevity of his treatment of it. Yet that very brevity was not without advantage, and he pleaded therefore that his addressees should 'suffer the word of exhortation'.